The Killing Compartments

The Killing Compartments
The Mentality of Mass Murder

Abram de Swaan

Yale UNIVERSITY PRESS
New Haven and London

Yale University Press books may be purchased in quantity for educational, business, or promotional use. For information, please e-mail sales.press@yale.edu (US office) or sales@yaleup.co.uk (UK office).

Designed by James Johnson.
Set in Ehrhardt Roman type by Integrated Publishing Solutions.
Printed in the United States of America.

Library of Congress Control Number: 2014949830
ISBN 978-0-300-20872-6

Catalogue records for this book are available from the Library of Congress and the British Library.

This paper meets the requirements of ANSI/NISO Z39.48–1992 (Permanence of Paper).

10 9 8 7 6 5 4 3 2 1

In memory of

Carrie de Swaan,

1946–2010

Contents

CONTENTS

Preface

More than twenty years ago by now, the phone rang. It was Nico Frijda, once my *Doktorvater*, as the German fondly call their thesis supervisor. "How come," he asked, "so many people hold such passionate feelings about faraway human beings they have never even met?"

Somehow the question stuck with me, and I wrote an essay on "Widening Circles of Identification," the gist of which is reproduced in this book. But shortly thereafter, Yugoslavia began to disintegrate with great mayhem and bloodshed. Only a year later, the genocide in Rwanda occurred. Unlike preceding episodes of mass annihilation, these instances happened right under the eyes of reporters, sometimes in front of TV cameras. They shocked readers and viewers all over the world. It seemed as if humankind had "learned nothing" from the Holocaust, which had happened half a century before. Of course, that lesson about not having learned anything could have been learned many times in the preceding fifty years, for there had been numerous instances of mass annihilation in the years since 1945. And after Yugoslavia and Rwanda there were more to come. I wrote a complementary essay, this time about

Rwanda, called "Widening Circles of Disidentification: On the Sociogenesis of Hatred," which also left its traces in this book.

When invited to give the Huizinga Lecture twelve years ago now, I chose to present an overview of mass killings in the past century entitled "Murder and the State." Many of these events, even some that took untold millions of lives, were unknown to this informed audience and had been to me, too, before I started delving into the subject.

How can such massive destruction occur in the contemporary world, even in apparently "modern" and "civilized" societies? Is it evidence of the "collapse of civilization" into chaos and violence, or is modern society, and civilization itself, barbaric at its very core, covered only by a frail veneer of civility? I think that apparently peaceful societies may sometimes veer onto a different track, one of increasing separation of people at every level, culminating in the deportation of the target population to the "killing compartments."

Another nagging question imposes itself: "How could they?" Are the killers just ordinary people who had the bad luck to end up in circumstances that transformed them into mass murderers? Or are they perhaps different from most other people, at least in some respects and to a certain degree?

Looking back, I think these questions have been with me most of my life, as they are with everyone for whom the Shoah was the formative event. This book was not planned from the outset as a historical survey and theoretical analysis of mass annihilation in the past century. It evolved that way under my hands. Only now it seems that the book had to be written in the form it finally took. I have tried to make sense and to avoid nonsense. I have come up with some answers—incomplete, tentative, but enlightening. There is no doubt that mass annihilation can also occur in contemporary societies. This is a most significant fact, ignored all too often, and it should be a central problem for the human sciences.

Anyone who is confronted with the disasters inflicted by human beings on other human beings is overcome by fear, rage, and grief. In the end, the greatest of these is grief, as mourning for lives destroyed may lead to greater respect for present and future human lives.

Reading the literature and writing this book was a lonely venture, but I would not have persevered without the help of my friends who gave me their comments and corrections: Boudewijn Chabot, Nico Frijda, Wouter Gomperts, Johan Goudsblom, Johan Heilbron, and Ton Zwaan. One far friend above all encouraged me throughout: Edmund Leites. My editors, Steve Wasserman and Laura Jones Dooley, made this a better book. I am much indebted to them all and to my companion of all these years, Cindy Kerseborn, who supported me when I needed it.

Several readers of the manuscript gave me their comments and corrections: Boudewijn Chabot, Nico Frijda, Wouter Gomperts, Johan Goudsblom, Johan Heilbron, and Ton Zwaan. One faraway friend above all encouraged me throughout: Edmund Leites. I am much indebted to each one of them.

Chapters 3, 5, and 6 of this book quote and elaborate on earlier essays published in my book *Bakens in niemandsland*.

CHAPTER I

Introduction

T HESE ARE PEACEFUL TIMES. Only rarely are people killed by their own kind, and only very, very rarely are they killed by other animals, microorganisms excepted. Nevertheless, even though the statistics should reassure, many people worry about lone killers, murderous gangs, and terrorist bands. At the same time, most people are vaguely aware that in this peaceful era, wars have killed combatants by the hundreds of thousands, even tens of millions. Yet mass violence against unarmed civilians has claimed three to four times as many lives in the past century as war: one hundred million at least, and possibly many more. These large-scale killings have required the efforts of hundreds of thousands of perpetrators. Such men (almost all were males) were ready to kill, indiscriminately, for many hours a day, for days and weeks at a stretch, and sometimes for months or even years.

Unlike common criminals who work outside the mainstream of society, in secret, on their own or with a few accomplices, mass murderers almost always worked in large teams, with full knowledge of the authorities and on their orders. Without exception, they operated within a supportive social context, most often firmly embedded in the institutions of the ruling regime. Unlike terrorists, the mass murderers usually did not want their deeds to be widely known.

The soldiers on opposing sides in a war are usually fairly evenly matched in weaponry, training, and coordination. In contrast, the perpetrators of mass extermination were armed, well-prepared, and organized; their mostly unarmed, untrained, and unorganized victims did not stand a chance against the men who came to kill them.

A tour d'horizon of merely the worst instances of mass annihilation in the past century reveals a score of episodes, many resulting in millions, even tens of millions, of casualties. At the close of the nineteenth century, German troops were busy exterminating the Hereros of South-West Africa (modern-day Namibia), taking eighty thousand lives; the Dutch subdued Aceh, with as many casualties; and under the auspices of King Leopold II of Belgium, regular military and mercenaries killed millions of Congolese in his privately owned Congo Free State. Between 1910 and 1920, a "revolutionary" civil war in Mexico claimed some two million civilian lives. Turkish special forces murdered roughly a million Armenian citizens during World War I. In the 1930s in the Soviet Union, the Great Terror took millions of lives, and millions of Ukrainians were deliberately starved. During the Rape of Nanking, Japanese invaders killed Chinese citizens by the hundreds of thousands, and in the entire course of World War II, they may have caused several million unarmed casualties in Asia.

In all this annihilation of human life, the Holocaust, the Nazi extermination of some six million European Jews and of so many other people, stands as the nadir. As the Nazi war effort collapsed, in central Europe about a million Germans were killed or succumbed from the hardships as around ten million were expelled. In 1947, at the time of independence and partition in India, a million people died in "communal riots," and some ten million were driven from their homes.

In China, under Chairman Mao between 1958 and 1962, during the Great Leap Forward, tens of millions of peasants were starved to death, and from 1966 on, the Cultural Revolution took a toll of perhaps a million lives. At about that time, in 1965, about a million "Communists" were killed in Indonesia following a military coup. The (West) Pakistani army murdered at least a million Bangladeshis in 1971, during the secession of East Pakistan. Between 1975 and 1979, the Khmer Rouge of Cambodia exterminated 1.7 million enemies of the revolution. In 1982, Guatemala's military junta turned a drawn-out antiguerrilla war into a campaign of expulsion in which a million Mayan Ixil people were driven from their lands and endured countless civilian casualties.

At the close of the twentieth century, amid bloodshed on all sides, Serbian troops massacred as many as ten thousand Bosnian Muslims. In 1995, in Rwanda, the Hutu Power movement resulted in the slaughter of almost a million Tutsis and "suspect" Hutus.

This list is neither complete nor even systematic. It conveys only a general idea of the incidence, scope, and diversity of episodes of mass annihilation in the past century. In all these instances, armed and organized men killed countless numbers of mostly unorganized and unarmed people. The violence in each case was massive. And it was asymmetric. Indeed, the asymmetry of force sets this bloodshed apart from another form of mass violence: the large-scale killing that goes on in wars between armed and organized fighters on either side, a more or less symmetric form of violence.[1] Military battle, between parties that are roughly equal in equipment and organization, remains outside the scope of this book. In the past century, this "regular warfare" (in reality there is not much that is regular about it) may have caused some thirty-five million casualties.

There is a third form of mass violence: the shelling and bombing en masse of unarmed civilians by cannon, from airplanes, or with missiles. This destruction, too, is asymmetric. The development of the rifle greatly increased the distance and speed of kill-ing (although for centuries bow and arrow matched them in this respect). From the mid-nineteenth century on, technological in-novations made it possible to kill ever-increasing numbers of non-combatants at greater distances with heavy cannon, far beyond the direct perception of the artillerists who manned them and hardly noticed the suffering they inflicted.

In World War I, the first bombings from the air inflicted ci-vilian casualties, and soon the distance between the airborne kill-ers and their victims on the ground grew again. In World War II, the Third Reich initiated the technique of bombing urban areas in order to kill large numbers of civilians. The Allied air forces re-taliated with vastly larger destructive impact against Germany and Japan. This long-distance annihilation reached a pinnacle with the firebombings of Tokyo and the atom bombs dropped on Hiroshima and Nagasaki. Allied bombings took 750,000 lives.

During the Cold War intercontinental ballistic missiles with nuclear warheads gave their operators the capacity to kill tens of millions up to six thousand miles away. Ballistic missiles can kill with frightening precision on a faraway continent while the spe-cialists in their operating rooms see only maps, graphs, statistics, and satellite images of what happens "on the ground." Although asymmetric, long-distance, mass violence is the greatest danger to the survival of the human species, so far, it has not made casualties in the same order of magnitude as the other forms of mass violence, quite likely precisely because of its well-nigh unlimited potential for destruction.

The even more recent airborne "drone" enables its manipula-tors to do the same on a much smaller and more precise scale. Such mechanized killings at great distance must affect the operators at the controls very differently than does the mass extermination at close range that is the subject of this book.[2] The ethical and legal status of such operations is poorly defined, and most important,

Western democracies have been the victorious perpetrators of this form of destruction, which makes for persistent moral ambiguity on the subject. Asymmetric mass violence at great distance falls beyond the scope of this book.

One other form of mass annihilation occurs as murder by omission, at a minimum as criminal negligence on a vast scale: famine. The British government certainly aggravated mass starvation among the Irish peasantry during the potato blight of the late 1840s. The British authorities in India followed a similar policy on a much larger scale by refusing aid or work to the rural population during the meager harvests of 1876–1879 and 1896–1902. The resulting death toll may have run into the tens of millions.[3] In the Ukraine in the 1930s under Joseph Stalin, again in the 1950s in Mao Zedong's China, and repeatedly in North Korea during years of scarcity from "natural" causes, the regime's henchmen requisitioned farmers' food stocks, thus preventing them from sowing for the next harvest while also stopping them from seeking relief elsewhere. These policies deliberately condemned rural families by the millions and tens of millions to a slow and excruciating death by starvation. They required, moreover, the deployment of huge numbers of party officials and police to take their stocks away from the peasants and keep them from leaving in search of food. Mass starvation under these conditions is a form of mass extermination, allowed to occur (or perpetrated) by well-established regimes as a form of rule by terror.

The subject here is mass annihilation—that is, massive, asymmetric violence at close range, where killers and victims are in direct confrontation.[4] It takes place most often in a context of war, civil war, revolution, or coup d'état. Such massive and violent confrontations aggravate existing hatreds, fears, and rage and provoke more violence.

Mass annihilation, mass extermination, and *mass murder* are in most respects broader terms than *genocide*, which was coined for purposes of international law. The UN Convention on Genocide of 1948 was meant to encourage early intervention by outside powers in order to prevent or stop mass killings and to bring the perpetrators to justice. Most instances of genocide are also instances of mass extermination. But many instances of mass extermination do not count as genocide under the convention, because some conditions do not apply: for example, the regime's "intent to destroy" cannot be proven, or the victims were killed for their political convictions or their class background rather than for belonging to a "national, ethnic, racial or religious group," as the convention has it.[5]

Many episodes of mass annihilation have been largely forgotten, and about most of them little is known. More often than not, a successor regime covers up what happened. The survivors must live with the perpetrators. They must be silent about the past and remain silent about the fact that they are silent, keep secret the fact that there is a secret, just as in official repression every mention of censorship is itself subject to censorship: an infinite regression of repression.

Only when the camp of the perpetrators was thoroughly defeated and some of them were brought to justice have the essential facts about the circumstances of these mass murders and those who committed them become known. A few of the many millions of victims survived to tell their story in memoirs or in court testimony. A rare bystander who witnessed the killings tried to alert the outside world or testified after it was safe to do so. Countless killers took an active part in these massacres, yet about them even less is known. As long as they were busy killing, they were in no mood to explain themselves. Even under the most fanatical regimes, the authorities tended to remain discreet about their extermination campaigns.[6] The perpetrators did better to remain silent, too: even among the military they were little esteemed, regarded at best as indispensable executioners. After the murderous regime collapsed or was defeated, the perpetrators had little reason to be candid about their deeds: they were likely to encounter social opprobrium, and they faced a (small) risk of arrest and judgment. Most of what we know about the perpetrators comes from the trials held against them, from testimonies by surviving victims and bystanders, from archival evidence, and from the defendants' own statements: before their judges they played down their acts and muted their convictions in order to appear as plain and colorless as they could and to pass as ordinary men.

Mass annihilation is the form of mass violence that has made by far the most casualties in the past century and in centuries before. In most instances, it occurred in a more or less demarcated context that was set up and maintained by the regime in power. Within that setting the perpetrators were encouraged and often compelled to humiliate, abuse, exploit, torture, and kill their victims, who lacked any means of defense. The killers acted in full confidence of impunity. They may have experienced an exhilarating sense of omnipotence, but in reality they could not act without the permission of their superiors. Their dominance was founded only on their obedience.

The perpetrators had to face their victims near at hand. They had to make themselves imperturbable against any appeal for mercy; they had to rid themselves of any inkling of compassion and push aside their stirrings of conscience or fears of later retribution. In other words, they had to ignore the humanity of their victims, to reduce them to objects of contempt and hatred, rightly to be destroyed. But many among them must also have had to ignore their own feelings of disgust, horror, and pity.

Even under such extremely asymmetric circumstances, perpetrators and victims constituted a social figuration, albeit one of utter inequality, perverse and distorted, but nonetheless complex for it, and with regularities of its own. The figuration imposed its demands on the perpetrators and its very different demands on the victims. There was, even in the killing compartments, social interaction among killers and victims, whether very brief or ongoing for many months.

The focus in this book is on the rank-and-file perpetrators who are in close contact with their victims. Their actions are explained first in the context of the situation in which perpetrators and victims find themselves at opposite ends. But a genocidal situation, no matter how insulated, does not stand on its own. In almost all instances, it is created and maintained by a regime bent on mass annihilation and can be understood only by considering the impact of that ruling regime.

The perpetrators, or genocidaires (from the French *génocidaires*, those who commit genocide), are in the service of this regime and are bound to realize its designs under the working conditions that it imposes on them. But we must widen our scope even more. A genocidal regime, any regime, comes to power and rules within the larger context of the domestic society and as a result of long-term developments in that society. Moreover, it interacts with foreign regimes in a changing international environment.

These very broad, long-run transformations may at first sight seem to be far removed from the daily experiences of someone trapped in a genocidal setting. But they are not. They affect the people who lived through those times. They instill collective memories and widely shared convictions—a collective mentality that may be less or more compatible with group hatred and group violence. Those who live under a genocidal regime thus take for granted that hostile groups exist and that certain people belong to one party and not to the other. To them it seems "natural" that "Muslims" constitute such a group, or "Communists" or "Armenians," rather than, say, "brunettes," "baritones," or "tailors." In fact, these categories, which emerged over long periods of time and once lay dormant, are resuscitated again by the regime for its own purposes; rarely are they invented from scratch.

If these hostile categories are the outcome of long-lasting societal processes, so, too, are the ways that people either refrain from or resort to physical violence. Over many generations, people in a society develop a certain widely shared *habitus*, a bundle of set habits that seem self-evident: they go without saying. Members of society acquire a shared mentality that need not be spelled out or reflected on: it is "just so."

Clearly, large-scale social transformations affect everyday individual behavior in a genocidal setting as well as in a peaceful one. The regime mediates between these levels by selecting and stressing certain elements in the society's common habitus and mentality and glossing over others that do not fit its designs. Critical to the creation of a genocidal setting is the regime's construction of an enemy group through selection from available historical themes. Also pertinent is the regime's justification of violence by picking the most convenient among the available moral arguments. Essential as well is the regime's effort of recruiting the killers, creating the killing compartments, and rounding up the target people.

If violence is not a natural given, once and for all, neither is enmity. Antagonisms are a perennial characteristic of social life. All group formation implies exclusion of others. At the psychological level, it implies both identification with one's own people and disidentification from others, who become outsiders. In chapter 3, the very long-term transformations of these identifications and disidentifications are detailed. Briefly put, over the centuries, they increased in scope and scale as human beings came to live in ever-larger social units, from hunter-gatherer bands to villages, cities, and nation-states. In the most recent stages, people developed strong identifications with and disidentifications from very large groupings, such as nations, ethnic groups, classes, races, and reli-

gions. It often almost seems as if people knew these countless remote strangers like their own kin and neighbors. This helps to explain at once the huge scale and the—almost intimate—emotional
intensity of contemporary mass conflicts.[7]

Mass annihilation is an explosion of collective violence. Thousands, perhaps tens of thousands of people are led to destroy hundreds of thousands, perhaps millions of people. But before that, most
of them may not have harmed a living soul. Once it is over, most of
them by far will never again physically hurt another person. Where
does this extreme violence come from, and how can it disappear
again, seemingly without a trace? It will not do to conclude either
that human nature is essentially violent and people just rein in
their rage almost all of the time or, on the contrary, that human beings are naturally peaceful and somehow are compelled or seduced
to act destructively.

Human violence has a natural and social history (the two are in-
separable). Through evolution, human beings have come to regulate
their impulses toward violence and their equally impulsive fears of
violence. They have done this by controlling one another and by in-
dividually managing their own impulses: this is the social regulation
of the individual regulation of violence. It is the subject of chapter 4.

We should note at the outset that this regulation, at least in
"Western" societies and in the very long term, has become more
encompassing, more even, stricter, and, within these limits, more
flexible. This is one aspect of what Norbert Elias calls the "civilizing processes." Genocidal regimes have succeeded in profoundly
altering this social and individual regulation of violence and fear.
They have done so in particular by creating killing compartments
where violence can and must be perpetrated with abandon and
impunity. Almost everywhere, the killing quickly becomes wild,
barbaric, and gory. The perpetrators consider it a dirty job that has
to be done. In the process, many become accustomed to the slaugh-

ter. They gradually lose whatever inhibitions held them back, and proceed either reluctantly or with mindless indifference or they become eager executioners out of rage, greed, and perhaps lust. Whatever their motives, so long as they comply, they help the regime accomplish its lethal objectives. In the killing compartments, the perpetrators go through a regression in service of the regime.

Chaotic and barbaric as mass violence may appear, it has a certain order. If it did not, the killers might turn against just anyone or even on one another, in any place, at any time. The targeted victims must be distinguished from the rest of the population, and the killing must in some way be separate from life as usual.

Distinctions and separations operate in all societies, at many levels. In the process leading toward mass annihilation, such dividing lines become starker and more pervasive. The target people are increasingly separated from the regime's people, in every respect. Mass annihilation occurs in societies that have become increasingly *compartmentalized* at all levels. *Mentally:* those in the dominant group come to identify more closely with each other as similar in all relevant respects, emotional, cognitive, and moral, and they *dis-identify* more sharply from others, who are perceived as different in all these respects. *Socially:* they will avoid interaction with these outsiders, who are thus increasingly isolated as a distinct category. *Institutionally:* the out-group is excluded from schools, hospitals, courts, commerce, public transport, administrative services, forcing them into seclusion and separation from society. *Politically:* the regime with its military, militias, and mass movements propagates, legitimizes, and enforces the separation of the targeted group. In the final stages, its members are rounded up and deported to separate compartments, where they are exterminated by the regime's killers. Pervasive compartmentalization allows people in other domains of society to function as if nothing has happened. Chapter 6 details this compartmentalizing process.

Once mass annihilation begins, the killers are more or less neatly separated from the rest of society in isolated killing sites. The killing might be the work of violence specialists in a closed corps, or outsiders might join the carnage, on their own or as a crowd. Four different modes of massive destruction can be distinguished, each characterized by a different degree and manner of compartmentalization of the killing sites and the killers.

The *conquerors' frenzy* of victorious armies on foreign soil, among an alien population, occurs far from home, largely unbeknown to the domestic public and perpetrated exclusively by the military.

When an established regime resorts to *rule by terror*, it employs professional violence specialists and a dedicated system of insulated detention and extermination sites.

In the *losers' triumph*, genocidal regimes facing imminent defeat by an enemy army surprisingly continue and perhaps intensify their campaign to annihilate the target group, even at the cost of undermining their effort in the war against their armed opponent.

In contrast, a *megapogrom* proceeds as a wave of apparently spontaneous deadly local riots, a free-for-all for whoever joins the slaughter of a vaguely defined target group. Major events, such as defeat in war or a threatened secession, provoke, synchronize, and concatenate these local events into one huge campaign of annihilation, condoned if not covertly or even openly encouraged, by the regime in power.

In chapter 7, this fourfold categorization anchors a discussion of a score of episodes of mass annihilation during the twentieth century.

Four levels of sociological analysis useful in understanding mass violence are detailed in chapter 8. *Macrosociological* (long-term, large-scale social) processes engender in people a widespread habitus and a shared mentality that may be more or less conducive to group hostility and violence. Such large-scale processes also shape a regime that in rare cases may turn toward mass annihilation. This concerns the *mesosociological* (mostly institutional) level of analysis. This annihilationist regime then creates and maintains the genocidal situation in which the perpetrators kill their victims. That is the subject of *microsociological* (small-group) analysis (and of social psychological experiment). An adequate understanding of genocidal episodes must take these three levels into account.

The fourth level of analysis, the level of *psychosociology,* concerns the perpetrators themselves. Are they merely and only the product of circumstance, of their immediate context, or do they have a biography of their own? Do they have particular motivations and inclinations that dispose them to become mass killers? There is much to be said in response to these questions, but it is only fair to warn you right away that no complete answer will be forthcoming. Each question raises many new questions; most must remain open, while some can be answered, in part. There are only uneasy answers.

In fact, there are two easy answers, but both are unsatisfactory. The first is that mass murderers are all beasts, monsters, or psychopaths. This is indeed the picture presented in war propaganda and sometimes in the popular mass media. Some perpetrators fit these descriptions, but they are a tiny minority. No reputable scholars believe that even a sizable minority of mass murderers were severely disturbed from the outset.[8]

The second response is that perpetrators are "ordinary men who commit extraordinary evil." In fact, this has been the prevailing consensus for almost half a century: it was their extraordinary situation that made these ordinary people into killers. This assertion is far less easy to refute than the first one, but this "situationist" view leaves out too much. It is the subject of chapter 2. There Hannah Arendt's notion of the banality of evil is critically reviewed. Following this is a reconsideration of Stanley Milgram's experiments on obedience to authority. The impact of their situation on people's readiness to comply with authority is now seen as much greater than was generally assumed before Milgram staged his famous demonstrations in the Yale social psychology laboratory. Next comes a reflection on Christopher Browning's historical research on the "ordinary Germans" of Battalion 101, one of the many Nazi extermination squads behind the Eastern Front. Browning's research indicates that loyalty to peers in the direct environment, too, plays a greater part than was formerly suspected. The chapter concludes with a reappraisal of the connection between mass annihilation and "modernity" or "democracy."

In the situationist view, ordinary people under extraordinary circumstances will commit extraordinary evil. And it directly follows that ordinary individuals, like you and me, under the same conditions would do the same thing.[9] In the most simplistic version, no further question need be asked.[10]

This "situation," however, can be understood only as the outcome of the policies of a genocidal regime that itself emerged in the context of broad, long-term developments. The generations that lived through these times acquired collective notions and common habits. Were some of them more prone to join the ranks of the killers, more readily recruited or more easily intimidated into participating? Or would everyone, "you" and "me" included, under the same circumstances automatically begin to kill and go on killing?

Paradoxically, Stanley Milgram's experiments, which are considered the touchstone of the situationist argument, also provide ample evidence for the importance of personal disposition in shaping behavior: as he conscientiously documented, numerous subjects refused to continue administering painful shocks and were very explicit in their reasons for their individual decision. Yet one interpretation has become dominant: "situation not disposition" has become the incantation that must dispel any thought of individual inclination and personal choice.

It is true that neither laboratory experiments nor historical research of judicial documents have shown which personality characteristics differentiate perpetrators from anyone else. But, then, the scholars have not searched very hard.

Genocidal killers are especially difficult to investigate. On the job they were completely inaccessible to outsiders. After the fact, they had every motive for hiding their past deeds. Most of what we know comes from judicial trials. Before their judges, the perpetrators tried to disavow any personal involvement in their genocidal work. They did their best to seem like average, uncommitted, ordinary men. If they did not always convince their judges, at least they succeeded in being portrayed that way in the scholarly literature.

If instead perpetrators are seen for what they are, as people with a past and with a personality of their own, three questions arise: Did they initially have certain characteristics that made them more likely to end up in a genocidal situation? How did they as genocidaires cope with that situation? And how, as postgenocidaires, did they adapt to the conditions after the episode of mass annihilation?

These are the questions raised in chapter 8. Even now, when we have evidence from so many trials of genocidal perpetrators, a growing collection of historical studies on perpetrators at work, and a considerable number of memoirs, biographies, and in-depth interviews, there is not much to go by. On the face of it, the killers succeeded in surviving long periods of mass slaughter with little personal damage. Apparently, most of them were capable of acting under those circumstances without moral misgivings, without a sense of personal accountability, and, above all, without pity. Maybe they formerly had such sentiments, perhaps they still experienced them, but it seems that they did not let these feelings get in the way of their genocidal work. This should be the point of departure in an attempt to reconstruct their personal dispositions, varied as they were. In this perspective, the perpetrators seem to fit, more or less, a pattern of stunted mentalization, familiar from the theory of early personality development.

Many perpetrators not only maintained themselves in the genocidal setting but, once it was all over, were able to adapt to a society in which very different conditions prevailed. This, too, demands certain qualifications (or disqualifications), abilities on the continuum from lying, denying, forgetting, deceiving oneself, distorting, avoiding, and simply making sure that the subject never comes up—once again, acting *as if nothing ever happened.*

Are we contemporary students of mass annihilation, whether historians, lawyers, or social scientists, in a position to understand, let alone evaluate, the available evidence, scanty as it is in most cases? After all, most of us grew up in times of peace, in secure and prosperous societies that for generations have been spared the violence of revolution, foreign invasion and occupation, civil war, or mass annihilation. Only some volunteered or were drafted to fight in foreign wars and thus have had firsthand experience with large-scale violence. Even such experiences of battle are far removed from mass annihilation, although every now and then soldiers commit acts of violence against unarmed bystanders: "collateral damage" at best, murderous frenzy against helpless civilians at worst. Finally, among the older generations there are the survivors (and perpetrators) of the mass murders by the Nazis and those who have survived other, more recent genocidal episodes. Yet the experience of inflicting violence and of fearing, fleeing, and suffering it, are far removed from the existence in the more secure, more affluent countries in this world. That may make mass annihilation even harder to understand.[11] Far removed from actual violence as contemporary citizens of stable states are, they need to believe that those who commit violence are either somehow exceptional—uniquely evil or uniquely diseased—or, on the contrary, that the perpetrators are people much like everyone else but that it is the uniquely evil force of extraordinary circumstance that brings them to their deeds.[12] Indeed, were it not for the state's effective restraints, people might harm and kill for many reasons, but they never do so for no reason at all.[13]

On the other hand, the present generations of scholars, untouched as they are by mass violence, are neither implicated as perpetrators nor involved as victims. That should free them to study the genocidal past with more detachment and avoid "undue" identification with the victims or equally undue disidentification from the perpetrators: they should steer clear of both the "engagement bias" and the "revulsion bias."[14] But this is just a methodological precept, not a method; it tells one what to aim for, not how to achieve it.

To that end, as Roy Baumeister counsels, "It is necessary to suspend one's sympathy for the victims and to make a serious, honest effort to look at events from the perpetrator's point of view."[15] This comes somewhat closer to suggesting a method, but it fails to explain how to accomplish that effort. Yet one way to do so might be to try and monitor the feelings that the victim's suffering and the perpetrator's atrocities evoke in the beholder, in oneself. Finding out through introspection how the accounts of the victims and the perpetrators affect one's own feelings may help to better understand their emotions.[16] A rare account of such methodological self-scrutiny is provided by Robert Jay Lifton, who indeed does try to empathize with the medical murderers he interviews, without ever identifying with them, trying all the while to keep the fate of their victims and his own moral convictions in mind: "Whatever empathy I mustered was in the service of something else: bearing witness."[17]

Even then, a major obstacle to understanding remains. It is assumed that perpetrators do feel and think and have a point of view. But maybe a good part of their mental functioning consists in not feeling, and not thinking and having no ideas of their own. That indeed is hard to reconstruct.

Once the genocidal episode came to an end, the regime and its perpetrators tried to hide what had occurred, destroy the evidence, impose complete silence, and prevent any attempt at revealing the facts. In that sense, every effort to reconstruct what happened, including this one, is an attempt to undo that repression and therefore is a partisan endeavor.

And, of course, in the last analysis, the scholarly detachment, even if it is doubled by an attempt to imagine the perpetrator's experience, remains a question of method, a scholarly effort, not insincere, but not entirely authentic either. In the end, there is no way I can deny my revulsion at the disasters human beings have inflicted on other human beings, nor is there any need for it.

CHAPTER 2

Ordinary Perpetrators and Modernity
The Situationist Consensus

A BROAD AND STRONG CONSENSUS PREVAILS in the social sciences about which personality traits distinguish genocidal perpetrators from other human beings: there are none. A small percentage of the killers, roughly the same as in society at large, say 5 percent, may indeed show psychopathologies that make them impervious to the suffering of others and even cause them to enjoy it.[1] The vast majority of genocidaires, however, display the same variety of traits and in roughly the same frequencies as the population at large. There is near unanimity among scholars, a rare exception in the human sciences, that nothing in their personality predisposes the perpetrators more than anyone else to commit their murderous acts. In the very titles of their books, the adherents of this view announce their conclusion: the killers are "ordinary men."[2] What must be explained is "how ordinary people commit extraordinary evil."

The argument follows a fixed itinerary. It begins with the psychological tests that were administered to the Nazi defendants at the Nuremberg trials by Allied psychologists and psychiatrists. The psychiatrist who investigated the overlords of the Nazi regime believed that some of them did indeed qualify as pathological cases.[3] These men had after all exerted themselves for years to see millions of people deported from home, worked to death in slave camps, and finished off by bullets or poison gas. They had been utterly devoted to Adolf Hitler and were fanatical anti-Semites. But the psychologists' tests showed nothing out of the ordinary, except in some cases an intelligence score above the average (but, one might add, that is not all that unusual among the holders of high corporate or administrative office).

The chiefs of the Nazi regime, each in his own way, were rather remarkable personalities. That psychological tests did not reflect any anomaly was seen not as a shortcoming of the tests but rather as evidence of the mental health of the persons tested.[4] They were, however, found to share high scores on certain traits that are not per se pathological: high ambition, overconfidence, and an "ambient" style of problem-solving.[5]

The Nuremberg defendants constituted the top of the Nazi hierarchy. Many thousands of Nazi criminals were tried by military tribunals in occupied Germany or by the courts of the separate Allied powers (not counting the tens of thousands sentenced by Soviet courts). The perpetrators of the Holocaust constituted a small minority among the accused Nazis. After 1948, in the German Federal Republic, they were not prosecuted in sizable numbers until the 1960s. Even so, out of the (roughly estimated) one hundred thousand perpetrators involved in the mass killings of Jews, only some seven hundred were tried and five hundred convicted by West German courts as of 1992.[6] It therefore took some time before the run-of-the-mill mass murderers became the subject of psychological research, based on judicial documents. Nevertheless, these trials did much to awaken the awareness of Nazi crimes and generated unique material on the perpetrators and the social context of their actions. Most subsequent historical research was based on this judiciary evidence.

If anything focused global attention on the Nazi crimes, it was the spectacular abduction of Adolf Eichmann from his hideout in Argentina and his subsequent trial, in the spring of 1961, before an Israeli court in Jerusalem. In most war crime trials, the defendants had presented themselves as average citizens, not especially motivated for their task, lukewarm at most in their ideological convictions, career-minded maybe, but not wildly ambitious, not much given to racial or ethnic hatred nor driven by passionate loyalties to the leader or the party. Strong motivations after all, might betray a personal commitment to their murderous task and bring their individual responsibility to the fore.

This camouflage strategy was brought to perfection by Eichmann's defender, Robert Servatius, who may not have fooled the prosecution or the judge, but certainly influenced some of those who reported on the trial, most notoriously Hannah Arendt (and, for that matter, the Dutch writer Harry Mulisch).[7] Even at the time, it was well known that Eichmann had been a fanatical Jew hunter who knew full well what fate lay in store for his prey. In interviews with Willem Sassen, his SS acquaintance in Argentina, which were excerpted in *Time* before the trial, expurgated by the Sassen family, Eichmann had said that he regretted nothing, but if they had killed all 10.3 million Jews, then he would have been satisfied: "I would say: 'All right, we have exterminated an enemy.'"[8] Arendt mentions that Eichmann during and after the war had repeatedly boasted: "I will jump into my grave laughing, because the fact that I have the death of five million Jews on my conscience gives me extraordinary satisfaction." Yet she dismisses this rather unusual confession as "rodomontade" (a boast) and adds: "Bragging was the vice that was Eichmann's undoing."[9] But as a matter of fact, Eichmann was not bragging; he was more or less accurate, and it was certainly not this vice that got him in trouble but the fact that he indeed had been pivotal in the extermination of many millions of Jews.

Arendt and many others who reported on the trial were enthralled by the fashionable notion of the time that the Nazi (and the Soviet) state was a mighty machine, manned by countless nameless, faceless bureaucrats and soldiers who were no more than cogs in the apparatus, obediently and unthinkingly doing whatever they were told, without much conviction of their own, except for loyalty to the system. But certainly in Eichmann's case, this was an expedient masquerade, set up by the defense, and it went together very well with the spirit of the times: "Befehl ist Befehl" (Orders are orders) had become the ironic watchword of the 1960s, implying the opposite: that people should never again hide behind their superiors' commands and that they should learn to judge for themselves and heed their individual conscience.[10]

Arendt depicts Eichmann as a pompous idiot, "genuinely incapable of uttering a single sentence that was not a cliché." Poking fun at his malapropisms, she observes with dead precision, "His inability to speak was closely connected with an inability to think, namely, to think from the standpoint of somebody else."[11]

Eichmann, whose efforts to expel, deport, and exterminate millions exceeded even the orders he received, who continued to the very last moment when even Heinrich Himmler had changed course, who said he despised colleagues who just followed orders, was the least apt example of an average bureaucrat, of just another number in the huge equation of the Nazi state.[12] Eichmann was totally devoted to Hitler and National Socialism, fanatically ambitious and without any trace of conscience or empathy regarding his victims even when he was directly confronted with their fate.

Were the perpetrators banal? Arendt's thesis on the "banality of evil" does not stand critical scrutiny, certainly not as applied to Adolf Eichmann or other Nazi leaders, nor for that matter to the rank-and-file killers. Her model might, however, fit the countless minor middlemen of the Holocaust: the administrators in the civil registry who passed on the names of the prospective victims, the local police who rounded them up, the engineers who transported them in cattle cars, the contractors who built the gas chambers and supplied the extermination camps . . . most of them, indeed, were in some sense banal.

It was Hannah Arendt's great, albeit not unique, accomplishment that she took the *idées reçues* of her epoch, combined them with widespread though unrealistic notions about Adolf Eichmann, and presented these musings as profoundly innovative insights all her own.[13] Her readers, being told with the seal of Arendt's authorial and philosophical rank, that what they had been thinking all along was novel and profound, piously gobbled it all up.

Not even Hannah Arendt herself believed in the *Banality of Evil*, as the subtitle of her book on Eichmann in Jerusalem has it.[14] She later corrected that catchy phrase, stating that she had meant to point out the banality of the evildoers.[15] But the words had already caught on and now probably express the greatest *bêtise* in the small but widely quoted repertoire of clichés about the Holocaust and about genocide in general.[16] The isolation, deportation, extreme exploitation, and final extermination of millions of people is not banal. Calling it that is frivolous.[17]

MILGRAM'S PUNISHING EXPERIMENT AND ITS AMBIGUOUS OUTCOMES

In the meantime and no doubt inspired by the Eichmann trial, a series of spectacular psychological experiments received rapt attention in the United States and across the world. Stanley Milgram had invited volunteers at Yale University to participate in what he presented to them as an educational experiment. They were told that they would be randomly assigned to the role of either "teacher" or "learner." In fact, all of them were made teachers and the learner was played by an actor, a plant. The teachers were expected to present the learner with a series of random words and administer an electrical shock each time he made an error in reproducing the sequence from memory. The setup was presented as an experiment about the effects of punishment by different teachers on memorization by the learner. As the "shocks" increased in strength, the actor playing the learner would simulate growing discomfort, and then signal more and more intense pain, until he fell silent. The electric shocks went from hardly perceptible to "dangerous" at 300 volts and beyond, up to 450 volts. Or so the subjects were led to believe.

Against all expectations, including Milgram's, two-thirds of the subjects went all the way and administered the highest and seemingly quite dangerous jolts. They did so under the adamant insistence of the researcher that they continue the experiment to the end. Most subjects protested, visibly and audibly torn between compassion and compliance. Nevertheless they went on to obey the experimenter and to shock the hapless learner. However, a considerable proportion did not obey: from one-third to four-fifths, depending on the staging of the experiment. Thus, there always remained a considerable share of naysayers who would ignore the researcher's adamant orders.

Apparently, the general expectation at the time had been that people would not obey if it went against their individual conscience. When it turned out that many or even most did, this finding became the overriding message from the experiment. But to people who would have thought from the outset that most people will do what they are told, Milgram finally proved that among a varying but sizable proportion of the test population, disobedience prevailed.[18]

Stanley Milgram made a film of his obedience experiments. In the very first scene, an ordinary man, undistinguished in every respect, duly starts out to do what the experimenter tells him to.

As the voltage increases, the teacher's uneasiness visibly mounts. Then, quite abruptly, he swivels on his chair to face the impassive experimenter, folds his arms across his chest, and squarely refuses to go on unless someone goes in and makes sure that the learner is all right. The experimenter tells him to continue with the arguments that are in his script. Finally, he says: "You have no choice." At that point, the teacher answers, "How do you mean? I have many choices." And he stops. An ordinary man, "just like you and me," under the same circumstances refused to inflict harm on another human being.

In another brief vignette, Milgram describes a woman who quietly complied as teacher until she noticed discomfort in the learner and equally quietly refused to continue. In the interview after the experiment she told Milgram that she grew up in Nazi Germany: "Perhaps we have seen too much pain."[19] Strangely enough, Milgram makes nothing much of these acts of resistance, even though many other subjects in his experiment refused to shock the "victim."

Conversely, quite a few teachers continued to give electric shocks to the very last, at a level that they were made to believe was very dangerous or even lethal. Some did so without any apparent misgivings or hesitations. These subjects just did as they were told to do, they said, and it was none of their responsibility. The entire episode left them unperturbed, or so it seemed.

Because the conditions in each experiment remained the same, the different outcomes must be attributed to the difference in personality of the subjects. That is the hidden side of Milgram's findings: personal dispositions are essential in determining what people do when a person in authority presses them to badly hurt (and possibly kill) another person. Stanley Milgram, the star witness for situationism, also supplied the evidence for its partial refutation.

The Milgram experiment is generally remembered as an indication that a great majority of ordinary people would commit atrocities if ordered to do so by a person in a position of authority. It is quite customary to conclude from these results that most people would collaborate with a real genocidal regime. But no one has drawn the same conclusion in the opposite direction and decided on exactly the same grounds that a very sizable minority, or even a majority, under a genocidal regime would join the resistance. Probably, the most sensible conclusion is that the outcomes of laboratory experiments must not be directly applied to real-life situations, either way.

Milgram did not find any significant differences between the compliers and the resisters. He recorded some elementary data about his subjects, such as their age, occupation, and education. There was a debriefing of individuals and a group meeting sometime after the experiment. But he left it at that.

The proportions of the two categories varied with the parameters that Milgram introduced in the setup of the experiment: the proportion of refusers increased when the element of authority was reduced (no lab coat; an ordinary room in a plain building; no experimenter present, just "other subjects"; the presence of other—planted—"teachers" who would refuse to go along with the experiment or on the contrary would comply ostentatiously), or if the element of empathy was intensified (a visible "learner"; the opportunity to hold his hand). This strongly suggests that the subject's reactions in the experiment are determined by the balance between the opposing tendencies of compliance and empathy. Reactions vary with the experimental setup but also between subjects in each experimental setting. Clearly, within a given setting the obedient and the defiant differ in the degree to which each is disposed to comply with authority and to empathize with a victim. And apparently these differences in personality could not be measured by the tests available at the time: "It is hard to relate performance to personality because we really do not know very much about how to measure personality."[20]

Milgram, and no doubt others who replicated his experiments, regularly came across subjects who "went all the way" without showing any reluctance or even uneasiness. Afterward one of them explained to Milgram: "I had to follow orders. That's how I figured it." This compliant participant argued that the victim brought punishment on himself for being "a more or less stubborn person." And yes, he could have stopped shocking the learner, if only the experimenter would have told him to.[21] What Milgram had stumbled on was the Rosetta stone of genocide studies: an innocent genocidaire. Someone with the mind of a mass murderer but without any guilt, who could have answered any question without shame of past crimes or fear of future punishment. However, after the presentation of a series of most enlightening thumbnail case descriptions, Milgram does not pursue this path further. It is a pity Milgram and his followers did not make more of an effort to go beyond the quantification of experimental data and try to explore in more depth the persons they dealt with.

Some people may have both a strong inclination to comply with the experimenter and a high tendency to empathize with the learner: they should experience increasingly strong inner conflict and get more and more upset as the experimental session goes on. Their readiness to administer shocks in the course of the experiment remains quite unpredictable, since two squarely opposed tendencies vie for primacy in their decisions. Other people might be less sensitive to authority or to the suffering of others, and they should not be much moved either way by the proceedings, but their choices, too, are hard to predict for lack of a strong motive either way. They are "lukewarm." The remaining two combinations, high compliance–low empathy and low compliance–high empathy, should allow us to predict with some confidence where the subject would end up on the shock scale in each experimental setting.

Paradoxically, after having demonstrated that obedience to

authority figures was much more common than many would have expected, Milgram's followers concluded that personal psychology was irrelevant in explaining compliance to authority. Supposedly, it depended on the characteristics of the situation alone. But this leaves unexplained that even within one and the same experimental context, a sizable proportion of subjects did go the other way. Because personal disposition was discarded as an explanation, such individual choices could only be relegated to error or chance.[22] Milgram's finding that there was no evidence for a systematic difference between naysayers and compliers was constructed as evidence for their similarity. Yet as we shall see, absence of evidence is not evidence of absence.

Milgram's experiment has been repeated many times, with all sorts of variations, but the main finding has been confirmed time and again: if an authority figure insists, many or most subjects will agree to inflict what they believe to be considerable suffering, even potentially mortal harm, on a third person.

This was and still is a most revealing experiment. But what exactly it reveals is not all that clear. The results are usually interpreted as strong evidence for a widespread tendency to obey authority figures such as psychology professors in white coats in the research laboratory of a prestigious university. And indeed, in the standard version of the experiment two-thirds of the subjects did go "all the way."

But did Milgram's subjects believe in the "reality" of the punishment that they inflicted on the student? That is in itself hard to credit. Nobody in their right mind would ever accept the idea that someone, anyone, would be electrocuted in the presence of certified researchers in the psychology lab on the campus of Yale University in New Haven, Connecticut. Nothing even remotely like that has ever occurred before or since.[23] A moment's reflection would have convinced the participants in the experiment that this could not be for real. Nevertheless, it is clear from Milgram's account that his subjects did take the situation very seriously and that many suffered intensely from having to inflict severe pain on the unfortunate "learner," in compliance with the experimenter's orders. But if the situation had been really "real," the compliant subjects would have risked electrocution themselves, since the penalty for murder in the state of Connecticut was still the electric chair; the defense that they were strongly pressured to administer lethal shocks, or that the experimenter had told them he assumed all responsibility, would not have absolved them. What is more, almost all adult citizens must have been aware of these facts. Inevitably, the thought must have crossed the subjects' minds at the time.[24]

Unquestionably, there was a gamelike aspect to the situation. The experiment must have been experienced by the "teacher" subjects as a very serious game. Apparently, the subjects were suspending their disbelief, just as the participants in a serious game tend to do. There were, moreover, some most significant ambiguities in the presentation of the experiment to the subjects: during the introductory talk, while the subjects had still to decide whether to participate, they were assured by the experimenter himself that there was "no danger" involved. During the session, the experimenter would answer every inquiry from a subject by saying that "no lasting damage" would result from the shocks.[25] But in the experimental room, the subjects sat in front of a console with labels under the rightmost buttons, the last ones to be pressed (375 volts and higher), which explicitly mentioned just that: "danger, severe shock." This ambiguity is all the more significant in that there are strong indications that the more the subjects increased the voltage, the more they trusted the experimenter's assertions that the learner would suffer no harm from it.[26]

Does the experiment show that the majority of people in real life are ready to electrocute someone if a person of authority tells them to? No. Does the experiment show that people can get carried away in an experimental situation and will do almost anything not to antagonize a person of authority, even act as if they were electrocuting a third person? Yes.

In other words, experiments are a kind of serious game. If the subject is "duped" in many respects (about the role of the experimenter, about the fake nature of the "learner victim," about the pseudo-shocks), this one aspect of the situation—that it was not entirely real, that it was all a sort of game—may not have eluded the participants.

Nowadays, ethics commissions would not allow the same or similar experiments to be carried out. Clearly, external moral constraints on psychological experimental research have become stricter. The strengthening of ethical canons in psychological experimentation is in and of itself a fascinating subject for sociological analysis, but not the most relevant in this context. Moreover, if the experiment were held today, chances are that a significant percentage of those invited to participate would have heard of Milgram's research and could no longer be made to go along with the suggestion of "reality" of the punishment inflicted by the subjects on the planted "learner."[27]

The psychologist Jerry Burger for that reason excluded from a later, meticulous replication experiment volunteers who had followed more than two college classes in psychology (since they were likely to have heard of the Milgram experiment) and in order to comply with the new ethics requirements, limited the shocks that could be administered to 150 volts instead of 450 volts. Burger applied a number of psychological tests to the subjects before the experiment. He found that people who were more disposed toward empathy and control were indeed slightly less prone to continue all the way to 150 volts. "However, the data were not entirely consistent or easily interpretable." Participants in the experiment who scored high on empathy were more reluctant to administer shocks but not less likely to continue until the end.[28]

Another psychologist, Thomas Blass, has reviewed the many replications of the Milgram experiment. He finds that major variations in the situational setup of the experiment did not much affect the outcome. However, some personality traits did make a difference in the participants' behavior: "authoritarianism" by one measure or another did make a difference, as did the aforementioned "trust" in the experimenter and, also, (lack of) empathy with the learner. Blass proposes an "interactionist" approach to the problem of obedience to authority that takes into account both situational and dispositional aspects.[29]

Milgram himself remained rather reserved in his interpretations.[30] But his experiment became a icon of modern self-consciousness: "If the situation demands it, everyone is a murderer." It was Milgram's objective to demonstrate how willingly most people comply with authority and, implicitly, with the enormous authority that science and scientists hold over ordinary people. Since then, writes Burger, "most social psychologists appear to agree on one point. The obedience studies are a dramatic demonstration of how individuals typically underestimate the power of situational forces when explaining another person's behavior."[31] Fifty years on, what stands out most is the authority that laboratory experiments hold, most of all, for scholars in the human sciences.

The next stop on this line is the Stanford prison experiment by Philip Zimbardo, in which a group of student volunteers was randomly divided into "prisoners" and "wardens." After just a few days of groupwise role playing, the students had begun to behave according to script, the prisoners becoming ever more submissive, the wardens more and more overbearing and sometimes quite unpleasant. At a colleague's insistence, Zimbardo called the

whole thing off "before it would have gone too far." It therefore remains an open question how far the groups would have gone, the
wardens in rudeness and the prisoners in subservience, whether the
participants on either side would have found ways to stop further
escalation, or whether they would have continued on the same slip-
pery slope. (This incrementalism, from "bad to worse," is of course
also a feature of the Milgram experiment with its shock buttons of
increasing intensity.) Zimbardo drew some drastic lessons from the
adventure: "Any deed that any human has ever committed, however horrible, is possible for any of us—under the right or wrong
situational circumstances. That knowledge does not excuse evil:
rather it democratizes it, sharing its blame among ordinary actors
rather than declaring it the province only of deviants and despots
—of Them but not Us." Sweeping as the statement is, it sums up
the radical situationist position and its moral stance very well.[32]

The central theme in Zimbardo's game was not so much "obedience to authority" but rather "conformism to the group," no
doubt an equally fundamental aspect of mass violence. Zimbardo's
experiment quite likely also concerned reactions to authority, this
time about an authority relinquishing his control and allowing at
least some of the students to misbehave. . . . The "wardens" must
have realized that the experimenter "let them do it" and the "prisoners" must have realized that he "let them have it." Zimbardo regularly interfered in the "experiment" by introducing new elements
or giving instructions to some participants.[33] Again, the situation
must be studied as a very serious game. But in this case, too, if
the students trusted that things would not be allowed to "really"
get out of hand, they were right in thinking so. The Milgram and
Zimbardo experiments are no doubt quite meaningful, the prison
experiment much less so than the shocking trials, but what they
mean remains an open question.

ORDINARY MEN OR ORDINARY GERMANS

The third phase in the discussion on genocidal perpetrators, after Arendt on Eichmann, and after Milgram's obedience experiment, came when students of mass violence began to explore the judicial documents on Nazi genocidaires. The pioneering and meticulous research by Christopher Browning produced the classic in this field: *Ordinary Men*. That title is followed by a subtitle: *Reserve Police Battalion 101 and the Final Solution in Poland*. The book's message is contained in this juxtaposition: the mass executions of millions of Jews in eastern Europe were in fact the work of "ordinary people." Browning makes his case convincingly. Most of his findings have been confirmed, and some vehemently criticized, by Daniel Goldhagen in his study of the same battalion, *Hitler's Willing Executioners: Ordinary Germans and the Holocaust*.

The evidence assembled by Browning, and by Goldhagen, is most perturbing in many respects. Most important, the recruits for Police Battalion 101 were not especially selected for their mission; they were recruited among somewhat elderly cohorts, not yet enlisted in any other uniformed service and quite unfit for front duties, let alone for the SS. The Hamburg policemen who initially were part of Reserve Police Battalion 101 were assigned to other units in the spring of 1941. The men left to participate in the executions were quite representative of the German (male) population in its entirety. The men expected to be recruited for police duty and had no idea beforehand of what lay in store for them.

On these points Browning and Goldhagen are in complete agreement. Their main difference may be gleaned from their subtitles: "ordinary" the men of Battalion 101 were, but were they ordinary "men," as Browning has it, or ordinary "Germans," in Goldhagen's words?

Under police interrogation in the 1960s, long after the war, most men of Battalion 101 denied any particular animosity against

Jews or a special commitment to Nazi ideals. They may well have wished to conceal the motivations that they brought to their killing assignment. Browning and Goldhagen have produced ample evidence of incidents of obscene and barbaric cruelty. Many men of Battalion 101 did not just follow the orders to kill by the thousands, according to schedule, but exceeded them on their own initiative. Even if later they denied strong anti-Semitic feelings, at the time these atrocities were committed with fanatic hatred and contempt of Jews.[34] In this respect, the draftees of Battalion 101 may have not been entirely "ordinary men."

It may be true that anti-Semitism in Germany in the early 1930s was no more endemic or vicious than in France and certainly not as rampant as in Austria or some east European countries.[35] But only in Nazi Germany was anti-Semitism crucial to the official ideology of the regime and were the institutions of the state mobilized for genocide.[36] Moreover, German culture had been traditionally authoritarian and militaristic, especially under Prussian influence. The sudden collapse of the German war effort in 1918 had spawned a subculture of accusation, resentment, and revenge among conservatives and veterans. The monopoly of violence in the Weimar Republic was eroded by the terrorist paramilitary Freikorps, while the hyperinflation of the 1920s and the global economic crisis of 1929 contributed to a climate of insecurity, despair, and rancor.[37] This was the context in which the Nazis grabbed power and Hitler spread his fanatical anti-Semitism. In these respects, Germany was indeed special, and so were the Germans, even "ordinary" Germans. If the Germans were different in these respects, they certainly were not unique. The German nation did produce genocidal perpetrators en masse, but it was not the only nation to do so either during World War II or in the twentieth century.

The conclusion must be that over a stretch of time an encompassing social situation may transform the dispositions of the people who live through that period. An authoritarian and militaristic tradition, defeat in war, political violence, and economic crisis, coupled with an endemic anti-Semitism that became state ideology, did affect the Germans of those days and may have rendered many among them more amenable to the massive killing of human beings whom they had been taught to consider "subhuman" and even "inhuman." But this does not make German anti-Semitism unique. Among some other nations hatred of Jews was at least as widespread, fanatical, and murderous. Browning and Goldhagen differ in essence about the weight that should be assigned to German anti-Semitism in explaining the annihilation of the Jews.

Even though the men of Battalion 101 were given a chance beforehand to excuse themselves from their assignment, only very few (twelve out of five hundred) took that opportunity. Browning, and following him other students of the "Holocaust by bullets" behind the Eastern Front, have shown that the overwhelming majority of men who were ordered to exterminate Jews and partisans did what they were told without much protest. They were supported in their task by Ukrainians, Latvians, Lithuanians, and other east Europeans who were as murderous or worse. Most of these Hiwis, short for *Hilfswilliger,* "willing helpers," were recruited among the Soviet prisoners of war from the border zones and thus spared almost certain death by starvation.

The case of Battalion 101, well documented as it is by now, is crucial for our understanding of genocidal behavior. It demonstrates the overriding effect of social context on individual choices and actions. It also shows the importance of a cultural background of shared convictions and sentiments regarding "other people": such collective notions create individual dispositions that may well facilitate murderous behavior as ordered. "Situation" and "disposition" are therefore not opposites. Dispositions are shaped by situations over time—in social processes, that is. Social processes, in turn, are the result of the myriads of interactions among people acting in good part according to their dispositions.

Central to the explanation of genocidal episodes is one particular kind of shared dispositions, deeply ingrained in the cultural context: groupwise identifications *with* and disidentifications *from* other human beings. These processes of identification and disidentification are the subject of chapter 3. The social psychological correlates of inclusion and exclusion are part of a much wider process of *societal and mental compartmentalization*, essential conditions for mass annihilation to occur, as is discussed in chapters 6 and 8.

What is known about Reserve Police Battalion 101 and similar extermination units of the Nazi regime comes almost entirely from judicial documents, reports on the police interrogation of former executioners.[38] Although these may be the best sources available, they still make for considerable distortion, with a systematic bias. Those who were interrogated had every interest to portray themselves as men who had no inkling of what they were being recruited for, who just happened to be picked for the job without any design or initiative of their own, who just did as they were told, and no more, without much conviction or diligence, without hatred for their victims (and without any pity either). They obeyed orders that they considered legal and binding, and they operated in time of war, when carnage occurred on both sides and one party's crimes justified the other side's misdeeds. They preferred to ignore the incommensurability of the total extermination of the Jews of Europe. They denied the incidents of wanton barbarity. They lied about their own part in them. Even those who had refrained from unrequired atrocities or tried to prevent their peers from committing them, who had avoided the shootings as much they could or who had incidentally helped some victims to escape, usually kept quiet about it to their interrogators because they did not want their fellow defendants to look worse in comparison.

Judicial evidence tends to reinforce the impression of depersonalization in the perpetrators. Before their judges, the men minimized their initiatives, convictions, emotions, ambitions, and desires. Their personalities pale in the process. They come to look more and more like Hannah Arendt's version of Eichmann, and for the same reasons he chose to present himself in that manner.

What is often lost in the trial documentation is the individual diversity in dealing with the genocidal situation. There was indeed a continuum of cooperation with the imposed project of extermination. Some men were "willing executioners," volunteering for the Jew hunt, eager to join the roundups and the shootings and given to haphazard cruelty (and sometimes equally random kindness, too, since unpredictable favors on a whim would even better display their supreme power over other human beings). Other men limited their participation to the tasks that were explicitly demanded from them, without much enthusiasm, but without objection either. And, finally, there were men who tried to exploit what little room for maneuver they perceived in order to stay away from the roundups, forced marches, and executions.

It is through these variations of comportment in one and the same situation that differences in individual personalities and dispositions are revealed. But even in the rare cases that individual behavior within the genocidal context has been documented, it is hard to infer from this evidence what the individual's dispositions were, and even harder to trace these personality characteristics back to earlier life experiences in childhood or adolescence. So far, this sort of research has not even been tried, neither for the perpetrators of the Holocaust nor for later instances of mass extermination.

A remarkable consensus across the fields of history, political science, sociology, and social psychology holds that genocidal per-

petrators as a group are not distinct in disposition from the population at large. It is the situation that turns people of diverse background and inclination into mass killers.

This apparently factual conclusion has had an enormous impact on moral thinking about "contemporary men and modern society." The vulgarization of the Arendt-Milgram-Browning tradition has led to the grand cliché of our times: potentially, all people
are genocidal perpetrators; they have just never been in a situation
where that would show.

The argument that the pressures of the social situation are
almost always uppermost, and for almost everyone, has a hidden
twist: apparently, if the great majority of human beings tend to
swiftly and completely adapt to their situation, obey authority and
conform to their peers, then this must be because of their inner disposition to do so in situations that elicit it. They are destined to be
malleable. But this vision of humanity implies an "oversocialized
conception of man" that glosses over the contradictory external
pressures and equally conflicting inner inclinations that human beings must cope with in one way or another.[39]

And yet, the scholars who have kept their cool all through the
descriptions of the most horrible atrocities become quite emotional
when they come to their blanket verdict on humankind. As be-
hooves all learned authors, they write in the third person throughout. There is no "I," no writer as a first person, in their text. There
is no "you" either, no reader to be addressed directly, in the second
person. But each time when these authors make their fateful statement, unfailingly in either the first or the last pages of their book,
an "I" and a "you" appear out of nowhere and they write: "*You
and I, under the same circumstances, might have done the same thing.*"
That is how "I" (that is, the author) and "you" (that is, the reader)
are introduced to each other. After that one sentence, the two will
not say another word to each other. But this should do: you and

I would have raped, tortured, shot, burned, gassed thousands of human beings . . . *under the same circumstances.*[40]

First of all, the fateful phrase: "If you and I had been in the same circumstances," is counterfactual and cannot be determined to be either true or false. Moreover, the same or even similar circumstances are extremely unlikely to recur in your or my life. The phrase is also counterintuitive, since people find it very hard to imagine themselves as mass executioners. Yet the idea that in a certain social context, in a given situation, some people will commit acts that they would not otherwise dream of is quite plausible. Some people are more likely to do so than others, and some will resist, even at considerable risk to themselves. Others may be willing and even eager to do what they are told. That does certainly depend on their situation of the moment, but not alone: it depends also on their prior experience and personal history, in one word, a term that has so often been declared out of bounds: on their personal *disposition*. And in other words: on their *particular personality*.

The argument that the situation alone entirely shapes behavior denies the actors' responsibility for their own choices and therefore goes a long way to exculpate them beforehand.[41] But the opposite position, that the actors' dispositions completely shape their actions, would likewise deny their responsibility. This reasoning is equally valid for both positions, but only in their deterministic version, when it is assumed that either situation or disposition fully dictates a person's behavior.

The point is that sometimes people are confronted with moral choices. They may not have been aware of it at the time, but still they had a moral decision to make. And the executioners made the wrong one. Those who have never been tried in this manner, for whom the bell never tolled, have been lucky so far and can continue to afford the belief that they would have known when the moment of truth had arrived and that they would then have made the right choice. Many perpetrators realize that they did not. That is the truth they must face and which many of them for most of their life try not to confront.

Mass Annihilation and Modernity

So far, the focus has been on the executioners, who found themselves trapped in genocidal situations to which most of them tried to adapt as well they could, while a very rare few managed to extricate themselves from the situation or simply refused its demands. But these situations had been created by the genocidal regime and its institutions: the army, the police, the militia, the civil registry, transport and communication networks, and the official media . . . . How could such regimes emerge and how did they operate?

Just as there formerly existed a naive tendency to regard the perpetrators as psychopathic monsters, so there was an equally simplistic view of genocidal regimes as a throwback to earlier, barbaric times. Neither notion is taken seriously in the scholarly literature, but authors use the one or the other view as a contrasting backdrop for their own arguments. Not surprisingly, when it comes to genocidal regimes, they argue that these were not at all atavistic; instead, they represent the essence of modernity.

During World War I, millions of young Europeans found themselves forced to annihilate those on the other side with machine guns and mustard gas. At the time, many asked themselves whether this had been a reversal into barbarism or, on the contrary, the product of industrial society, the bureaucratic state, rational planning, and mass politics—in a word, of the Modern Age. The subsequent emergence of Communist, Fascist, and National Socialist regimes made that question even more urgent.

The debate has a long and respectable pedigree. One of the

more recent voices is that of Zygmunt Bauman, who published a reflection on genocide that gained him wide renown: *Modernity and the Holocaust.* The core message of his book is that the Holocaust is not some aberration of contemporary civilization but "a characteristically modern phenomenon that cannot be understood out of the context or cultural tendencies and technical achievements of modernity." Not only have the modern state and modern bureaucracy brought domestic peace and a defense against outside attack, but they also contain at their very core the potential of murderous destruction. Moreover, according to Bauman, the civilizing process, in its drive toward evermore pervasive rationality, is essentially a two-sided phenomenon. It not only promotes humane and lawful modes of social existence, but also facilitates the "rationalization" of the unrestrained use of violence, devoid of any moral calculus or ethical inhibition.[42]

There is no denying, if anybody wanted to deny it, that the Holocaust occurred in this, contemporary world. The same applies to the vast extermination campaigns in Soviet Russia and Communist China and so many other exterminatory episodes in the most recent past. In fact, similar mass killings may be going on, somewhere in the world, at this very moment.

The problem is that words like *modernity, civilization,* and *rationality* are so all-encompassing that they refer to almost any aspect of contemporary society. By themselves, they cover everything and therefore explain nothing. All too easily a "critique of modernity" slides into a blanket condemnation of contemporary society and its inhabitants, us: People may think that they came a long way, that they know better than their ancestors. (In one respect they do: our contemporaries have some knowledge of what came before, whereas their ancestors knew nothing about their future, today's present.) People may want to believe that they live in a better, more reasonable, more knowledgeable world, but behold, all this is no more than arrogance, hubris, pride, according to this critique of modernity.

Bauman set out to define the implications of the Holocaust for an understanding of present society. He especially hoped to change sociology at its very core. After all, the reality of the Holocaust completely transforms, or should transform, our conception of present-day society. Bauman may not completely have succeeded in this task, but he did signal its urgency to a broad readership. And he is correct in pointing out that the reality of the Holocaust and of subsequent genocides has hardly left an imprint on the discipline of sociology.

According to Bauman, sociologists identify themselves with scientific culture and therefore prefer to avoid any references to ethical considerations. This is part of their very methodology: "Sociology promoted, as its own criteria of propriety, the same principles of rational action it visualized as constitutive of its object."[43] None of this is fair; only a small minority of social scientists are committed to rational choice theory. Most sociologists, rational choice theorists included, are wedded to democratic, egalitarian, and emancipatory ideals and that commitment often shines through in their work.

Bauman was increasingly carried away by a vision: the horrendous image of a cool, planned and premeditated, calculating, bureaucratic, dispassionate, deliberate, impersonal campaign to industrially destroy millions of lives in specially designed death factories and efficiently dispose of the remnants. Indeed, this is one aspect of the Nazi destruction of the Jews and so many other people. It reflects in fact the modernist side of the National Socialists' own imagery about their project of annihilation, a fantasy that they turned into reality, but only partly so.[44]

The Nazi *Endlösung* (Final Solution) was mostly a sequence of ad hoc and improvised measures in reaction to challenges and opportunities that the quickly moving war theater presented.[45] This is one aspect that Bauman mostly leaves out, as the German sociologist Hans Joas remarks in an address in his honor.[46] The actual destruction of the Jews on the killing sites most often was unrestrained, wild, barbaric. Murder was not enough; Jews had to be made to suffer before being killed.[47] Only a part of the Holocaust took place in the gas chambers in Poland. It began as an endless succession of mass executions: as a "Holocaust by bullets," carried out by special extermination squads behind the Eastern Front.[48] The extermination camps that were set up as industrial slaughterhouses for human beings were the scene of obscene savagery and gory barbarity. All this Bauman chooses to ignore.[49]

According to historian Dan Stone, "There is a certain perverse comfort to be derived from believing that it was the procedures of a disciplinary, medicalized, rationalized society which led inexorably to the death-world of Auschwitz. The indictment of rational society helps blind us (willingly, if unconsciously) to the extreme violence and, worse, the desire for violence, which characterized the Holocaust experience [of the killers]."[50]

Once again, there are particularly modern elements in the Holocaust, as there are in preceding and subsequent instances of mass annihilation.[51] Sociologist Randall Collins points out that Germany was among the most modern societies of the early twentieth century, in many respects ahead of Britain and the United States on the four dimensions of modernity he distinguishes: bureaucratization, democratization, secularization, and capitalist industrialization. However, according to Collins, "The rise of the Nazis to power in Germany was the result of a contingent factor that cut across the processes of modernization." What brought the Nazis to power was not anti-Semitism, which by the early twentieth century had subsided in Germany (though it was rampant in Austria and eastern Europe), but defeat in World War I and the subsequent economic crisis.[52]

Bauman's strongest case for an omnipresent genocidal tendency in modernity of course refers to the Nazi Holocaust. (The Soviet terror would come in second.) Other instances of mass violence were too obviously brutal and chaotic to be cited in evidence of the modernity thesis. At times, Bauman wanders from the Holocaust to other genocidal episodes, commenting in passing on Rwanda or Congo, and concluding his *Postmodern Ethics* with the famous slogan: "The modern era has been founded on genocide, and has proceeded through more genocide."[53] It is, once again, a rhetorical flourish that shocks people into awareness of the cold and calculated destruction of human life that has gone on in the recent and very recent past. But it explains nothing about "modernity" or about "genocide," or about the connections between the two. One might maintain with more justice that moral indignation about genocide emerged only in modernity and that the Spanish extermination of the Indians of Mexico was the first instance of a genocidal campaign that ran into broad moral opposition on the side of the victors, rather than just among the defeated.[54]

In the footsteps of Hannah Arendt, who used Eichmann as an example of man under totalitarianism, Zygmunt Bauman deals with the Holocaust as a case that should demonstrate his general theses on modernity. In order to do so, he can point to many disturbing elements in the rational ideas and bureaucratic practices prevalent in contemporary society, but he also has to ignore the barbaric and regressive aspects of the genocidal enterprise. The kindest qualification of his scholarly approach is that it is underresearched and overtheorized.

Sociologist Michael Mann certainly cannot be blamed for having skimped on his research. His works excel in combining thorough historical investigation with broad and clear sociological theorizing. On the subject of mass annihilation, Mann takes a view that squarely contradicts the main thesis of Rudolph Rummel, an early statistician and chronicler of genocide in the twentieth century. Rummel apodictically begins his final volume, *Death by Government,* with the motto: "Power kills. Absolute power kills absolutely."[55] In contrast, Mann entitles his study *The Dark Side of Democracy: Explaining Ethnic Cleansing* and sets out to explain the ethnocides and, in one grand stroke, the genocides of the twentieth century: "*Murderous cleansing is modern, because it is the dark side of democracy.*"[56]

Mann has a point. Although democracy is essentially a procedure for the people to select its leaders peacefully while safeguarding minority rights, elections have often been the occasion for popular and sometimes quite bloody violence against minorities. Political scientist Ward Berenschot has shown how in Gujarat, India, "ward bosses" in cahoots with local thugs provoked violent riots in order to close the ranks of the Hindu or Muslim voters behind their respective leaders.[57] Such pre-electoral ethnic riots are not uncommon in other democracies, too.

Equally, the fall of authoritarian or dictatorial regimes may open the way for political entrepreneurs to rally support by creating antagonism between groups of different ethnic, religious, or class backgrounds. Such was the case in Yugoslavia after the fall of Marshal Tito, and in Iraq after Saddam Hussein. However, these constellations are not quite "democratic" but "predemocratic" at best. It is the politicians' populist appeal that incites violent passions against rival groups and prompts those in turn to close their ranks against their opponents.

Finally, according to Mann, campaigns of murderous ethnic cleansing were committed by "settler democracies" in North America, Australia, and South Africa, "more so than by more authoritarian colonial governments." That statement is refuted by a long series of genocidal campaigns, among them Leopold II of Belgium's men against the Congolese, Germans in South-West Africa against the Hereros, and the Russians against the Kyrgyz Kazakhs in Central Asia—authoritarian regimes all, which outmurdered their democratic counterparts by far.[58]

Other objections to Mann's view of "settler democracies" can be raised. These murders and massacres were often the work of local settler militias in frontier areas without the support of the—remote—national government (and without much opposition from it either).[59] Citizens who thought of themselves as "progressive" and "enlightened" objected to these massacres. Such gross slaughter they considered a throwback to a barbarous past that went squarely against the moral and legal accomplishments of modern times. Would the "project of modernity"—which is what its critics like to call it—not rather entail transforming the "underdeveloped aboriginals" through conversion, education, health care, and job training into citizens fit for full inclusion and ready to earn their wages in the labor market? In other words, the concept of modernity is so wide as to embrace both genocide and the welfare state. The practice of democracy has been more compatible with the welfare state but has been flexible enough to allow at its margins at times murderous ethnic cleansing and colonial savagery.

Michael Mann recognizes that the regimes of Stalin and Hitler (and Mao and Pol Pot, for that matter) "were dictatorships, not democracies, though they did emerge out of would-be democratizing contexts, which they then exploited."[60] This sentence is hard to fathom and probably without meaning. By now, the connection implied in the very title of the book has become quite tenuous.[61] On the other hand, Mann presents an enlightening discussion of the interplay between ethnic, religious, or class divisions and the process by which one of these dimensions "trumps" the others and comes to determine the course of violent strife and mass killings.

Mann provides rich and exact descriptions of many instances of mass annihilation in the twentieth century, but in the attempt to fit these into an overall explanatory framework he has "overtheorized" his case. His argument carries an ideological charge (and the italics are Mann's): *"ordinary people are brought by normal social structures into committing murderous ethnic cleansing."* In this context, the term *normal social structures* is surprising: very few students would call Hitler's execution squads and annihilation camps "normal social structures," or for that matter Pol Pot's Cambodian killing fields, or the Rwandan Hutu Power gangs. But the first words, "ordinary people," are by now very familiar from the literature on mass annihilation. Mann restates his position with the wording that has become standard by now: "Placed in comparable situations and similar social constituencies, you or I might also commit murderous ethnic cleansing."[62]

What is at stake is the verdict on modernity, according to Mann: "There is something in modernity releasing this particular evil on a mass scale." That "something" does not just stand for "racism," "fanaticism," or "blind obedience" or "depersonalized bureaucracy." That would be still too comfortable. The culprit is much closer to home; it hides in the very core of what most of us stand for: democracy. Even worse, it hides in us, in almost all of us: "We are almost all capable of such evil—perhaps even of enjoying it."[63]

This theme resounds in the contemporary literature on the Holocaust. It is the refrain in many a lament on the condition of modern humanity. The unanimity with which it is advanced and received must point to a deeper layer of meaning that resonates among a very broad, educated contemporary public.

I do not believe, as does French theorist Charlotte Lacoste, that the hidden objective is to absolve the perpetrators of genocide from blame by normalizing or "banalizing" them: if they are just like us, and we are "good people," then they must be good people, too.[64] But Lacoste is right in signaling a tendency to spread the blame and pin the guilt not just on the genocidal regimes and their killers but on the entire era to which they belonged, and even on the human species as a whole: modernity, with all its ordinary people.

CHAPTER 3

Widening Circles of Identification and Disidentification

The scope of identification is expanding.
—Norbert Elias

I
N EVERY EPISODE OF MASS ANNIHILATION, the perpetrators commit deadly violence against their victims. This immediately raises two fundamental questions. The first: How do such heavily charged divisions between large groupings of human beings arise? And the second: Is there a universal human disposition to act violently, and if so, how is it regulated? This chapter is devoted to the first question, the next chapter to the question of human violence.

People have very strong feelings, not only about their kin and close acquaintances, but about thousands, millions of remote and unknown people whom they have never met and may never meet. They may feel loyal and connected to those distant strangers, or conversely they may hate and despise them without ever having come across one of them. Such categorical long-distance feelings concern one's nation versus the enemy nation, one's ethnic, racial, or religious group versus people of another faith, race, or ethnic origin, and, until recently, one's class as opposed to the other class.

Why should people entertain such strongly held notions and

emotions about others they have never met and may well never meet? In many respects, it is as if they have known their counterparts closely and for a long time.

For the greater part of human history, most people did not even know about the existence of the vast majority of other human beings on the planet. When, indeed, they were even conscious of the presence of others, they usually did not care one way or another. If they were anything like contemporary hunters and gatherers, Neolithic peoples must have been highly aware only of neighboring bands as competitors for food, as partners in trade, and in the exchange of young women or sometimes young men. By the same token, they also feared them as potential attackers, robbers, rapists, abductors, and killers. Most likely, they did sense a similarity and most often some mutual affinity with those nearby groups. Such mixed feelings could quickly turn into open hostility at the slightest threat or provocation.

As hostilities persisted and group boundaries became firmer, "we-feelings" and "they-feelings" hardened. The others might be perceived as people who did not belong in one's own ranks and were completely alien in every important respect. Such intergroup processes are quite familiar. What is less obvious is the development in scope of these "we-feelings" and "they-feelings" over very long periods of time. The strong passions that distant strangers may evoke, up to the point of self-sacrificing loyalty for one's own kind and murderous hatred for the alien but anonymous enemy, is an outcome of this transformation of sentiment and opinion. The process is best described in terms of "widening circles of identification and disidentification."

In episodes of mass annihilation it sometimes appears as if the killers murder indiscriminately. But it is very rare that they attack "their own kind." When men kill, and kill en masse, they usually have a clear idea whom they are after and take pains to make sure they kill the right ones. Mass violence, per definition, is aimed at very large numbers of potential victims. The target population must be identified beforehand, and it must be defined in more than mere cognitive terms; the designation must also carry an intensely emotional charge. The killers must be ready to rob, torture, rape, or murder their victims, but first of all they should be able to recognize them.

When armed and organized men confront an alien population, everyone in their sights belongs to the other camp and is therefore a legitimate target. Thus, early in the twentieth century, German colonial troops exterminated almost the entire Herero nation in modern-day Namibia. In the 1930s, the victorious Japanese invaders in China killed everyone they encountered, as long as they looked Chinese to them. The victims, mostly unarmed civilians, were classified from the outset as an "enemy population," belonging in a different moral and emotional compartment.

And yet, just as often, the killers have lived together with their enemies for generations, in many cases quite peacefully, to all appearances. Thus, Cambodian peasants did not seem to carry profound grudges against urban dwellers, nor did Javanese or Balinese peasants appear to be overtly hostile to their neighbors in the Communist movement. Croats and Serbs, before the dissolution of Yugoslavia, freely intermingled, and so did Hutu and Tutsi peasants in their Rwandese villages. In these instances, the killers had to be careful that they did not attack the wrong person, one of their own. Hostile feelings, if there were any, had remained mostly hidden, but once the killing began, all sense of solidarity and compassion seemed to vanish completely. A few years after the massacres occurred, it again appeared as if all had been forgotten and hardly any signs of hatred or resentment came to the surface.

A genocidal regime singles out certain groups of the population as the object of mass hatred. It must then make an intensive and sustained effort to spread this message of hatred among "the regime's own people." But it can do so only if its propaganda connects with widespread ideas and emotions about the target population, with themes that have constantly circulated in the common culture, whether they have lain dormant or been in the forefront all along. It is this "raw material" that is processed in a campaign of hate propaganda. Hazy popular notions must be absolutized (the targeted people are not just "worse," they are "totally evil"); essentialized (no matter what the targeted people say or do, it is what they *are*, their immutable essence, that sets them apart as especially detestable); and generalized (each and every one of them is odious; there are no exceptions). Once the killers begin their work, they act out sentiments and convictions that are widespread among the regime's people.

IDENTIFICATION, DISIDENTIFICATION, AND GROUP FORMATION

Social identification is a mental activity in which some people come to be perceived as "more like us" and others as more "unlike us," in most or all morally and emotionally relevant aspects. In other words, it is about similarities and differences that matter for those concerned. Such a process of identification and disidentification occurs as its psychological correlate in the course of group formation, as part of the dialectics of inclusion and exclusion. It always proceeds in a dynamics of competition. It is both a cognitive and an emotional process: perceived similarities or differences provide a basis for emotional involvement and detachment and vice versa.[1]

Because social identifications are an aspect of group relations, they evolve with the transformations of human society. Identifications based on kinship may be as old as humankind, and those depending on physical proximity as old as sedentary agriculture, while others have evolved in the past few centuries, being grounded in relatively recent social formations, such as class, nation, ethnicity, or race.

A sense of identification as such is not an emotion but, rather, a person's disposition to be affected by the actions and vicissitudes of others with whom that person identifies. It is, in the words of the psychologist of the emotions Nico Frijda, a "concern," a necessary condition for emotions to occur: "No concern, no emotion."[2]

Sigmund Freud saw identification at work in "the earliest expression of an emotional tie with another person."[3] In the Freudian perspective, identification often comes with "projection": impulses and feelings that are unacceptable to the person are disavowed and attributed to other persons ("the object"): "I am not jealous of her, she envies me." This is called "projective identification," and it helps to explain not only how hostility increases between groups but also one group's tendency to perceive the other group, no matter how powerless it may seem to an outside observer, as the threatening and aggressive party. As the anthropologist Howard F. Stein writes: "The enemy is perceived through projection, as embodying the disavowed characteristics of one's own group, resulting in a psycho-cultural gap." The menace from the hostile group that has been constructed in this manner next serves to strengthen the cohesion in one's own group. Stein speaks of "adversary symbiosis."[4]

Often, the genocidal regime depicts its designated victims as filled with hatred, lusting for power, and murderous, as the real aggressor threatening the regime and its people, who are the true victims. Political scientist Donald Horowitz has shown how rumors serve to "project onto the future victims of violence the very impulses entertained by those who will victimize them."[5]

The mechanism of identification thus elicits a sense of similarity and closeness, while disavowal and projection may evoke a sense of difference and distance: a sense of "disidentification." It involves the idealization of one's own kind, the disavowal of "unacceptable" characteristics in one's own circle, and the projection of such characteristics onto "others" who must therefore be avoided or excluded, chased away or killed. Minor differences just as often may drive disidentification: Freud called this the "narcissism of small differences."[6] These trivial distinctions can be expanded into the essential characteristic that make the "we-group" vastly superior and the "they-group" utterly despicable.

One of the first social scientists to adopt the psychoanalytic notion of identification and elaborate on it was political scientist Harold Lasswell, in 1930.[7] Lasswell began by widening the circle of social or "mutual" identification beyond the narrow scope of primary relations: "Of great political relevance is *mutual identification*, whose distinguishing mark is the inclusion of persons within the field of reference of the symbol who are beyond face-to-face experience of any one person."[8] Such a "field of reference" might encompass, for example, all Americans, dead or living. Already in early infancy, symbols and meanings are manipulated in such a way that the child comes to identify with the state and with all those others who identify with the same object: "Indeed, it is the interlocking character of identification which reasonably insures the incorporation of the state symbol into the child's conception of himself."[9] And Lasswell elaborates this argument until the question arises whether a "world identification" can emerge, an identification with all human beings on earth: "Shall we speak of the 'World Minimum' and expect active sentiments to crystallize about it?"[10]

Lasswell's connection between the intimate identification processes of early childhood and the broader dynamics of social identification explains much of the emotional intensity of bonding in larger human groups. Psychiatrist Vamik Volkan, writing about early identifications, stresses not only the positive bonds with one's own people but also their complement, the disidentification from the others: "I hold that children learn to take satisfaction in the properties, both real and intangible, that they share with their own group, and regard what is shared by members of another group as far less desirable—even 'bad'—especially if the other ethnic or national group is seen as hostile or is rejected by the adults in their own group."[11]

People's identifications, and their emotions in general, develop in the course of their lives, within their social context. But identifications and other mental states, as they prevail in society as a whole, evolve in the course of the history of that society. It was the Dutch historian Johan Huizinga who suggested that human emotions might develop in a specific direction in a given society and during a particular epoch, such as the late Middle Ages in northwestern Europe.[12] Taking Huizinga's depiction of the exuberant medieval personality as his point of departure, Norbert Elias set out to provide a "sociogenesis" of the more "civilized" personality types that were prevalent by the early twentieth century and whose discontents were so vividly portrayed by Freud. Elias writes about the "civilizing process" that occurred in Europe in the course of half a millennium. Civilization, in Elias's view, is the outcome of historical processes. Under different circumstances it could well break down in a reversal toward decivilization or barbarization. This, according to Elias, was what happened when Nazism became ascendant in Germany.[13]

In Elias's account, transformations of personal habitus are inextricably interwoven with transformations in the surrounding society. The most important of these was the formation of states, "with and against one another," in a European system of states. Within the evolving framework of this state system, markets and networks of exchange further developed. In some of these emerging states, notably in France, a "court society" emerged, which imposed much more demanding restraints on the regulation of violent, sexual, and other bodily impulses than had been prevalent among the knightly warriors of an earlier epoch. It is in this context that the "chains of interdependence" among people lengthened and strengthened. The increasing and expanding interdependencies promoted a sense of mutual identification in the people who made up these chains. This civilizing process went together with wider and stronger social identifications. People came to consider one another as more similar and, in many respects, as more equal than they did before.

Primal Identifications: Kinship and Proximity

For the largest part by far of their time on earth, human beings have lived in small bands based on kinship. The circle of identification may have spanned from a few dozen to at the most a few hundred people who knew one another face to face and were probably quite aware of the kin relations that connected them. In an evolutionary perspective, selection may have operated to strengthen kinship altruism, familial loyalties, and identification along bloodlines.

Only in the past few hundred generations, some five to ten thousand years ago, another principle of social organization came to predominate alongside kinship ties: physical proximity. When human beings began to practice sedentary agriculture, they settled near neighbors who often were only remotely related or even no kin at all. In the village, as the primordial unit of social organization in agrarian society, the two principles of identification, the bonds of kinship and of neighborhood, interfered or concurred with each other. Both kinds of bond helped to instill the mutual confidence necessary for collective efforts in defense, policing, irrigation, building, and so forth. The village thus represented a new kind of survival unit, one that acquired its cohesion in collective action against external enemies and against nature. At any moment, clan loyalties that transcend village borders might come into conflict with the bonds of village proximity.[14] The persistent institution of the blood feud provides an example of such conflicting loyalties.[15]

It must have required a sustained effort to develop a sense of identification among villagers who were not necessarily related by blood. Collective action, especially collective defense against outside attacks, was of the essence in providing the experiences and memories of shared achievement and common interest: a new "we-feeling" emerged, pitching "our village" against "their" neighboring villages. As the essential unit of survival and defense, the village was also the primary unit in the competition with rivaling villages.

To this day, in the religious rhetoric of the unity among the faithful, two kinds of metaphors prevail. Both are aimed at increasing their mutual identification. The first refers to relations of blood and kinship: an almighty father, merciful mother, brothers and sisters in faith, children of one father. . . . But the other imagery suggests proximity: neighbors. The vocabulary is of course taken from the reality of agrarian societies and must in turn have served to reinforce the villagers' identifications through religious sanctions. Thus, in the course of a few millennia human beings developed the symbols and rituals, the forms and rhythms, that could instill mutual identifications at the village level.

In military-agrarian regimes, peasant villages initially came under priestly rule. In the course of time, one after another they were taken over by warriors.[16] In the process, the nature of identifications among the villagers also changed: they became brothers and sisters in one faith, against heretics and infidels; and they became subjects of one ruler against those of a hostile lord. The two circles of identification—of faith and rule—far exceeded the village community, but it is questionable whether these wider connections meant much in everyday peasant existence.

Three other networks emerged in these military-agrarian societies, each encompassing a much more extensive domain than that of the village: one was dynastic, the second monastic, the third military. Ruling clans intermarried and inherited, forming lasting dynasties with extensive networks based on the organizing principle of kinship. Villagers may have identified with some ruling family in terms of symbolic kinship (children of a ruler-father). All that has survived until today is the propaganda spread by the rulers themselves; whether their peasant subjects in fact identified with them can no longer be ascertained, but it is not very likely: for survival they continued to depend on the family circle and the village community; what happened at the more encompassing level where the rulers operated mattered little in their lives.[17] For the ruling elites themselves, by contrast, their mutual identifications must have been most meaningful in the reciprocal recognition among rivals of equal standing and in the joint exclusion of the common people as unworthy and without honor.

The second kind of network, the monastic order kept together by religious bonds, extended at least as far as did dynastic connections: monastic orders used religious symbolism to instill a sense of identification, much fortified by the imagery of brothers and sisters devoted to a common, divine father, a mother of god, and their son. But actual kinship played no role in the monastic orders; on the contrary, like military organizations, religious bureaucracies tried to prevent kinship cliques from forming in their midst, for fear that they might clash with the organization's hierarchical ties.[18] Nor did common origins, or past geographic proximity, matter much.

Whether and to what degree the common peasants shared an emotional identification with their remote fellow believers is again hard to assess. There is only the official propaganda to go by, since almost all sources on premodern history were written by clerics. This is why historians and historical sociologists must practice methodological anticlericalism.[19]

A third kind of network in which specific identifications emerged consisted of the military. In armies, too, other bonds prevailed than those of kin or proximity alone. The mutual identifications of warriors were much fortified by "the negation of the negation," the solidarity instilled by excluding and fighting a common enemy: the enemy of one's enemy must be one's friend.

Of course, still other forms of identification may be found in predominantly agrarian societies, such as the mutual identification of guild members in the early modern cities. But for the vast majority of people, the bounds of kin and geographic proximity remained by far the most important lines of identification: blood and soil determined who were considered "one's own people," who were perceived as more or less "the same," with whom one commiserated, in short, with whom one identified. Beyond the circle of the family or the village, identifications as a rule were much weaker, since they concerned strangers, who were perceived as different and usually as inferior. As long as there were no interests involved, one needed not be concerned with these outsiders; ignorance and indifference prevailed. Only when their interests were at stake, people became concerned and "interested" in the strangers. They might come to see them as quite different, and therefore most often less worthy in every sense, and they might well develop a collective sense of disidentification from them.

The great religions of the world all offer a repertory of concepts to convey the idea of one humanity, or at least a community of faith that one day might encompass all of humanity. All these religions contain the commandment to help a needy stranger. But proclamation of the faith by itself could and cannot create new, more encompassing identifications or persuade people to take care of suffering strangers. That happens only when social conditions, the mutual dependencies among people, allow it. Once they do, widely circulating concepts in religion (or science) sensitize people to what can, may, and must be done. Since they know that most others are familiar with the same ideas, these will help them to coordinate their efforts, to orientate their collective action.

The effective unit of survival, defense, and thus of competition was the village. Rare were the conflicts that pitched the body of believers against the infidels; the peasants usually stayed outside those religious battles. Almost all of the struggles in which they did engage set against one another believers in one and the same faith. But even if they barely touched the lives of the common peasants, monastic orders represented a new principle of social organization. Religion, moreover, offered a rich vocabulary for strengthening loyalties among the villagers. Finally, the great proselytizing religions, Christendom, Buddhism, and Islam, provided a conceptual repertoire for conceiving of humankind, or at least of the body of believers, as a single entity uniting human beings who were all God's creatures. But, in essence, people continued to live together in circles of kinship and proximity, in clans and villages, and identified with their peers accordingly, as relatives and neighbors.

In predominantly agrarian societies, clans could expand into feudal coalitions that might now be called "tribes" or "ethnicities." These were large associations for mutual protection and advantage, led by blood-related warriors: the Guelphs and Ghibellines of southern Germany and Italy in the twelfth century, for example, or the Hoekse (Hook) and the Kabeljauwse (Cod) in the Netherlands of the fifteenth century. In recent times, similar armed factions have fought each other off and on in large parts of Africa and the Middle East. Such clan coalitions operate within the framework of a state apparatus still under construction, without surrendering their military capabilities.

Even in cities, affective identification may have been limited mainly to extended families and neighborhoods. A relatively new form of solidarity emerged where guilds and other corporations were formed, "brotherhoods" that reactivated the symbolism of fraternal identifications. In merchant towns especially, people of different origin mingled. Quite often the townsfolk associated these "minorities" with much larger, religious entities, the Jews with Jewry, the Muslims with Islam, the Calvinists with the Reformation, and so forth. These symbolic links might then lead to disidentification from the outsiders, sometimes to their exclusion, and every once in a while to expulsions, pogroms, and massacres.[20] But at other times, such demarcation lines remained dormant, irrelevant in daily encounters, work, and trade.

In any constellation, instilling and maintaining collective identifications requires a continuous effort. What inspired and sustained people's identification with a specific social entity more than anything else was the experience that it represented the unit of survival for its members, that their physical security and material existence depended on it.[21]

Emerging Nation States and Widening Circles of Identification

The next major restructuring of identificatory emotions occurred with the rise of the nation-state in the past few hundred years. It gained momentum only with the emergence of an urban-industrial mode of existence and the advent of mass politics: for the first time, people on a large scale began to identify with others, not on the basis of kinship or proximity, or of membership in a narrowly circumscribed network of dynastic, monastic, military, or corporate ties, but on the basis of a much more encompassing common denominator: the nation. Members of one nation "imagine"—as Benedict Anderson has it—a shared past and a common destiny.[22] They do not trace their origins back to a common ancestor, even though the metaphor for the revered founder of the nation evokes the father of a very extended family. The national territory (the "father-" or "motherland")—represented as contiguous, closed, and immutable—evokes the image of a vastly extended proximity.

In the long-term process of state formation and industrializa-

tion, the essential unit of survival and defense—the unit of competition, that is—came to be the national state. And it is at this level of
integration that the dynamics of identification, the process of inclusion and exclusion, are now reproduced. The very essence of true
Frenchhood may be forever indefinable, but if it is grasped in the context of rivalry with the neighboring nations, the English and the Germans, it suddenly becomes more tangible as "other-than-English" or
"counter-German."[23] The dialectics of identification and "discrimi-
native separation" is repeated in a new order of magnitude, and at
a higher level of social integration, the nation.

Seen in this perspective, as a recent stage in a very long-term
development, nationalism, or classism and even racism, is not just
divisive and exclusive but also unifying and inclusive, as it tran-
scends the parochial identifications of clan and village society
to build relatively new and vastly extended webs of human solidarity at the price of an equally rigorous exclusion of the others,
the complement to their unity. Again, it required an immense
effort of symbolization, communication, and education to super-
impose these new, national identifications on the preceding identifications of kin and proximity. Members of one nation do not
know each other and yet they know that they are similar: they are
strangers to one another and yet familiar. The rest of humanity are
aliens. Much the same might be said about identifications along
lines of class or race, which both have much more clearly demarcated complements: proletariat and bourgeoisie, *Herrenvolk* and
Untermenschen.

The advent of industrial production, of the urban mode of life,
and of mass politics has increased the sense of familiarity, of proximity, and of interdependence between the participants in one political
economy. And it has led to new structures of identification: classes,
races, and nations, as well as ethnic and religious groupings.

In mass politics—which is not necessarily the same as democratic politics—political entrepreneurs operate to mobilize one or another structure of identification, defining and redefining their appeal until they hit upon a version that works. With the resurgence of all sorts of nationalisms in Eastern Europe and parts of the former Soviet Union, it appeared as if deeply ingrained, timeless group loyalties after a period of Communist repression finally returned to resume their unavoidable hold on people's minds. That was indeed the account presented by the nationalist activists themselves. But in every modern state there are categories that do not fit the self-definition of the state with its nation, that straddle political borders or differ from the nation's mainstream in religion, language, and history. And yet, these distinctions and the corresponding identifications remain dormant in the vast majority of cases.

What explains the resurgence of ethnic identifications in formerly Communist countries is not their immanent unavoidability but the disintegration of the Communist state apparatus and the resulting chaos, which forced people to find new forms of organization to help them ward off social degradation, material expropriation, or physical threats and to compete for the newly vacant positions of power and profit. Under those circumstances, activist politicians by trial and error seek to kindle those identifications that will evoke the greatest response—that is, the strongest popular support. Such experiments in finding the most effective common denominator will occur most intensively during times of transition and upheaval, when struggles for position are intensified and the lines of competition are being redrawn, as happened, for example, after the collapse of Yugoslavia and Iraq.

Even though the symbolic vocabulary refers to large human aggregates, such as nation, race, class, and country, it usually carries connotations of intensely emotional, primary relations, for example, of a parental figure defending and protecting its children, or of brothers and sisters united in one faith and one endeavor. And even though it is a phenomenon of mass politics, the structuring and reinforcing of these identifications do not occur only or even primarily in very large settings, such as mass meetings or media broadcasts. That is where the vocabulary and symbolism is reactivated and radiated far and wide. But much of the restructuring of identification actually proceeds not by radiation but rather through conduction—that is, by face-to-face contacts in primary settings: in the family and among peers. In other words, small groups constitute the matrix for the restructuring of large-scale identifications, and sometimes such primary groups are formed especially for that purpose.

Extensive and greatly enlarged "social figurations" are usually quickly reduced to primary group relations that then come to stand for the encompassing object as a *pars pro toto:* soldiers and terrorists report that what matters after fighting has gone on for a while is not the abstract and idealized nation, and not the army, the party, or the movement—that is, not the enlarged figurations—but rather the comrades in their own platoon or activist cell. In other words, identifications—even of a most encompassing and abstract nature, for example, with America, the proletariat, the Communist Party, or the Aryan race—apparently survive and flourish more readily in a much more compact, face-to-face setting: in the social context, therefore, that represents the same scope and intensity of interaction as the early human bands in which identifications originally evolved.

Children learn to identify with larger social settings, especially of a religious, class, national, or ethnic character, in the primary settings of the family and the school class. And the most emotional scenes in many families are those that concern precisely such apparently general and abstract categories of identification. In other words, this is often how parenthood, and especially fatherhood, is "done" or "enacted": by mobilizing much larger and encompassing symbols in the service of parental authority. "No one will deface the flag in this house," "You wear your cross to school with pride, no matter what they call you," or "We worked hard all of our life and we are proud of it." After all, the vocabulary and symbolism of class, faith, nationhood, and race is much richer and more persuasive than any parent could improvise in a family argument; and it is always available, ready for use by parents (and later, with a vengeance, by adolescent youths in a counterauthoritarian mobilization).

In order to understand the enormous impact of these rather new and abstract vocabularies, we should realize that they are invoked mostly in primary settings, taking their emotional charge from intimate relations, which then spills over to the larger context. In other words, people may not be so ready to die for the nation, but they may be ready to kill in order to avenge a slight that they believe has been inflicted on their parents' honor or to come to the aid of a comrade-in-arms and not be seen as a coward by their peers.

The reduction of grand identifications to small settings may also be analyzed from a more materialist perspective: class, nation, faith, and race have been symbolic denominators that in the recent past have almost invariably been carried by mass movements. Even though their emotional impact may largely be actualized and reinforced at the level of the primary group, their motivational effect may also be aroused by the social opportunities these movements create. Every movement holds a promise of leadership; it offers cadre positions, chances of power and prestige, within the movement itself. For those who are part of this social movement and share the identifications it represents, such positions are all the more rewarding because they are felt to be "righteous"; ambition is not felt to be in any way self-serving but a service to the cause. Even plain membership, with its insignia and festive gatherings, may lift one above the outsiders.

Successful movements allow enterprising individuals to increase their social and commercial contacts within the new network, to find jobs, customers, and employees within its ranks. And once the movement succeeds in conquering strongholds in the machinery of the state, or even establishes a state apparatus of its own, career and business opportunities are the members' rewards. Many social movements, no matter how marginal and millenarian they may appear to outsiders, to their followers represent a long shot at a great reward, a high-risk–high-profit strategy. The movement may prompt its adherents to overestimate the chances of success: a manipulation of expectations that is an almost indispensable condition for collective action to get under way.[24] Moreover, many of the adherents may simply have no chance at all of increasing their power, prestige, or profit outside the movement.

Thus, members of the militia are assured of a small job and some pay, and of prestige in the immediate environment. Once the struggle gets under way, they may plunder shops, expel tenants and owners, take over their property or their job. Once the movement is victorious, they may partake in the spoils of power. When these beliefs and expectations are shared and reinforced by one's family or peers, the ambition becomes righteous aspiration, serving the cause; and the greed becomes a righteous claim, the wages of serving that same lofty cause.

But if these passions are to be effectively mobilized, the right denominator must be found, one that pitches one unit of competition most effectively against another, and after it is found, it must be maintained, reinforced with all the resources of mass communication and organization, and intensified in the affective hothouse of the primary group.

Social identifications are at once inclusive and exclusive, and identifications with very large social entities represent a relatively recent phenomenon in human history, one that for all its exclusiveness also entails an enlarging and unifying momentum, above and beyond the older identifications of kin and proximity.

Yet social identifications, no matter how intensely held, are

essentially multiple and unstable. For most individuals they encompass the family and the village, the peer group and the neighborhood, and the larger entities of class or nation, with all the contradictions these multiple identifications imply. Perhaps, human
beings in the present era need to identify with alternating intensi-
ties on all these levels. Sports provide a telling example: local identifications are mobilized in the early stages of the tournament, and
as the season proceeds, loyalties shift to much broader regional entities, until in international encounters, the fans identify with their
national team or even find themselves suddenly identifying at the
continental level with a neighboring country that participates when
the matches for the world championship are being played.

A global identification, with humanity in its entirety, differs
from all other social identifications in one decisive aspect: it appears all-inclusive, as if no human beings are left to be excluded.
The dialectics of inclusion and exclusion, the dynamics of competition have apparently come to a halt. Except, of course, that those
diehards who still reject the universal embrace must now be excluded from this peace of almost everyone with almost everyone.
Moreover, other threats will be evoked to mobilize the mechanism
of identification again: enemies from outer space or a threat that,
even though it emanates from human agency, nevertheless threat-
ens humanity in its entirety: nuclear disaster or environmental
catastrophe. Thus it is still possible to hate in the name of world
peace and the united human race the warmongers, the polluters, or
anyone who rejects values presented as universal.

Such human-produced threats to humanity, or at least the
awareness of them, are again recent phenomena, dating back a generation or two at the most. Antinuclear or environmental movements
operate best by singling out identifiable wrongdoers to mobilize the
global dialectics of inclusion-exclusion and competition.

There are underlying long-term processes that aid in the development of global identifications. Norbert Elias stresses the im-

portance of domestic pacification through state monopolization of violence and the attendant lengthening and strengthening of the chains of interdependence among human beings in contemporary society. And as the rhythms of urban life and mass culture spread across the continent, people in many respects become more similar and find it easier to recognize one another as more or less "the same."

This development did not always proceed in one, outward path of forever-widening identifications. Sometimes the process must have reversed itself. Richard Jobson, traveling in West Africa around 1620, relates how an African trader offered him women for sale as slaves:

> Hee shewed unto mee, certaine young blacke women, who were standing by themselves, and had white strings crosse their bodies, which hee told me were slaves, brought for me to buy, I made answer, We were a people, who did not deale in any such commodities, neither did wee buy or sell one another, or any that had our owne shapes; he seemed to marvell much at it, and told us, it was the only merchandize, they carried downe into the countrey, where they fetcht all their salt, and that they were solde there to white men, who earnestly desired them, especially such young women, as hee had brought for us: we answered, They were another kinde of people different from us.[25]

Jobson refused the offer, since "neither did wee buy or sell one another," and the women "had our owne shapes," which can only mean that he ignored differences in race and gender for a common humanity, whereas he distanced himself from the—Portuguese—slave traders on moral grounds as "they were another kinde of people different from us." In later years British complicity in the great Atlantic slave trade would require thorough disidentification from the Africans.

In a fascinating essay, historian Thomas Haskell has attempted to explain the emergence of what he calls the "humanitarian sensibility" as it manifested itself in the antislavery movement of the early nineteenth century. As a "market-orientated form of life" spread among the bourgeoisie of the Western world, affecting its perception and cognitive style, and promoting "a certain calculating, moderately assertive style of conduct," it also "taught people to keep their promises" and "to attend to the remote consequences of their actions."[26] This "recipe knowledge," as Haskell calls it, then spread among the working class in capitalist-industrial society. The changes in cognitive style were prompted by transformations in society. They bring about a restructuring of what Frijda has called "concerns" in individual human beings, at the same time preparing for identifications of even wider scope, encompassing all of humanity. But such global identifications remain tenuous and tentative. They may be undone by more pressing concerns manifesting themselves in the inner circles of identification. Because the dynamics of competition and exclusion operate only marginally, these global identifications may never become charged with the intensity that characterizes the identifications with primary groups or even with the large subdivisions of humanity that now hold sway over human minds.[27] And yet, human beings find it increasingly difficult to deny the awareness of their essential equality.

Citizens of contemporary nation-states have over centuries learned to share and care in huge networks of identification. By the same token, they have learned to exclude and despise equally vast human conglomerates in complementary networks of disidentification. This sets the stage, not only for the rule of law and the welfare state, but also for rare but catastrophic episodes of mass annihilation.

IGNORANCE AND INDIFFERENCE, IDENTIFICATION AND DISIDENTIFICATION

Identification and disidentification are not each other's opposites; rather, they occupy two sides of an emotional triangle, with ignorance and indifference at its base. The vast majority of human beings are completely unknown to one another. Throughout history, most people were unaware of the very existence of the greater part of their fellow human beings, and only in the past few centuries has this begun to change at an accelerating pace. But even today, when most people are at least vaguely aware of other people in distant lands, indifference prevails, sometimes coupled with diffuse, not very strongly held fantasies.

For people even to begin to have feelings at all about distant strangers, they must first find out about their existence, and if next they are to hate them, they must first be told about the hateful characteristics of these aliens. All this would be a rather vacuous and sterile exercise, if there were no actual interdependencies between the one group and the other. The abject habits of the Ludimango, the ways in which the men exploit the women, their cannibalism, the roasting alive of deer and fowl, the teasing to death of eels, cats, and bulls, the torturing of adolescent boys, the excision of young girls, the burning of widows—none of it will much excite other groups so long as they have no business with the Ludimango.

It is the transformation of social relations that brings with it the transformation of sentiment, in a double movement of identification and disidentification that supersedes prior unawareness and indifference. The increase in scope of these emotional concerns corresponds with the increase in scale of social relations, brought about by conquest, conversion, and trade. The Atlantic slave trade is one critical instance of trading and raiding relations that shaped new patterns of identification and, much more so, disidentifications.

When European merchant slavers and their African raiding accomplices hunted down, deported, sold, and exploited some ten million Africans and their descendants in the New World, they did so precisely because they needed them, not as raw material or as fodder, but as workers, as human laborers, as sentient, competent human beings who would understand orders, anticipate reward and punishment, master the demanding crafts of plantation agriculture and the subtle skills of domestic service. In other words, the slave traders and the owners at once had to identify with their victims as similarly equipped human beings and to disidentify from them as beings with similar sentiments, of moral value, with a human soul.

Chattel slavery was a concomitant of the rise of the modern world system—the emergence of the great Atlantic trading triangle between Europe, Africa, and the Americas. To transform Africans into slaves required massive social and emotional work. They had to be recognized as human beings and to be excluded as "cattle," as "apes" (still the species closest to humans), as quasi-animals, as subhuman beings. At the very best they were considered "childlike"—that is, "not yet" completely human, but undeniably on their way to full humanity under the tutelage of stern but benevolent guardians.

The theme of slavery is raised here in passing only, to demonstrate the two double movements that constitute the dynamics of the widening scale of emotional concerns. With the emergence of the triangular Atlantic trade, a social figuration of larger scale than before emerged. This increase in the reach of social relations was accompanied by the emergence of sentiments of widening scope. The twofold socioemotional process of identification and disidentification overcame earlier unawareness and indifference. Plantation slavery was one great training ground for mass deportation, massive exploitation, and extreme deprivation, increasingly legitimated with racist theories. It also provided one of the first instances of the socioemotional work of identification and disidentification on a transcontinental scale.

Not only when it comes to massive exploitation, but even more so when it is about mass annihilation, these patterns of identification and disidentification define the target group to be victimized and the others, "the regime's people," who profit from it. The perpetrators do their work in accordance with these patterns of affective separation, which are reinforced by the regime and widely shared by its people.

CHAPTER 4

The Transformations of Violence in Human History

THESE DAYS, WHEN PEOPLE THINK OF EVIL, they do not so much associate it with rebellion against God: apostasy, heresy, idolatry, and blasphemy, sorcery or superstition. Their thoughts turn to the harm human beings inflict on one another. The concept of evil has shifted from vertical to horizontal. Nowadays, the worst evil that people can commit is violence: torture, rape, and murder. Violent crime on a mass scale, genocide, is considered the epitome of evil, the Holocaust the low point of history.[1] Yet, at the horizon, a third form of evil emerges: crimes against the natural environment.

But so far, mass extermination is considered the most abominable crime. New legal concepts of global jurisdiction—war crimes, genocide, and crimes against humanity—have been developed to prosecute and punish it. This strong and almost universal rejection of violent behavior makes it all the more difficult to study the subject of mass extermination without taking up moral or political positions. What is more, some discussions of mass violence, which may at first appear to be entirely motivated by scientific considerations, barely hide an almost theological preoccupation with the

Origins of Evil and the Fall of Man. Ethology, the scientific study of animal behavior, has become today's theodicy, the modern explanation of the presence of evil in the world. But then, *ethology* is an anagram of *theology*.

The Prehistory of Violence

Anthropologist Richard Wrangham and science writer Dale Peterson published a book with the suggestive title *Demonic Males,* in which the authors trace the violent tendencies of human males back to their hominid ancestors, as they can still be observed, it is thought, in contemporary chimpanzees. Interestingly, for many years aggression among these apes was almost entirely overlooked, even by observers in the field, paramount among them Jane Goodall.[2] Violent behavior, when observed among chimpanzees in the zoo, was long considered an artifact of captivity.[3] Thus, these seemingly harmonious simian troupes seemed to hold a promise for a more peaceful human mode of existence: human beings, and young adult male humans especially, had only to return to their more natural and pacific ways.

The Fall of Chimpanzee came with a young researcher's observation, in 1974, of a very violent incident in the colony Goodall had studied since the early 1960s.[4] From there, it was downhill all the way. One destructive episode after another was reported, not just between competing males, but also by adult males against their mates, and finally by—mostly—male raiding parties against adjacent groups: the chimpanzees had changed places in the theodicy.[5] Humans from now on were considered cursed forever by their violent evolutionary origins in the *Pan* family.

But even in Wrangham and Peterson's book, there is hope: in the last chapter, the bonobos appear as the ethological promise of human salvation. Among them, solidary females time and again succeed in getting the better of solitary males. The females maintain harmonious relations with their female kin by continual grooming, licking, and rubbing of all sorts. Frans de Waal has confirmed this assessment with *Our Inner Ape,* which chronicles his own observations of captive bonobos and chimpanzees. It once used to be said that the human kind existed somewhere between Beasts and Angels. Today it is located halfway between chimpanzees and bonobos.

Perhaps the most important lesson to be drawn is that of the variability in primate behavior: two species that are very closely related, chimpanzees and bonobos, and that live in immediately adjacent habitats, nevertheless display widely divergent social arrangements and have entirely different repertoires of violence and violence control. There might even be cultural differences between them in this respect, group traits that parents teach their offspring.

All this research certainly makes more plausible the notion that violent behavior is at the very least a possibility of human beings, especially of young adult males. This potential may lie dormant, it may never be activated, and it may even be entirely absent in some individuals, but most human beings can resort to violence, and quite a few sometimes do. That does not mean that they must or that they need constantly to control an urge to attack or defend. It just means that under certain conditions human beings can behave quite violently toward each other. This capacity for violence may indeed have very deep evolutionary roots. And so, by the way, may the capacity to control violent impulses and to collaborate peacefully. Randall Collins brings the debate to the neuropsychological turf by reversing the standard notion: "Humans are hard-wired for interactional entrainment and solidarity; and this is what makes violence so difficult."[6] In fact, for most people sustained violent action requires prior preparation and training, an appropriate setting, and considerable effort to overcome the inhibitions against it.[7] Just as human beings can interact quite violently, they obviously also can interact to prevent or quell such violence. As among other apes, both the violent episodes and their regulation are essentially social phenomena that occur in a group context. Even in the most aggressive communities, actual violent confrontations occur only sparsely, even though the danger is constantly present and must be permanently guarded against.

There clearly are some genetic traits that incite to violence and others that restrain the urge to attack, just as there are strong genetic determinants that evoke empathy and others that limit or quell it. In other words, a selective equilibrium prevails in every vertebrate species, and an emotional balance in every specimen.

Much of what I have said may sound perfectly obvious, and indeed it should be. But I am afraid that quite a few opposite statements on the same subject might have sounded equally obvious (to a less informed audience), whereas they are wrong.

"Under certain conditions human beings can behave quite violently toward one another." The key question is: "Under what conditions?" (And the obverse question is equally valid: "Under what conditions will humans behave peacefully toward one another?") Of course, at this level of generality, the question cannot be answered. It will have to be broken down, and even then, only partial answers may be forthcoming.

The notion that once upon a time human beings lived in peace with one another ("just like their simian forebears") until something occurred that ended this harmony proves stubborn. Before the introduction of tools, people must have been devoid of aggression, goes the argument. Maybe it was the turn to hunting and the craving for meat that made men into killers. Perhaps it was the introduction of property or the accumulation of capital that provoked violence.[8] Equally plausibly, it could have been the appearance of statelike institutions that unchained collective aggression. Or was it the encounter with Western civilization that turned peaceful peoples into raiders and killers? No, it must have been modernity that robbed human beings of their natural compassion and, whenever the regime required it, could turn them into murderous automatons. As Karl Marx long ago pointed out when introducing the subject of primitive accumulation, all these speculations evoke as many metaphors for the Fall from Grace.[9]

There is in fact abundant evidence for the omnipresence of rape, robbery, arson, and murder in prehistoric societies, including the wholesale slaughter of one group by another (which is especially relevant for our purpose). Anthropologist Lawrence Keeley has inventoried the evidence from ethnology and archaeology in *War Before Civilization* and comes to a rather bleak judgment about stateless societies: "The primitive world was certainly not more peaceful than the modern one. The only reasonable conclusion is that wars are actually more frequent in non-state societies than they are in state societies—especially modern nations."[10]

And in his final chapter, Keeley concludes:

> The facts recovered by ethnographers and archaeologists indicate unequivocally that primitive and prehistoric warfare was just as terrible and effective as the historic and civilized version. War is hell, whether it is fought with wooden spears or napalm. Peaceful prestate societies are very rare; warfare between them was very frequent, and most adult men saw combat repeatedly in a lifetime—in fact, primitive warfare was much more deadly than that conducted between civilized states, because of the greater frequency of combat and the more merciless way it was conducted. Primitive war was very efficient at inflicting damage through the destruction of property, especially means of production and shelter, and inducing terror by frequently visiting sudden death and mutilating its victims.[11]

In his *War in Human Civilization,* an appropriate title for a companion volume to Keeley's, Azar Gat surveys warfare in the course of human history. No lack of material there.

As Gat points out, stateless, irregular, and small group warfare consisted mostly in raids: frequent, brief, but therefore no less murderous confrontations. "Group fighting grew in scale with the growth in size of the human groups themselves." He summarizes the secular development of warfare:

> Before the state, too, there was some difference in in-group and out-group killing, with the former modulated in small-scale, Paleolithic human societies by successively extending and weakening kin circles, up to the regional groups of hundreds or, at most, a few thousand. In agricultural societies these onion-like kin circles grew larger, although anarchy, voluntary participation, and small numbers continued to dominate both internal and external fighting. Political organization, however, vastly magnified the difference between the two "forms" of fighting, casting the latter—constituted as war—in the mold of the state's most characteristic attribute.

As a result, Gat maintains, "overall mortality rates evidently decreased with the growth of the state and the transition from '*warre*' to 'war.'" That was, of course, a result of the state's capacity to monopolize violence within its territory and to protect the inhabitants against one another and against violent outsiders.[12]

This rather regular warfare was mostly a matter of organized combat between two more or less equally matched parties of armed men. Yet a different kind of violence occurred time and again, also perpetrated by armed men, but against vanquished opponents or entirely defenseless populations: "mass annihilation."

And just as the gradual emergence of states or, rather, the formation of a system of states led to fewer casualties of war (on the whole and in the long run), it may not necessarily have mitigated the frequency and lethality of massacres. Organized armies of well-equipped soldiers, expedited by a distant state, could overcome the resistance of less coordinated and poorly equipped fighters outside the state system with relative ease, and once they had defeated these enemy forces, they could plunder, rape, rob, torture, and kill without encountering much resistance. And so the conquerors did, all too often. Yet in most cases, hardly any testimony or material evidence survived to remind later generations of the carnage wreaked by these victorious armies.

Since their earliest beginnings, people have perpetrated large massacres upon their own species. Nearly every war, every battle ended in pillage, arson, rape of the defeated women and the enslavement or extermination of the surviving enemies. Archaeologist Bill Leadbetter concludes, after a long enumeration of genocides in ancient history: "Modernity may have brought genocide to new ideologies and technologies, but the phenomenon itself may well be as old as civilization itself."[13]

MASS ANNIHILATION IN HISTORY

From biblical times and antiquity to the Middle Ages, from the onset of the Modern Age to the present, from the Occident to the Orient, countless examples are known of wholesale slaughter by onrushing conquerors and established rulers of the people they had defeated or subjected.[14] The Israelites, the Greeks, and the Romans proudly chronicled the massacres they committed on defeated nations, most often exaggerating the number of victims they made in their hour of triumph. Homer lets Agamemnon say to Menelaus about the defeated Trojans: "No, we are not going to leave a single one of them alive, down to the babies in their mothers' wombs— not even they must live. The whole people must be wiped out of existence, and none be left to think of them and shed a tear."[15]

Most surveys of mass violence before the Modern Age begin with biblical tales of carnage among the vanquished, followed by ancient reports on the massacre of defeated nations in classical times.[17] Striking in most of these summaries is the gap between antiquity and the late Middle Ages, a lacuna of more than a thousand years. This was, by all accounts, a period of continual battles that usually ended in wholesale plunder, arson, mass rape, and massacre. The scale of warfare was still much smaller than in present times, if only because the logistics of the period would not allow large armies to carry on prolonged campaigns: the soldiers lived off the land they traversed, and this by itself provoked plunder, murder, and famine. Once the enemy had been defeated, the vanquished opponents were often killed in great numbers and the local population was robbed, expelled, or slaughtered, after the women had been raped. Only slavery could save the defeated from being killed on the spot. Such bloodbaths, frequent as they were, certainly can be considered "mass annihilation," since the victors were armed and organized, whereas the defeated warriors and the unarmed population could hardly put up any resistance. Was it *genocide* in the contemporary sense? The terms *nation, race, ethnicity,* and *religion,* which legally define *genocide,* if they were current at all, did not yet carry the connotations they have acquired in recent times. But the annihilation of an entire group because its members were considered different in one sense or another was commonplace throughout the Dark Ages. The murder weapons were, of course, not as advanced as in present times, but even in the very recent past, millions were killed in a few months' time with stones, clubs, iron rods, and machetes, or with small arms and shotguns. The major difference was that administrative techniques in these bygone centuries were still rudimentary, and civil registries or death lists for the targeted population hardly existed. The victorious soldiers killed whomever they found on their way, with little ado. Local people who had sided with the conquerors, hoping to share in the spoils, joined in the carnage. The killers were no less savage than their modern successors, possibly even more barbarous and maybe less systematic and detached. The numbers of their victims ran in the thousands and tens of thousands, occasionally in the hundreds of thousands or millions.

The victims were literally innumerable, the witnesses may not even have dared to count them, and the survivors had other things on their mind. The killers prided themselves in their deeds, and the chroniclers honored them by vastly inflating the number of victims.[17] Thus, the Assyrians erected triumphal monuments to commemorate the massacres they had wreaked. Among the earliest well-documented accounts of slaughter on a grand scale are the chronicles of the Crusades, the occasion for pogroms against the Jews and for massive bloodbaths among the Muslims in the Holy Land. "[The] crusaders rode in blood to the knees and bridles of their horses," relates Raymond of Aguilers in his exultant account of the capture of Jerusalem in 1099: "In my opinion this was poetic justice that the Temple of Solomon should receive the blood of pagans who blasphemed God there for many years. . . . A new day, new gladness, new and everlasting happiness, and the fulfillment of our toil and love brought forth new words and songs for all."[18]

Christians also fought other Christians. Calling the opponents "heretics" was enough to overcome the bond of common creed. One of the bloodiest sectarian campaigns was the twenty-year crusade against the Albigensians of southern France that began in 1209.[19]

On the other side of the subcontinent, on the eastern borders of Europe, the infidels attacked. There loomed the threat of Genghis Khan and his Mongols, who had conquered a good part of Asia in a series of bloody massacres that made his name proverbial to this very day, in the West as well.[20] Asians fought Asians: in the southeastern part of the continent the Vietnamese massacred the Cham; in the Far East, Japanese slaughtered Koreans.[21]

The European conquest of the Americas ushered in a new era, also in mass extermination. The Spanish conquerors' superiority in armament and organization was so vast that, after the Aztec armies had been defeated, the Indians were "defenseless," even when they fought to survive. Moreover, the importation of slaves from Africa made the Indians seem redundant and took away the Spaniards' economic hesitations to kill them off. The ensuing bloodshed took millions of lives. Contagious disease, especially smallpox, killed even more Indians, since these infectious microparasites were new to the Americas. The indigenous population had not had a chance to build up immunity against them. Earlier, a similar fate had decimated the population of Europe, when cholera and bubonic plague reached it in successive waves during the fourteenth century, traveling with the merchants (and the lice and rats) on the trade routes from Asia.

Whereas Indians were killed en masse by "germs and steel," more than ten million Africans were caught, sold into slavery, shipped across the Atlantic, and sold once again to work the plantations of the Americas under the worst conditions, from generation to generation, for centuries. Although a million or more may have succumbed during the countless transatlantic passages and many died from infection, hunger, exhaustion, and violent punishment, this chapter in the history of the West does not count as an instance of mass annihilation. Slavery was not a system of destruction but one of exploitation. In terms of human suffering it was immeasurable.

One of the most contested issues concerns the fate of the Indians of North America. Some scholars, such as David Stannard, author of *American Holocaust,* consider their fate a clear case of genocide.[22] Others contend that only a few thousand Indians have been expressly murdered in the course of the nineteenth century, by settler militias or army units.[23] Many North American Indian tribes fiercely fought US troops or local posses, and although they could not match their enemy in logistics and equipment, they certainly did not succumb as "unarmed and unorganized" victims. Nevertheless, these uneven battles were called the Indian Wars. In the end, the Indians never stood a chance against the superior numbers, logistics, and organization of the white conquerors who, initially at least, had the better weapons.

Many, many more Indians than were killed outright became the victims of "inadvertent omission" at the very least, "criminal neglect" in the worst case: expropriation of the ancestral hunting grounds, deportation, compulsory labor, infectious disease, deliberate starvation, along with the attendant demoralization and alcoholism.[24]

Episodes of local extermination also occurred in Australia, New Zealand, and Tasmania.[25] Similar mass annihilation was perpetrated by other European conquerors in the course of the nineteenth century, for example by the kaiser's soldiers in Namibia and Kenya, or the Dutch colonial army in Indonesian Aceh, or on an even larger scale by the czars' armies in Central Asia and the Caucasus, or by the mercenaries of King Leopold II of Belgium in the Congo "free state."[26] Probably these colonial campaigns around the turn of the nineteenth century were all the more lethal since the Japanese, Russian, Belgian, and German conquerors were latecomers at the great feast of European expansion and all the more in a hurry to consolidate their conquests. But the other European colonial powers also committed massacres on a vast scale.

Little has been documented about most of these episodes, and what little is known has conveniently been ignored. Outside the sphere of European conquest and settlement even less is remembered (by Westerners). The conquering spree of the Zulu king Shaka in 1826 stands out as an extraordinarily bloody campaign, in part because Shaka took no prisoners. Apparently, he needed no slaves. He overran a good part of the territories surrounding his realm with a strategy of utter terror and the wholesale extermination of his defeated enemies and their kin. Although the sources are unreliable, his victims are estimated in the tens of thousands.[27] One reason that Shaka's tale survives in the margins of Western memory is that he operated in a territory bordering on land settled by whites and that he at times successfully confronted European troops. This was not a case of lethal Western expansionism but of mass annihilation by indigenous conquerors. Many other genocidal campaigns by native peoples in Africa, or for that matter Asia or the Americas, must have remained completely unknown for lack of chroniclers who wrote down the events for posterity.

Western testimony of atrocities by indigenous warriors who battled the European invaders served to legitimize colonial expeditions against the "primitives" and "barbarians." But quite often they were based, at least in part, on fact. Large-scale massacres were no exception outside the Western sphere of influence, and they certainly did not occur only in the struggle against European conquerors. Blanket denial of the massacres perpetrated by indigenous warriors against other native peoples, or against the colonizers, amounts to an essentially sentimental embrace of the "innocent Other," in the name of anti-imperialism or a critique of "modernity."

One of the most lethal instances of mass extermination in modern times has almost completely disappeared from memory: the Taiping Rebellion, which ravaged great parts of southern China from 1850 to 1864 and—even by the most prudent estimate—cost some twenty million lives.[28] The worshippers of God's Chinese son, Hong Xiuquan, were inspired by the teachings of Christian evangelists and incorporated some elements from the Gospels in their own millenarian vision. The Taiping rebels wanted to introduce Western innovations, but they also hoped to restore the world of the old Ming dynasty (1368–1644), when China was ruled by indigenous Han emperors instead of the Manchu rulers of the Qing dynasty (1644–1912). Rural misery, ruthless official oppression, and inspiration from their new leader and his teachings incited the peasants to revolt in huge numbers. An unparalleled rebellion resulted. The derelict Qing emperor clung to his power and even employed British advisers to combat the desperate peasants. It was essentially an unequal civil war between ragtag peasant troops and the emperor's antiquated army. The incredibly high casualty numbers were caused by the systematic practice of massacring all defeated warriors along with anyone else who happened to be within reach.[29] And also, the armies on the march survived by plundering the crops and stocks, causing famine wherever they appeared. Of course, until the twentieth century, it was part of the normal course of war that armies had to feed themselves by ransacking the lands they marched through, causing mass starvation among the peasants.

Similar millenarian peasant rebellions had occurred from time to time in East Asia, for example, the Ikko-ikki rebellion in Japan in the fifteenth and sixteenth centuries and the Tonghak movement at the turn of the nineteenth century in Korea.[30]

Time and again, superiority in organization and logistics, even more than advanced weaponry, facilitated the conquest of remote territories and the subsequent massacre of resistant or resigned populations. Back home, the public hardly knew about the destruction that went on and cared even less. The indigenous populations were seen as obstacles on the way to progress who needed to be civilized with a firm hand or, if they foolhardily continued to resist, had to be wiped out. In extreme cases, entire populations were exterminated.

Colonial conquest by its very nature occurred in a sharply demarcated compartment, far from home, against an unfamiliar population, considered alien and inferior, that could not make itself heard, let alone vindicate its rights before public opinion or in the courts of law of the colonizing society. The conquerors knew that their deeds would remain mostly unnoticed at home. Even had their acts become known, they would have been broadly condoned. The perpetrators were rightly confident that they could act with impunity in their enclave of asymmetric violence.

Throughout most of recorded history, the more blood the victors shed, the greater their glory. Only in the past few centuries do the murderers prefer to pass over the bloodshed silently or to minimize the numbers. Even the most fanatic neo-Nazis of today do not flaunt the murderous achievements of Hitlerism but—against all evidence—deny them. What is especially modern about mass annihilation is not so much its vast scale but the horror it has inspired among contemporaries.

These genocidal episodes occurred wherever armed men overcame local resistance and went into a conquerors' frenzy of arson, rape, plunder, and massacre. What made the difference in the nineteenth and twentieth centuries was that the victors' home societies had long since become more pacified and accordingly more civilized: mores had become a bit gentler, sensibilities had become somewhat more refined, and the rule of law had been established, to a degree. But none of this appeared to count in the distinct compartment of colonial conquest. There, quite often, the warriors could afford and needed to let their inhibitions go: to "regress in the service of the regime."

Many contemporary authors stress the "modern" quality of these settlers' massacres and colonial expeditions, sometimes going so far as to declare mass extermination a characteristic feature of modernity. Historian Ben Kiernan has signaled that in almost all modern genocides four themes are evoked. The first two are clearly antimodernist: a claim to the heritage of antiquity and the idealization of agriculture. The two other themes are ethnic purity and the necessity of conquest.[31] Even the German Nazis idealized an almost mythical Germania, as Tacitus had described it, and glorified a pure German Herrenvolk that was to rid humanity of "world Jewry" and would then rule the Slavs of eastern and central Europe as serfs on huge agrarian estates. Similar archaic fantasies are to be found in an equally modernistic ideology, the Khmer Rouge doctrine of restoring the glories of the ancient kingdom of Angkor Wat.

Mass violence has occurred throughout human history, and the scale of that violence was congruent with the scale of social organization that prevailed at the time. More than anything else, the formation of states and the emergence of a state system shaped the mode and the scope of violence. In the long run and in a broad view, individual, incidental violence has decreased, especially in the West. Collective, sustained violence, such as war and mass extermination, has occurred less frequently, but when it occurred, it was even bloodier than before. Administrative capacity, logistic resources, military technology, and propaganda have enormously increased the state's potential for waging genocidal campaigns.[32]

States are the greatest killers of human beings in the modern world. It is not even the state at war with its armed enemies that kills most. Most victims of state violence are unarmed civilians, or defeated and disarmed enemy soldiers.[33]

Not every mass murder was a genocide in the formal sense of the 1948 UN Treaty on Genocide. In many instances the regime's "intent to destroy" cannot be demonstrated, or its objective was not the complete or even partial destruction of the target group. In other cases the intended victims were not singled out for their supposed racial or ethnic origins, for their religion or nationality, but because of their political convictions ("politicide") or class background ("classicide"). Those two denominators were especially pertinent under Communist regimes, bent on destroying political opposition and the propertied classes. Finally, some mass killings had no other motive than to sow random terror among the domestic population or a foreign, defeated people, in order to paralyze all resistance.

Rudolph Rummel coined the term *democide*, literally the "murder of a population," to denote not only genocide but also politicide, classicide, and massive terror killings.[34] In Rummel's terms, democide presupposes the direct involvement of the state in the preparation and perpetration of the killings.

Although the UN Convention on the Prevention and Punishment of the Crime of Genocide does not mention it, in everyday usage, *genocide* implies large-scale annihilation perpetrated by a state, which all UN signatories were and which all perpetrators of genocide were.[35] This omission alone may explain much of the confusion around the concept and the assessment of genocide. The direct involvement of the state's military, police, or special services and of the governing party's militias can in most cases be established beyond any doubt. Much harder to demonstrate is "the intent to destroy, in whole or in part," especially since the highest echelons of the regime are often careful to cover up their involvement to the outside world, for example, by avoiding all paper trails.[36] Sometimes, rebellious troops, militias, or even loose criminal gangs or bands of thugs are the executors of mass murder, and the state plays no visible role. Yet, even in those instances, mass killings are the direct result of incitement by local politicians and gang leaders. The violence usually occurs with the tacit consent and covert encouragement of the government in power.[37] In the Convention on Genocide the term *genocide* also covers "causing serious mental harm," again with the intent to destroy in whole or in part the target group. However, the term *mass annihilation* and its synonyms in this book imply in all cases "serious bodily harm," which invariably is accompanied by "mental harm," but they do not cover mental harm without actual physical damage.[38]

Terms such as *genocide* or, for that matter, *politicide* and *democide* refer to annihilation on a very large scale, with many more victims than even the worst serial killer, operating on his own, ever made. Even a vast terrorist attack, such as the destruction of the Twin Towers in New York on September 11, 2001, does not qualify as genocide: there was no intent to destroy a specific group. Nor does it come under the terms of Rummel's *democide*. His definition does include mass killings with the sole intent to terrorize a population, but only when direct involvement by a state can be demonstrated. The effect of 9/11, in full peacetime, in a country that for almost two centuries had not been attacked by foreign troops on its own soil, was devastating. But on the scale of contemporary mass destruction, the number of casualties was quite small.

The term *mass annihilation* in the present context refers to killings on a very large scale, from many thousands to tens of millions. Moreover, it refers to the killing by armed and organized personnel of human beings who lack any means to effectively defend themselves. And third, it implies that the killers operate in a supportive context, almost always with direct support from the ruling regime. These three criteria—quantity, asymmetry, and a supportive context— together define the term *mass annihilation*.[39] Other criteria, such as the intent behind the killings or the nature of the target group, are to be assessed for each particular episode. The term *genocide* is reserved for those instances of mass annihilation that fall under the UN definition, but the terms *genocidal* and *genocidaire* are used more broadly, in reference to mass annihilation and its perpetrators.

What is "very large scale" or "mass" killing? One person killed is one too many. But our subject is the murder of many thousands, of tens or hundreds of thousands, millions, even tens of millions of human beings.

In the chapters that follow, the selection of cases is pragmatic. In most instances mentioned here, the casualties number hundreds of thousands and more, sometimes many, many more. But instances of mass murder on a smaller scale are also included when they appear pertinent for one reason or another. Other episodes in which apparently hundreds of thousands, even millions of lives were lost, for example, imperial Russian depredations in Central Asia, are mentioned in passing only, for lack of accessible sources.

Having thus demarcated the boundaries of my subject, I will try in what follows to impose some order on the perplexing complexity and variety of mass annihilation. But first, one case is described in detail to convey a more informed impression of the course of events in one exemplary instance: the mass murders in Rwanda in 1994.

CHAPTER 5

Rwanda

Self-Destructive Destruction

T HE MASS ANNIHILATION OF TUTSIS and "suspect" Hutus by the Hutu Power movement in Rwanda in the spring of 1994 came as a complete shock to the outside world, even though there had been many ominous precedents in the recent history of the countries in the African Great Lakes region. However, the major world powers preferred to ignore the insistent and alarming warnings by reporters and foreign observers. Once the violence broke out, foreign governments chose to disregard their "Responsibility to Protect."[1]

One of the most recent instances of mass annihilation, the Rwandan genocide is by now very well documented. This is for several reasons. Not only was the genocidal regime completely defeated, but its perpetrators were rounded up by the hundreds of thousands under the victorious regime of the Tutsi Rwandan Patriotic Front (RPF). In addition, some major defendants were tried by the UN International Criminal Tribunal for Rwanda in Arusha, Tanzania, and by regular courts in other countries. Many suspects have been interviewed, and the trials have yielded massive documentation. Moreover, reporters and scholars have published their accounts, and social scientists have reported on their field research among perpetrators and victims in Rwanda. The Rwandan case, of course, was unique, but it does permit us to identify trends that were quite similar in other episodes of mass annihilation.

In Africa, as elsewhere, European conquest and trade led to expanding networks of expropriation and exchange. Small kingdoms and roaming clans were brought under the direct or indirect authority of the colonizers and forced into larger political and economic entities. The European powers ruled over colonies much vaster in surface than the political units Africans had been accustomed to. The new rulers brought different kingdoms and very divergent groups of people under a single colonial authority. Even so, the new colonial borders often cut right across territories that had once been united under a single indigenous ruler or that were inhabited by people who felt they belonged together, whereas other groups that felt no mutual affinity were forced to live in the same administrative area. Thus, the lines of identification and disidentification were continually redrawn. The European conquerors, on their part, redefined indigenous peoples, often shaping them into "tribes" modeled on a smaller scale after the nations that had emerged in Europe. Group divisions that soon came to look "natural" and "perennial" in many cases had emerged only recently and in fact were more fluid and changing than they were made to appear. Equally, the opposition between "native" or "indigenous" people and alien "immigrants" or "invaders" masked a historical reality of continuous movement of people across large areas.[2] Sustained and intensive social work on all sides was required to rebuild people's identifications and disidentifications, to create the sharp opposition between groups that prepared the ground for massive violence of one side against the other. As in other parts of Africa, intellectuals played a conspicuous role in this effort.[3]

The episode of mass annihilation in Rwanda displays the vicissitudes of one such opposition between groups of people and shows how it was socially constructed over time. Since the seventeenth century, the territories that are now known as Rwanda and Burundi had each been ruled by a royal family with its court elite, while the kingdoms of Buganda and Bunyoro occupied the area to the north, which is now known as Uganda. By the end of the nineteenth century, the region had been divided up by European colonial powers. The northern part of the region was under British rule as Uganda, and the Germans acquired Rwanda, Burundi, and Tanganyika. King Leopold II of Belgium ruled and exploited the Congo through his private company, the Congo Free State. After the defeat of the Germans in World War I, Great Britain kept Uganda. Belgium (which had taken over the Congo from Leopold II in 1908) obtained Rwanda and Burundi under a mandate from the League of Nations.

In 1959, Hutus rebelled against Belgian rule and the privileged position the colonial rulers ascribed to the Tutsi: a massacre of Tutsis ensued. After independence came, in 1962, the Rwandese Hutus revolted and again killed countless Tutsis. In neighboring Burundi, a Tutsi minority government carried out massacres of rebellious Hutus in 1972. The worst came in the spring of 1994, when in three months' time the Hutu Power regime in Rwanda exterminated about eight hundred thousand Tutsis and "disloyal" Hutus with guns, clubs, and machetes in one of the starkest instances of genocide in the twentieth century.

Initially, Western opinion perceived the mass killings in Rwanda as a spontaneous and catastrophic outburst of long-simmering "tribal hatred." There is now ample evidence that the mass extermination of Rwandan citizens was the culmination of a carefully prepared, well-organized, bureaucratic campaign, using modern means of mass communication, propaganda, civil administration, and military logistics, even though the actual slaughter was carried out mainly with the traditional peasants' weapon, the machete.

The courtly elites of the traditional kingdoms were known as Tutsis, and the colonial powers sought the support of these aristocrats for their rule in Rwanda and Burundi, where the great majority of the population consisted of Hutu peasants. Under colonial rule, however, the meaning of Hutu and Tutsi and the relations between these groupings were thoroughly transformed. The categorization of Rwandese and Burundese into Tutsi and Hutu underwent a series of changes over the decades and entailed a multiplicity of overlapping meanings that are almost impossible to disentangle, variable over time and from one community to another. The encompassing social context was one of political and economic transformations toward a larger scale of interdependence.

The precolonial kingdoms of the lands in the Great Lakes region had been quite stable and intricate political systems. Each kingdom exerted considerable power over large parts of the region. The monarch had much say in the appointment of the "provincial" chiefs.[4] However, these so-called central kingdoms did not exert much impact on daily life in the villages and held little sway in the minds of their subjects.[5]

Since the seventeenth century, large swaths of Rwanda had been ruled by the Nyiginya dynasty. The kings maintained their position by granting land to competing aristocratic clans that grew in size and power until another round of internal strife would decimate their ranks again. The aristocrats, mostly pastoralists, were called Tutsi, and they called the common peasants Hutu, which then carried the meaning of *boor,* in the triple sense of a peasant, a person of lowly origin, and a rough or uncouth person. The term *Tutsi* gradually came to mean not only herder but also a person of high status and a warrior.[6]

The kingdom was torn by incessant struggles between kinship associations and regional alliances, between "blood" and "soil" groupings, and it remained divided until the German invasion at the end of the nineteenth century. As Jan Vansina writes in his history of the Nyiginya kingdom, "One must therefore conclude that Rwanda as a fully centralized state is a colonial creation."[7]

Clearly, in the past century and a half, the region of the Great Lakes went through major social transformations, much accelerated during the colonial and postcolonial era, from essentially segmented and decentralized polities and economies to the much more centralized states and markets of contemporary Uganda, Rwanda, and Burundi. But this process, far from being exceptional on the African continent, was the normal course of state formation and economic development there.[8] Thus, on its own, the increase of scale in the social organization of Rwanda cannot serve to explain the extraordinary (although not unique) massacres that occurred there. It constitutes one, necessary, condition for these developments.

Exceptional in Africa is the Rwandan state apparatus, which is quite solid and finely branched into "communes," each with their own "burgomaster," further divided into "sectors" with a "councillor," and finally subdivided into "cellules" with a "responsible." This tiered system allows the leadership to disseminate orders from above and to mobilize the population for the traditional corvée labor.[9] Precisely these compulsory collective duties would take a sinister turn in the spring of 1994.

The social transformations of the past century formed the context for a transformation of emotional concerns. The conceptual pair Hutu-Tutsi gradually shifted meaning and emotional significance. The connotations of these terms have retained a baffling complexity as over time one layer has been superimposed over another and they all continue to reverberate in recent usage.

Contemporary scholars are unanimous in rejecting earlier interpretations of Hutu and Tutsi as fixed racial categories. But, paradoxically, this is exactly what the words had come to mean in Rwandese politics in the twentieth century. Earlier scholarly writings had introduced the racialist theories that were fashionable in Europe around 1900 to the German administration of the area. Racialist thinking equally influenced the Belgian colonial administration and many Rwandese intellectuals of the time.

Early missionaries and ethnographers chose as their informants almost exclusively court aristocrats who identified themselves as Tutsi and who suggested that their peers had always been in command as a hereditary ruling group. This most likely was a retroactive fiction of the sort that established oligarchies are wont to provide (and come to believe themselves after one or two generations). The early German anthropologists characterized this hereditary ruling class as "Hamites," with certain physical characteristics, a "somatic norm image," as the cultural geographer Harry Hoetink terms it: a tall frame; a high forehead; narrow, elongated hands and feet; and a long, thin nose.[10] All these traits were contrasted with the features of the Hutu peasant class, of "Bantu" stock: a flat, broad nose and a short, stocky build. The members of the ruling group gladly accepted the images that the foreign experts presented them with.

The images are reminiscent of nineteenth-century racialist theories about the French aristocracy, which was said to be of "Germanic" stock, tall, blue-eyed, and blond, as contrasted to the common people of France, who were portrayed as swarthy, short, and stocky and of Celtic origin, according to the racist theorists of the day, foremost among them Count Arthur de Gobineau (1816–1882). In his wake, German anthropologists speculated that the original population of the lake kingdoms (Uganda, Rwanda, and Burundi) were of Bantu or "Negroid" origin, whereas the Tutsi were assigned to the "Ethiopid" or "Nilotic" stock that descended from "Hamitic" or "Semitic" roots.[11] In his study of the mass killings, the political scientist Mahmood Mamdani states: "It was an idea shared by rival colonists, Belgians, Germans, English, all of whom were convinced that wherever in Africa there was evidence of organized state life, there the ruling groups must have come from elsewhere. These mobile groups were known as the Hamites, and the notion that they were the hidden hand behind every bit of civilization was known as the 'Hamitic hypothesis.'"[12]

The Belgians adopted the German scholarly view and carried it into administrative practice. Already under German rule, Tutsis were privileged and allowed to attend school. The Belgian authorities, in accordance with their policy of "local self-rule," favored indigenous officials as local administrators, many of them recruited from the court aristocracy that was identified with the Tutsis (even though a considerable proportion was considered to be of Hutu origin). From 1933 on, they set up a municipal civil registry containing file cards of all citizens with a photograph and the mention of their ethnic affiliation.[13]

Contemporary scholars have completely refuted these categorizations of their predecessors. First of all, no evidence has been found for an invasion by Tutsi pastoralists and for their settlement among the Bantu peoples of the Great Lakes region. Second, because their linguistic, religious, and cultural practices are almost completely identical and the distribution of their physical traits does not correspond with the current categories, scholars now incline toward the opinion that Tutsi and Hutu must have belonged to one and the same cultural and endogamic entity for many centuries and that they may well belong to the same genetic grouping.[14]

In his study of Rwanda, Lucien R. Bäck comments: "The fact that Hutu and Tutsi speak one language and share a common culture suggest that they must have lived together for much longer than merely a few centuries, if they are not actually of common stock."[15] And as late as 1988, the ethnic divide was by no means the single and universal cleavage in rural Rwanda. Even in "mixed company" of Hutus and Tutsis, peasants allowed themselves ethnic jokes, "inoffensives plaisanteries," as village politics pitched the locals against outsider officials, rather than one ethnic group against another. But this was soon to change under the impact of ethnic conflagrations in neighboring Burundi and propaganda in the Rwandese media.[16] Contemporary Tutsis reject the binary, hereditary division between Tutsi and Hutu, preferring to apply political and socioeconomic distinctions. This may well be a public stance. The very denial of inborn differences between the two groups was what most enraged the ideologues of Hutu Power. At present, their "ethnic amnesia as rational choice" certainly serves the ruling Tutsi elites to legitimize their position.[17]

An Interlude on the Identification of the Others

Identifications *with* and disidentifications *from* other people presuppose first of all an identification *of* the others. The affective and moral categories require a prior cognitive, or pseudo-cognitive, construction. In Rwanda, up to the present, this has occurred in everyday interactions on the basis of reputation, experience, intuition, and impressions. From the 1920s on, informal practices were complemented with administrative techniques for identification: civil registries, identity papers, passports, photos, and so forth. But this did not foreclose continual questioning of who were Tutsis, who were Hutus, and how to tell the difference between them. On the contrary, as we shall see, precisely the most fanatic proponents of a hereditary division between Tutsis and Hutus were obsessed with the possibility of Tutsis posing as Hutus in order to confuse and divide them. Apparently, even today, even for people whose life vocation consists of applying the distinction, it is very difficult to make a determination by looks alone. Instead, they rely on identification cards, which are based on the civil registry, even as they deplore that these cards have been tampered with for generations. Intermarriage has been common for centuries, and people are classified as Hutu or Tutsi according to paternal descent, but people have often presented themselves as being descended from one or the other grouping as best suited the situation. This practice has rendered all classification essentially uncertain. Despite this, during the Rwandan genocide, the Hutu Power murder squads killed countless Rwandese on the mere suspicion of having Tutsi roots or of having connections and loyalties with Tutsis.

All divisions that have an effect in society, even those that closely correspond to readily observable somatic distinctions and may well be based on genetic differences, are "essentially social." That is, they are reconstructed and elaborated in the stories people tell each other, and they are re-created and enforced in measures taken by the authorities. Moreover, certain distinct physical characteristics may be "inherited" from one generation to another that are based only in part on genetics: a good example is body length, which is closely correlated with superior nutrition and less childhood disease. Until very recently, and in many regions of the world, adequate nutrition was a privilege of the rich, who passed on their fortune and their height to their offspring. A clear skin, a firm glance, an upright posture, a resounding voice, a vigorous stride—in brief, an entire "habitus" that seems to completely characterize physical appearance, and especially to mark the contrast between the appearances of the mighty and the lowly—may be passed down from parents to children and yet, in first instance, lack any genetic foundation.

Not only are the rich richer, but they are also more beautiful. Rich people can more easily select healthy, well-shaped mates, tall, without socially undesirable blemishes or deformities, and in so doing reproduce a socially more desirable phenotype. Thus, there may be significant, inherited differences in physical appearance between social groups that originate not in different genetic stock but in socially inherited differences in wealth, prestige, and power. Next, through the social process of sexual selection—that is, by selective mating—these social differences may in the end *cause* genetic divergence between the various endogamic groups.[18] Finally, a single somatic norm type may very well be absent, and nevertheless the social group may still be recognizable, because of "family likeness," both in the literal and in the Wittgensteinian sense.[19] There may even be a series of mutually quite different somatic types, each of which is considered characteristic for the group, each representing a node in the network of family likenesses and possibly originating in a specific intermarrying network. The latter seems to be the case with European Jews: they do not look alike at all, and yet some do strike interested observers as "very Jewish"—that is, as displaying a family likeness to one of the dozen or so of "Jewish types" the observers have memorized in the form of a Gestalt. Moreover, people may not look that much alike in their features but may act alike, have a similar habitus in speech, gesticulation, gait, bearing, and dress, all of which strongly suggests somatic likeness. Thus it may be that some Tutsis look quite Tutsi, which means at the same time, unlike Hutu, without this implying that they are of different genetic stock. There may well be several distinct Tutsi types. Every Tutsi type would be the result of socially inherited differences in nurture and socialization, reinforced by selective intermarriage, with minor but visible genetic differentiation as the end result. This would explain how Rwandese can sometimes "correctly" identify Tutsis and therefore also Hutus but that often they cannot decide or make mistaken assignments. It would also explain a major paradox in the Hutu Power propaganda: on the one hand, Tutsis are said to be very different from Hutus, including in appearance, for reasons of genetic inheritance, but on the other hand, they are accused of forever trying to pass as Hutu for sinister reasons of their own, and succeeding quite well at it.

Quite often, the fact that it is hard to distinguish a target group from the rest of the population is interpreted, not as evidence that the difference might not be all that great, but on the contrary as even further proof of the evil nature of the enemy, who are capable of passing as the regime's people in order to sow confusion and protect themselves. Genocidal regimes are constantly worried about "Hutu peasants manipulated by their Tutsi spouses" or "Khmer bodies with a Vietnamese mind." Even SS men had to pass a genealogical test before marrying to ensure that no un-Aryan stain would contaminate their offspring.

In the case of Rwanda, in the past hundred years or so, scholars have time and again reignited the controversy over the origins of Hutus and Tutsis. The contested Hutu-Tutsi distinction eventually was instrumental in a series of human catastrophes, culminating in the genocide of the Rwandan Tutsis.

HUTUS AND TUTSIS: FROM PERSONAL IDENTIFICATIONS TO GENERAL DISIDENTIFICATIONS

But what did the terms refer to initially? What did they mean before they were absorbed in the European and colonial discourse of physical anthropology, introduced in the Great Lakes region political and administrative vocabulary, and then adopted in the nationalist and racist rhetoric of the Hutu Power movement?

For lack of written sources, these precolonial connotations are difficult to reconstruct. The few informants who still remembered the older meanings of the terms had unwittingly absorbed the connotations that became current under German, Belgian, and postcolonial rule. In 1986, anthropologist Liisa Malkki interrogated elderly Hutu refugees who had fled the bloody repression by the Tutsi-dominated regime in Burundi after the insurrection of 1972. They were convinced that the Tutsi were foreigners who had arrived from "the Nile" and from "Somalia" and that they were not Bantus but "Hamites."[20]

The Tutsis had invaded Rwanda and conquered the land that once belonged to the Hutus. They did so not simply by violent means: "The Tutsi, possessed of 'innate cleverness' in the art of deception, *tricked* the original inhabitants of Burundi into servitude by the gift of cows." And as a result, the Hutus "became their slaves." In fact, there existed a clientele relation or debt bondage between the mostly Tutsi cattle-owning pastoralists who lent cows to mostly Hutu peasants and received some produce and labor services in return. That relation was embedded in a network of political authority that transformed the economic exchange into a bond of servitude.

These debt obligations initially were carried collectively by the entire lineage, the *umuheto,* but gradually were replaced by obligations upon individual peasants.[21] As René Lemarchand writes in his study of conflict in Burundi, "In the latter sense, Hutu refers to a 'social subordinate' in relation to someone higher up the pecking order. . . . 'Social son' is perhaps even more accurate, since it denotes not just social inferiority but a measure of affectivity. . . . Thus a Tutsi cast in the role of client vis à vis a wealthier patron would be referred to as 'Hutu,' even though his cultural identity remained Tutsi."[22] These bonds became increasingly oppressive and exploitative under colonial rule. In the process, the notion of a specific, local, face-to-face relationship between two persons was transformed into the concept of a generalized and decontextualized relation between two timeless, irreconcilably hostile categories. This was accomplished by introducing the mythical history of conquest by the "alien Tutsis" and their subjection of the "indigenous Hutus." In this latest version, all Tutsis were said to be the descendants of alien conquerors and exploiters of the Hutus. All present-day Tutsis were believed to be trying to regain their political and economic predominance by any means. This lust for power has become the essence of the Tutsi character. Surprisingly, in this account the Tutsis are superior to the Hutus, in some respects: they are more intelligent and more loyal to their own kind. Tutsi women are more attractive. However, these properties only serve the Tutsi thirst for power. Hutu men are lured into marrying Tutsi women, so that the wives can be made to spy on their husbands and betray them to their relatives. The Hutus describe themselves as "primitive," "naive," and "uncivilized," compared to the Tutsis, but also as "simple," "frugal," and "honest" people. The small Twa minority is mostly ignored or "idealized as natives."[23]

THE MOBILIZATION OF FANTASY

The Hutu respondents in the Tanzanian refugee camps of the mid-1980s may have been "naive," dilettante partisans, but their themes were echoed almost word for word by the ideologues of the Hutu Power review *Kangura* and the propagandists of radio Mille Collines in the Rwanda of the early 1990s. In this respect, the ideologues of the extreme Hutu "nationalist" militia, Interahamwe, did not invent their stereotypes but exaggerated and intensified notions that had for many years circulated widely among the Hutu.

Starting with its first issue, *Kangura* reprocessed the familiar themes of the Tutsis as devious manipulators, of Tutsi women as treacherous seductresses, all for the sake of power. In these texts reverberates the repetitive drone, the insistent hyperbole of hypnotic rhetoric:

> Every Hutu should be aware that the Tutsi woman, wherever she may be, works in the pay of her Tutsi nation. As a consequence, every Hutu is a traitor
> —if he marries a Tutsi woman;
> —if he lives with a Tutsi woman;
> —who hires a Tutsi as his secretary or supports her . . . .
> Every Hutu should know that every Tutsi is dishonest in business. He has no other goal than the supremacy of his nation.[24]

Here there is one major opposition, between Tutsi and Hutu, and a minor opposition, between men and women. As the repetition of the word "every" drives home relentlessly, these oppositions are all-embracing and admit of no exception.

An additional element is introduced: "The Hutu must stop pitying the Tutsi."[25] This is an almost literal exhortation to dis-identification, which nevertheless assumes that identification has occurred previously, at least among some Hutu. At this point, the disturbing invective *inyenzi*, surfaces, to be translated by the familiar *cafard*, or "cockroach." Cockroaches keep on coming, they keep on eating, and the peasant must keep on killing them. By now, the Tutsis have been transformed into a general category, dissociated from any particular social figuration, decontextualized and detemporalized. Identification *of* the Tutsis, disidentification *from* the Tutsis, and avoidance of all identification *with* the Tutsis—these are the necessary conditions for establishing a *Hutu Power* identity. Through projection, all evil but still human characteristics have been assigned to the Tutsis; through exaggeration, the Tutsis have been demonized into the superhuman embodiment of evil; and finally, through dehumanization, they have been reduced to vermin. At this point, the stereotype of the "others" is complete. The evil traits are not a matter of degree: they represent *absolute* evil. They permit no exception and apply to all "others": they are *generalized.* And, third, it is immaterial what the "others" do, or say, or seem; these traits are inherent in the being of the "others": they are *essentialized.*[26] The process of disidentification is complete; it has gone even beyond hatred and achieved a semblance of dispassionate destructiveness.

And yet, a complementary process of identification continues, creating an equally absolute, categorical, and essentialized self-stereotype of the Hutus. They should be bound by mutual loyalty, regardless of location or rank: "Every Hutu should consider another Hutu as his brother. If tomorrow one of the volcanoes were to erupt, the Hutus from Rukiga could come and live in Nduga and become by this very fact one of the people there. And if he expected a famine in Nduga, a Hutu from Nduga can go and stay in Rukiga and becomes one of them. But no matter what he does, a Hutu cannot become a Tutsi, nor the inverse."[27]

Such were the messages that were incessantly relayed by the new medium, radio. In the late 1980s, the government had distributed receivers in large numbers among the peasant population. As elsewhere in Africa, people now carried them about wherever they went, closely pressed to their heads.

THE GENOCIDE IN RWANDA

Over the years, in Rwanda, and in Burundi, the circles of identification and disidentification had widened from the scope of village and lineage to generalized categories of Tutsis and Hutus on a national and even transnational scale. In everyday life, ties of kinship and proximity frequently cut across the Tutsi-Hutu divide, because of intermarriage and social mingling. On the other hand, neither side had forgotten the oppression under the monarchy and the bloodbaths that followed independence.[28] The memory remained as a silent undercurrent in all interaction between the two groupings and may well have made for an ambivalence of sentiment in these contacts. Such were the slumbering emotions that the Interahamwe propagandists set out to awaken, radicalize, and fanaticize.

In field research on the memory of the events of 1994, ten years or so after the events, Hutu respondents—both villagers and convicted perpetrators—consistently denied animosity toward their Tutsi relatives or acquaintances.[29] This was partly lip service to the Rwandan Patriotic Front regime's repression of any expression of hostility toward Tutsis (and vice versa). In part, it may be an idealization of circumstances before the war and the genocide occurred. But there is no doubt that the incessant hate-mongering before and during the period of genocide echoed and reinforced feelings shared by a large part of the Hutu population to varying degrees. Hatred may have been only one motive in the killings, but paradoxically the killing itself reinforced the hatred, transforming the self-image of the perpetrator into that of a justified killer who acted out of legitimate hatred for his detestable victims.[30]

The Interahamwe propagandists set out to overcome the ambivalent emotions prevalent at the local level and to hammer them into a monolithic hatred among all Hutus for all Tutsis at the national level. They never entirely achieved that objective, but their effort was necessary to unleash the genocide, albeit not sufficient by itself.

Equally important were the tense relations between Rwanda and neighboring Burundi: the two governments (or, rather, their leaders) had just reached an understanding when their two presidents were killed in an assault on their airplane as it landed in Kigali on April 6, 1994. The death of Juvénal Habyarimana, the president of Rwanda, was the signal for a countrywide annihilation campaign by the Interahamwe movement of extreme Hutu nationalists with strong support from inside the regime. French units had trained the Presidential Guard even as it was engaging in terror executions. Later it was to take the lead in the mass annihilation.[31]

The Rwandan Patriotic Front had been making raids into northern Rwanda since 1990. The RPF consisted of Tutsi refugees from the massacres of 1959 and after, who had lived in exile in Uganda and fought there in the victorious rebel ranks of Yoweri Museveni. By early 1994, the RPF held large swaths of Rwandan territory. The mass annihilation of their fellow Tutsis prompted them to advance all the more rapidly. When the RPF army threatened to take the capital, Kigali, and appeared on the verge of routing the Hutu troops, France once again came to their aid with Operation Turquoise. After three months of genocide, with the rest of the world watching passively, these French units were finally dispatched with the official mission to stop the killings. In vain they attempted to prevent the occupation of Kigali by the RPF and to create a safe zone for the Hutu troops. They did succeed in helping the Hutu army and the Interahamwe escape across the border to Bikavu in eastern Congo.[32] A huge mass of Hutu refugees, implicated in the killings or just fearful of the approaching Tutsi forces, followed the Hutu troops across the border. In Bikavu, the genocidaires continued their murderous raids on the local Banyamalenge people, former Tutsi émigrés and their descendants. This led to an invasion of eastern Congo by the new Rwandese government and to the subsequent ousting of the Congolese president of thirty-two years, Mobutu Sese Seko. He was replaced by Laurent Kabila, initially a protégé of the Tutsi regime. Since then, incessant banditry and civil strife have continued to cause death and destruction in eastern Congo, at the costs of millions of lives. These events have registered almost no effect on international opinion throughout the almost twenty years that the bloodshed has continued.

Although all genocidal regimes depict their targeted victims as the real threat and themselves as the potential victims, in the case of Rwanda it would be frivolous not to try to distinguish people's realistic fears of a military conquest by the RPF from fantasies about the demonic nature of the Tutsis who lived in Rwanda at the time.

By 1990, the RPF did constitute a real military threat in the northern provinces of Rwanda, where its soldiers committed many atrocities against the local Hutu population.[33] And, of course, all the time, in neighboring Burundi the Tutsi minority had controlled the government and the army and had harshly suppressed the Hutu majority, culminating in the 1972 massacre of Hutus, and subsequent bloodshed.[34] In addition, there was the understandable fear that Tutsis in Rwanda might form a fifth column once the RPF had advanced from the north. Moreover, refugees and defeated Rwandese units, many of them wounded or disabled, returned from the fighting in the north and spread hatred of the RPF in their villages.[35]

The target population of a genocidal hate campaign need not constitute a threat in any "real" sense: the Jews in Germany did not; the Kulaks in the Soviet Union might have been expropriated instead of exterminated; and it is hard to see how the victims of the Cultural Revolution in China threatened the Communist regime. In this sense, the relative autonomy of collective fantasy is vindicated, especially when it is kindled by the regime's propaganda.

In Rwanda, as with many other instances of mass annihilation, the dialectics of identification and disidentification were played out within a specific political context of external threat and domestic disintegration. Tutsi troops from Uganda had invaded Rwanda and were confronted by Hutu government forces. Relations with the Tutsi-dominated government in Burundi, to the south, were uneasy at best. In the meantime, the semiautonomous Interahamwe militias were condoned, supported, and often trained and equipped by the regular army but were not entirely under the control of the Hutu-dominated Rwandese government. People fleeing the RPF forces in the north and refugees from Burundi in the south—together numbering more than a million—greatly increased the strain on the resources of Rwandan society.

Everyone in Rwanda (and Burundi) had sufficient cause to fear violent attacks once the state could or would no longer ensure personal safety. The moderate wing of the Hutu "interim" government in Rwanda was trapped between the Hutu Power movement on the one hand and the threat of the RPF army in the north. The Tutsi regime in Burundi, almost completely controlled by the army, could not afford to relinquish its minority monopoly without the danger of being swept aside by the Hutu majority. Each country lived in fear that what had occurred in the neighboring state might next happen there, with the help of the adjacent regime. And with each round of violence, new memories supplied the raw material for subsequent anxieties about the intentions of the complementary group. Thus the stage was set for the next conflagration.

The domestic context was one of a disintegrating state monopoly of violence, the international context one of insecure relations with the adjacent countries. Economic circumstances were equally dismal: an extreme scarcity of the one indispensable economic resource, land. Rwanda's population had increased from 1.6 million people in 1934 to 7.1 million in 1990. In 1997, after the genocide and the exodus of Hutu refugees, the population had dropped to 5.5 million. By 2010, it almost doubled again, to 10.6 million. This density has long created a fierce competition for arable plots.[36] Rwanda, at the time with 407 inhabitants per square kilometer (and 574 per square kilometer of arable land), is not only one the most densely populated areas in the world but a region with few alternatives to agriculture. This lent all conflict of interest an especially explosive zero-sum quality: the land that one person wins is necessarily lost by another. It thus becomes hard to imagine that mutual compromise and consent between rival sides might ever profit all parties concerned. This is the material base for the often extreme "either-or" character of mutual perceptions. Moreover, in 1993, the price of coffee, one of Rwanda's main export commodities, had dropped dramatically, by 70 percent, causing great financial strain in a country already among the poorest in the world.[37]

In Rwanda, the relation between the Hutu Power movement and government circles was intricate and intimate. The militia were covertly supported by the state, even if sometimes publicly rebuked. In the end the government condoned the genocide and the army participated in the mass killings. But the massacres had been prepared long before in an orchestrated campaign that followed the fault-lines of preexisting and widespread patterns of identification and disidentification that had been evolving for almost a century.

The threat of a Tutsi invasion from the north radicalized the Hutu Power movement. Once the killings began, they hastened the onslaught by the Tutsi troops of the RPF. But civilian Tutsis in Rwanda do not seem to have organized themselves against the menace of the Hutu extremists or in support of the RPF invasion.

In fact, in many villages, when the bloodshed began right after the downing of the presidential airplane, local notables set up mixed Hutu and Tutsi patrols to keep the peace. Only when the regime convoked all prefects to a meeting at which it proclaimed the extermination of the Tutsi population and imposed compliance did most village authorities abandon their resistance to the bloodshed.

And yet, notwithstanding the incessant drone of the Hutu Power propaganda machine, the great majority of rank-and-file perpetrators after the fact dismissed the impact of the hate campaign against the Tutsis.[38] It was, they insisted, not so much out of ethnic hatred that they killed, but out of fear of the Interahamwe squads that forced them to either join the killers or be killed themselves. And many of the civilian perpetrators explained that since there was a war going on, every Tutsi had to be killed: men, women, children, even infants in the womb. This was, they said, their way of resisting the advancing armies of the RPF. Members of the militia and regular soldiers explained that they were killing Tutsi civilians en masse "before they would go to the front" to fight the RPF.[39] Most never went, and many who had been at the front deserted and returned home to join in the massacre of unarmed Tutsi.

Through the intricate system of surveillance and corvée service that stretched into every hamlet, local notables knew who among the villagers could be bullied into joining the killing squads and who might refuse. They told the Hutu Power squads whom to approach. This hidden selection, almost completely ignored in studies of mass annihilation, goes a long way toward explaining how some people ended up as mass killers and some did not, including in other genocidal episodes.

Money helped, sometimes, to avoid killing or being killed. Some people got off lightly, paying off the killers with a round of banana beer or some bills, so as to be left in peace.[40] These were usually people with some prestige and means, businessmen for example, who were less easily intimidated and could afford a round of bribes. But many others were forced to join the murderers or be murdered themselves. Other Hutus, caught protecting or hiding Tutsis, were forced to kill those they had hidden with their own hands or suffer death themselves at the hands of the genocidaires.

A position of authority could be a liability. Officials stood out among the villagers, and the killers often singled them out, humiliating, intimidating, or attacking them so as to force them to incite the villagers against the Tutsis. Many complied under duress, a few stood their ground, and some needed no prodding to lead the attacks on the Tutsis.

Were the killers "ordinary Hutu"? Yes, in the sense that, except for the Interahamwe and the Presidential Guard, they had not been especially indoctrinated or trained for mass murder. Although they behaved outrageously in the extreme, there is no indication that there were more psychopaths and criminals in their ranks than among the general population. To all appearances, the vast majority of murderers indeed seemed "ordinary Hutu."[41] In one and the same situation, some participated eagerly, others reluctantly, still others indifferently. But what made them join at all and then act in one way rather than another has not been established, nor did researchers try hard to find out.

The number of perpetrators in the Rwandese genocide was huge. Estimates vary between one hundred thousand and three million. But the best approximation might be about two hundred thousand; about a quarter of those carried out 90 percent of the murders.[42] Most of those were soldiers or members of the Interahamwe. In general, the perpetrators tended to be young males with no or few children, poor, landless, and unemployed. Local circumstances varied enormously, but nowhere was there a shortage of killers. It was indeed a "génocide populaire."[43] The gangs tried to get as many people as possible to come with them and often persuaded or compelled the new "joiners" to kill with their bare hands.[44]

Women did come and watch the massacres, egging on the men and stripping the corpses of anything they could use. Some women joined in the actual killing, and a few were among the worst perpetrators. Clearly, greed was a major motivation. So was anger about the RPF invasion and fear that the old, Tutsi-dominated monarchy might be restored. Finally, many joined in the killing out of obedience to a village authority and out of conformity to their peers from the same community.

Many more Hutus did not join the killing. Those who were pressured to kill, and refused to do so, risked being killed themselves. Even so, there were those who took enormous risks to help Tutsis they knew and sometimes even those they had never met before.[45] Some helpers were actually members of the killer gangs, willingly or unwillingly. Apparently the circumstances allowed for self-selection, and people did make choices that could carry very different consequences.

There is no reason to assume that the helpers were not just as "ordinary" Rwandese as the perpetrators are said to be. Clearly, the term *ordinariness* does not discriminate the eager killers from the reluctant accomplices or the valiant rescuers, or from those who managed to remain aloof. The expression covers the entire diversity in personal histories, individual dispositions, and social positions that make all the difference in one and the same genocidal context.

The genocidal campaign started with Interahamwe and regular military in army trucks descending on a village in the early morning hours, carrying with them lists of local Tutsi families who were then rounded up with the assistance of the local mayor, or *préfet*.

The local authorities knew who in their community counted as Tutsi and where they lived. In their turn, these officials were under pressure from their superiors and under threat from the militias and army units. Sometimes the Tutsi families were marched to a nearby grove to be shot; more often they were assembled in the village church to be exterminated with machine guns and hand grenades.

These were the more "orderly" massacres, carried out by soldiers and militiamen specialized in violence and operating in an occupational compartment of their own.

In contrast, quite often loosely organized killer squads made their own decisions whom to go after, sometimes quite arbitrarily: the most common accusation was that "the accused was Tutsi, looked Tutsi, or supported Tutsi."[46] After the victims had been singled out, many of them were humiliated, robbed, and abused in every which way. And even then, they were made to pay for the privilege of being killed instantly by bullet rather than being tortured or raped first and then slowly hacked to pieces with a machete.[47] "The killings were physically intimate," writes anthropologist Lee Ann Fujii in *Killing Neighbors*.[48] Murders were carried out with clubs, hoes, axes, hammers, spears, swords—in short, the tools Rwandese peasants had at hand. The victims were thrown, alive or dead, in nearby latrines and cesspools. The atmosphere was one of unceasing horror and frenzy, but also of a gruesome carnival, with the killers running around in masks and covered with banana leaves so as to spread panic and avoid being recognized. They banged on cans and blew whistles to intimidate their victims and make merry.[49]

The bloody feast usually began once the marauders gathered before a Tutsi house to taunt and scare the inhabitants while drinking palm beer. Next, if the owner seemed powerless against their jeers and insults, they became more daring and would attack his cow, at last killing and eating it. Since the owner appeared unable to counter such humiliation or protect his property, obviously he would not be capable of protecting his family and himself. Excited by the palm beer and a rare meal of meat, the marauders would recklessly invade the house, taking whatever they could lay hands on and attacking the women. After they had robbed and beaten the man of the house, violated his womenfolk, depriving them of all dignity, their targets were now worthless and had to be murdered to prove it. Moreover, alive the family might someday accuse their attackers and demand restitution. Apparently, the killers feared that at some point they might be held accountable. This is also why they tried to create as many accomplices as possible by forcing people to watch and join in and, when their turn came, to kill.[50]

The killers operated in large groups, and a few did most of the killing; the others were pressed to watch, and bystanders were pulled over to look on. All this served to extend the circle of accomplices, obliterate individual responsibility, and create a solidarity between the killers and "their people." On the other hand, because the perpetrators expressly acted in public view, they left evidence and witnesses of their deeds that would make it easier to prosecute them in the future. But apparently, they acted at once out of fear for retribution and in the delusion of impunity, even as the RPF was fast approaching.

The entire murderous masquerade served the purposes of the Hutu Power regime, which had set its mind on the extermination of the indigenous Tutsi. The perpetrators let themselves go in wild and barbaric acts of destruction, which, no matter how uninhibited, still were functional in the realization of the objectives of the genocidal regime: a clear instance of *collective regression in the service of the regime*.[51] Usually, they would herd a large group of Tutsis into a church or school, so as to kill them more efficiently. But first, the victims were made to suffer, for example, by cutting their Achilles' tendons to prevent them from fleeing, even when they were too young or too old to run. Only then were hand grenades thrown into the crowd, maiming many before killing them.[52]

The Rwandan genocide also was an instance of autodestructive destruction, since the genocidaires were busy killing unarmed and unorganized Tutsis but put up little resistance against the heavily armed and tightly organized RPF on its march toward Kigali: "We could not fight with the [RPF] soldiers. We fought those we could fight."[53]

Though the Rwandese government forces faced a stronger opponent and were powerless to expel the invaders, they made little effort to defend what ground they could still hold. Instead, facing defeat, the Hutu Power regime used its scarce resources to deal once and for all with its Tutsi citizens and annihilate them to the very last soul: it was "now or never," even if it was the last thing the Hutu Power regime would ever do.[54] In fact, by mid-May, when the RPF's onslaught could no longer be halted, when some three-fourths of Rwanda's Tutsis had already been murdered, and most civilian perpetrators had already tired of the killings, urgent calls were broadcast to continue the massacres to the very last Tutsi. This makes the Rwandese genocide a prime example of a specific mode of mass annihilation: a *losers' triumph*, a delirium of annihilation at the time of imminent military defeat.[55] Even if the regime was about to lose the war, the destruction of the enemies of the Hutu race would be its grand victory in the face of history. The Rwandan case is a telling instance (there are more examples) of this paradoxical last effort to exterminate the unarmed and unorganized enemy en masse, rather than make an all-out attempt to prevent defeat at the hands of an armed, organized, and advancing enemy.

Before the genocidal violence burst forth, Tutsis and Hutus frequently mingled, attending the same schools, hospitals, and churches. In that sense, Rwandese society on the eve of the genocide was not thoroughly compartmentalized along ethnic lines. The Hutu Power regime carried on a relentless propaganda campaign to stir up hatred against the Tutsi but never tried to put in place institutional separations.

Once the mass killing started, the perpetrators made little effort to hide their acts. When Tutsis were rounded up to be killed, they were held not in isolated camps or execution sites but in churches and schools right in the middle of the village.[56] The murders usually occurred not in separate, shielded killing compartments but in public and even with ostentation. Nor did most killers operate as closed units of professional violence specialists, distinct from the civilian population. On the contrary, any Hutu who wanted to could join the massacre, if not actually pressed to do so. In all these respects the mass annihilation occurred under conditions of low compartmentalization in Rwandese society.[57]

As members of their communities and cells, Rwandese peasants were accustomed to being called every now and then for corvée duty. That is how many Hutus interpreted the order by the authorities to go and cleanse the area of Tutsis. They went about the work as a compulsory *boulot*, a job they were told to do. Initially many were reluctant and had to overcome a fear and loathing of bloodshed and murder, but gradually the task became easier to perform. In the early morning they marched together through the fields with their machetes on their shoulder, as if they were going to clear away the bush, and at night they returned home after a day's work. Some nights there might be a village feast where the victims' cows were slaughtered and their meat divided among the revelers, with much drinking and laughter.[58] This is how convicted and jailed perpetrators told their story to Jean Hatzfeld, author of *Machete Season*.

In other villages young men assembled to seek out area Tutsis, threaten them, steal their belongings, and then slaughter and eat their cows. Next, they would arm themselves and dress up. After gathering as a group, with their clubs and machetes, their shouts and songs, in their masks and costumes, surrounded by a small crowd of onlookers, they would pursue their human targets to finish them off. In the process, the killers collectively created a mobile, temporary killing compartment in which anything was allowed, where moral precepts counted no more, and where they goaded one another into a furor that drove them to kill, even as the act of killing whipped up their furor even further.

After a day's action, the killers went home and took up their everyday activities, as peacefully as ever. The next day they might join again in the hectic excitement of the killer band.[59] In this respect they resemble sports fans who, quite innocently, collectively create a scene of ecstasy and abandon; when one of them steps out of the crowd, he may be as sober and quiet as ever—that is, until he moves back into the charmed circle. Like them, the murderers always operated in groups, but they acted within a compartment of wild cruelty that the ruling regime had encouraged and even compelled them to collectively create.

In many instances of mass killings in public, observers have noted the ostentatiously obscene cruelty, the theatrical, even festive staging of the murders, and interpreted it as evidence of the barbarization of the perpetrators. (Several similar episodes are discussed in chapter 7.) But the theatrics of destruction may also serve a function: to demarcate the location and the moment as an extraordinary occasion in which all normality is suspended, to create a clearly distinct killing compartment in the absence of organizational separation and physical seclusion.

CHAPTER 6

Genocidal Regimes and the Compartmentalization of Society

THROUGHOUT HUMAN HISTORY, armed men in groups have killed, not just their armed and coordinated enemies in battle, but in even larger numbers unorganized and unarmed men, women, and children who were helpless against their violence. Mass annihilation is, alas, not the exception. Through the ages, it has occurred time and again, mostly in times of war, civil war, insurrection, or in their aftermath. In modern times it may have happened less frequently, but when it has, it has often been on an even larger scale. The key factor in this transformation of mass extermination is the emergence of states, in a system of states.

STATE FORMATION AND GENOCIDAL REGIMES

As states increasingly succeeded in monopolizing the means of violence in their territory, they accumulated a capacity for destruction unequaled by any institution except rival states. Within each territory this monopolization of violence brought about pacification, as domestic violent competitors were successively defeated. At the same time, states as monopolists of violence threatened the violence monopoly of rival states. In the modern age, "states make war and war makes states."[1] This ongoing competition created a potential for large-scale, violent conflict between states, more devastating than any other type of collision. By the same token, this concentration of the means of violence gave the state an unequaled capacity to repress its own citizenry.

And yet, the domestic monopolization of violence by the state also created the basic conditions for the civilizing processes that Norbert Elias discussed. Physical violence receded from everyday life. As a result, people no longer needed to be constantly on the alert against attack. They, especially the young men among them, could also less afford to fight, to wound or kill others. Their fighting skills diminished. The vast majority of people became less prone to physical violence, less prepared for it, and less competent to use it, but better at controlling their own inclinations to use force. The social regulation of the self-regulation of violent impulses grew stronger and more encompassing, in every individual life and for more and more individuals.[2] In Western societies especially, the murder rate steadily declined.[3] Violence increasingly became the province of specialists, of soldiers, police (and criminals, too). They had increasingly effective arms at their disposal, and in ever greater quantities.

This process of state formation went together with an encompassing transformation of the people within the state's reach into citizens of the state, through the incessant exertion of what the sociologist Pierre Bourdieu calls "symbolic violence."[4] The emergence of states, especially nation-states, also transformed the knowledge, the judgment, and the feelings that people had about one another. The circles of identification widened to embrace the entire nation, all the state's people. The circles of disidentification similarly broadened to refer to other, competing, nations in their entirety or to groups within the nation's borders that were nevertheless considered alien. If the nation was not the sole common denominator of identification and disidentification, then creed, race, or class might be superimposed on it or even come in its stead. What matters is that the social organization of sentiment greatly increased the scope of both inclusion and exclusion, of solidarity and hostility, of identification and disidentification.

This is the broad context in which many episodes of mass annihilation occurred in the nineteenth and twentieth centuries. Mass annihilation is a special kind of violence, very asymmetrical and on a very large scale: organized and armed men kill large numbers of people who are without arms and without coordination, and they do so within a framework of institutional support or, at the very least, of condonation. Such violence occurs more readily in the context of societies that are highly compartmentalized: the target group becomes more and more separated from the dominant group in society, in every sense and at every level.

Asymmetric mass violence occurs most often in the shadow of war: in the aftermath of victory, or on the eve of defeat. In times of war, inhibitions against violent and impulsive behavior tend to break down. As long as soldiers fight a more or less symmetric enemy that stands its ground, the opportunity to engage in wanton slaughter does not occur. It is only when they face defenseless people—defeated enemies or unarmed civilians—that the chance presents itself.[5] Once they are brutalized by battle, soldiers are more likely to inflict atrocities on people who represent no threat to them. Many fighters are enraged by what the enemy did to them or their comrades in arms. This impels them to take revenge, and then, all too often, anyone who belongs to the enemy's people will do. War decivilizes. It dulls empathy; it prepares one to remain untouched by the suffering of others and to inflict such suffering oneself, with equanimity or even elation.

War is the perennial metaphor invoked in mass annihilation. Not only does war facilitate mass killing, but it also helps to legitimize it. Even when there is no actual war, the metaphor of war alone serves to justify eliminating the enemy, if only in self-defense or in the defense of one's country and the cherished symbols that go with it: if we do not now act against them, and once and for all, then they will act against us, and finish us off first. Nations that have experienced bloody conflict in the preceding generation are more prone to start another round and will resort more easily to violence against unarmed and unorganized "opponents."

In almost all instances, a regime depicts its genocidal campaign against a helpless target group, even though it is entirely one-sided, as a symmetrical battle against enemies who might well get the upper hand if they are not destroyed before they get the chance. Metaphors of contagion and infestation are equally common in this context: the opponent is like a disease, a virus, or bacteria, or like a parasite or an insect, that must be eradicated before it destroys the host body.[6]

COMPARTMENTALIZATION

A state is behind almost every instance of mass annihilation. Time and again states have committed or condoned annihilation campaigns within and beyond their borders. The state's monopolization of violence may over time have resulted in the further civilization of society. Yet at times, these more civilized ways nevertheless have excluded from protection entire categories of citizens, who, in extreme cases, have been exposed to all the violent resources of the state's monopoly. The regime may mobilize the entire machinery of the state to persecute and even annihilate its target group, and this can be done more thoroughly than could have been achieved in societies where the state apparatus did not so completely monopolize the means of violence.

Regimes that resort to mass annihilation do so mostly under conditions of advanced compartmentalization, a separation of the regime's people from the target group in every sense and at every level. The targeted people must first be demarcated, they must be registered, and they must be isolated and made the object of a persistent campaign of vilification and dehumanization. The rest of the population is incited to hate and loathe them. This is the social work of "disidentification." It proceeds by actualizing long-standing (and often long dormant) prejudices, by activating stereotypes—in sum, through disidentification as an active process. This entails explicit propaganda campaigns, provocations, shaming rituals, public humiliation, and allegations of villainous manipulation and conspiracy for which not only the supposed wrongdoers but the target group as a whole is held responsible. Stalinist and Nazi show trials are of course telling examples of this practice. The prospective victims are portrayed as the actual threat, the regime's population as the intended victim: it is the regime that acts out of self-defense and to protect its population. This is the other face of a simultaneous campaign to strengthen positive identifications among that part of the population that is under the regime's protection. It serves to make those citizens into "the regime's own people." What is required at this point is a theory, yet unwritten, of the symbolic violence that engenders physical violence and of the symbolic violence that is engendered by physical violence.

As compartmentalization progresses, people tend to become increasingly opinionated and aroused about the target population while also becoming quite indifferent about what is actually done to them ("which, anyway, is their just dessert"). Whatever impulses they would rather not own up to in themselves they now are ready to ascribe to the target population (a proclivity called "projective identification"): lust, greed, a thirst for power, cunning, and evil designs toward the regime's population combined with favoritism toward their own kind, as well as weakness, cowardice, sloth, and squalor. It now seems better not to consort with the target people, not to be seen with them, to avoid them even in private. This may come from sincere personal aversion but also out of fear of being tarred with the same brush. "Bystanders also learn and change as a result of their own action—or inaction. . . . To reduce their own feelings of empathic distress and guilt, passive bystanders will distance themselves from the victims." These people must be deserving of their fate and therefore should be devalued.[7] Because daily contacts become fewer, stereotypes and slander become harder to correct. Of course, most of the regime's people know a few of the target people personally, and more often than not, those acquaintances do not appear at all like the official model: they are "good" people, apparently the exception that confirms the rule. So, almost every outsider is an exception to at least one insider.

There is in this compartmentalizing process a close interplay between official state doctrine, propaganda, and public ritual and, on the other hand, personal perception and sentiment. In this sense, the relation between the regime and its citizens is very intimate indeed.

Subsequently, compartmentalization enters the "legal" sphere and becomes institutionalized. The targeted outsiders are barred from schools or hospitals, relegated to their own "reserved" institutions, excluded from educational and medical care. They may also be assigned on government orders to special living areas, "ghettos" in the same city, "homelands" or "reservations" in the same land. They will be allowed to use common, public spaces only at certain times; they may be subject to a special curfew. In order to prevent spontaneous contact between the regime's people and the target group, and to further humiliate them, the excluded may have to wear special marks, unless they are identifiable at first sight as targeted people, for example, by the color of their skin. All these aspects of the compartmentalization process are well conveyed by the South African term *apartheid*.

When actual deportation begins, compartmentalization is carried to its next phase. The targeted people may first be isolated in special zones or transported to shielded areas such as internment camps, in order to concentrate and more perfectly control them. Special units are assigned the task to round up, deport, segregate, and sequester the target population: *out of sight is out of mind.*

At this point, the stage is set for the extermination of the intended victims. Specific areas may be screened off from the uninitiated so that torture and murder may proceed unnoticed by, but not unbeknownst to, the broader population: it is a public secret, private knowledge. The regime's people suspect what is going on and are duly intimidated; they dare not mention it openly, let alone hold the regime accountable in public.[8] They know that they may be punished, but not exactly for what, and so, out of fear, they police themselves.[9]

The violence against the target people is carried out in dedicated sites of annihilation. Here, the killing squads do their work. The professionalization of mass murder is in itself a token of advanced compartmentalization: the regime can do without the participation of civilians, and the regime's people remain shielded from confrontation with mass destruction. The paradigm is German society under Nazism, for it was the most compartmentalized of annihilation campaigns in these respects, Indonesia and Rwanda during their episode of mass annihilation much less so.[10]

In societies that have gone through a relatively prolonged period of domestic peace and little or no foreign warfare, the aversion toward violence and the incompetence in coping with it and applying it may have grown accordingly. This is a basic assumption of Elias's theory of civilizing processes. Under those conditions, brutal, open violence against the target group will meet with indignation and disgust among a good part of the population, even if it finds itself not directly threatened. A regime that is about to initiate large-scale persecutions, deportations, and killings must somehow shield its population from perceiving the harm it intends to inflict on the target group. It will therefore make an effort to further compartmentalize society.

When it comes to the actual campaign of annihilation, in most instances the killing proceeds in remote, isolated locations, "hinter den Kulissen," as Elias calls it, "behind the wings," to spare the sensitivities of the regime's population and possibly to protect the identity of the perpetrators and thus ensure their impunity. Both phases of the Nazi Holocaust, the extermination by bullets and the extermination by gas, took place in remote zones of the Ukraine and eastern Poland, far from the heart of Germany and from the occupied countries of western Europe.

But even in these most thoroughly compartmentalized episodes of mass annihilation, what went on did not remain entirely secret. Thus, the men in the extermination squads of Police Battalion 101 were visited by their wives, who attended the executions; Wehrmacht soldiers came to watch the rows of naked Jews being gunned down, and quite a few lent a helping hand.[11] Many of the Gentile villagers helped search the victims for coins and jewels and returned later to rob the corpses of whatever remained of value.[12] As for the extermination camps, a witness stated: "Secrecy? Good heavens, there was no secrecy about Treblinka; all the Poles between here and Warsaw must have known it, and lived off the proceeds. All the peasants came to barter, the Warsaw whores did business with the Ukrainians—it was a circus for all of them."[13] And the camp commander, Franz Stangl, told his interviewer Gitta Sereny: "The whole place stank to high heaven from kilometers away. For two weeks after coming through there—or 'visiting' there—many used to say they couldn't eat. But no, they saw nothing and knew nothing, of course."[14]

Even so, the Nazi SS went to extremes to try and keep the final destination of the European Jews a secret. They did this to facilitate the deportations as well as to avoid antagonizing the rest of the population. When defeat appeared unavoidable, they did what they could to destroy all traces of their activities and to escape captivity at the hands of the Allies.

The annihilation of so many millions of people could not proceed in perfect secrecy, not even under the most compartmentalized conditions. When compartmentalization has been less complete, secrecy has been even less assured. At the other extreme of the spectrum are the massacres in Rwanda or the deadly South Asian riots during Partition, where the killer gangs rounded up spectators to make them witnesses and accomplices of their deeds. In a sense, with their conspicuous provocations and cruelties, performed in front of the crowd, they created the killing compartments on the spot through perverse rituals of atrocity: either one sided with the murderers or one risked being put on the side of the victims. Most people by far must have tried to stay as far as possible away from these killings and therefore are never mentioned in the reports.

Under conditions of advanced compartmentalization, the menial work of murder is left to specialists, usually military men, militia members, police, and a sprinkling of medical people and lawyers. Common criminals, too, can be of use, so long as they maintain a minimum of discipline and obey their superiors. The target group is further separated from the regime's population: "fraternization" is strictly forbidden, no succor should be given those who are taken from their homes, and those who might be tempted to help the prospective victims risk the same fate. People who are found hiding targeted persons or protecting them in any way may themselves be killed on the spot.[15]

Even as the process of compartmentalization is carried to its completion, in a psychological and social as well as a spatial and temporal sense, the separation is never perfect, and the sequence does not proceed in every case neatly from the first stage to the last. Often the killing sites are visible, even accessible, to the rest of the population. Yet even then, compartmentalization continues, at least in a mental and social sense. Passersby avoid interaction with the victims, try not to identify with them, and ignore them as much as possible. In the words of German sociologist Wolfgang Sofsky: "The indifferent are by no means innocent of the facts. They know as much as they want to know, and what they don't know they do not want to know. But that means that they do indeed know enough to know that they want to know no more."[16] In brief: "They make themselves not know."[17]

In many episodes of mass annihilation the rest of society maintains its pacified ways, and the vast majority of citizens continues to be protected by law, custom, and etiquette. Just as it would not occur to the butcher to use a knife outside the shop or on anything but animal flesh, the police and the guards would not dream of attacking anyone who does not belong to the designated category or of brutalizing their victims outside the spaces marked off for the purpose. Obviously, what occurs under these conditions is the bureaucratization of barbarism. The most barbarous acts are perpetrated, sometimes in a calculated and detached manner, sometimes wildly, with passion, lust, and abandon. What matters is that the barbarism occurs in demarcated spaces, in delineated episodes, well separated from the rest of society, from the everyday existence of the regime's citizens. The barbarity is compartmentalized.

The writer Mark Danner quotes witnesses of the "Bosnia Genocide":

> Western and his colleagues were struck not only by the cruelty of these abuses but by their *systematic* nature; they very rapidly came to understand that though the Serb soldiers and, especially, the "paramilitary" troops responsible for "mopping up" were committing wildly sadistic acts of brutality under the influence

of alcohol, their officers were making rational, systematic use of terror as a method of war. Rather than being a regrettable but unavoidable concomitant of combat, rapes and mass executions and mutilations here served as an essential part of it.[18]

Here, the wildness and brutality are let loose, or maybe even instilled, and at the same time instrumentalized for specific purposes, within demarcated spaces, and at appointed times: an archipelago of enclaves where cruelty reigns as all the while it is being reined in.[19]

At times, under the conditions of state monopolized violence, a certain level of civilization is maintained in almost all respects and for the vast majority of the population while nevertheless the regime isolates a target group, separates it in every respect from the dominant group, and, in the extreme case, creates and maintains compartments of destruction and barbarism, in meticulous isolation, almost invisible and well-nigh unmentionable. It is as if the civilizing process continues in one part of society but takes the opposite turn in another part: in the compartments where the target group is isolated and destroyed, a process of barbarization, a *de*civilizing process takes place. Norbert Elias speaks in this context of a "collapse of civilization."[20] It is more precise to describe the process as one of *local* decivilization, occurring wherever and whenever the regime and its henchmen deport, concentrate, and exterminate their victims. Within the confines of these compartments, civilization has been suspended, under carefully controlled conditions decivilization is allowed to proceed, barbarism is deliberately provoked and unleashed against the target population.

Decivilization may be described at the mental and social level as a breakdown of civilized canons of interaction, as a regression into a prior, more primitive, less structured stage of existence. The killers in their murderous enclaves go through a *regression in the service of the regime*.[21] Brutalized and coarsened, they still act within the confines and the conditions that the regime has imposed on them so as to realize its objectives. The regime has mobilized barbarism for its own purposes and carefully encapsulated it into special compartments of local decivilization.[22] Even wild destructiveness has been made instrumental, functional in the regime's campaign against its designated enemies.[23]

Civilization has not broken down everywhere or in all respects, the social order has not fallen to pieces, barbarism has not spread all over, and decivilization has occurred only in well-defined episodes and spaces. The civilizing process has taken a different track, one of *dyscivilization,* allowing for isolated and localized sites of decivilization.[24] In many respects the state continues to function in a bureaucratic, planned, "modern," and even "rational" manner. But within this framework it has arranged for encapsulated reservations of atrocity.

Compartmentalization is the social arrangement and the psychic defense mechanism par excellence in a society where targeted groups are excluded from the protection of the state and from the solidarity of the other citizens and where they are mistreated and murdered in enclaves of atrocity, while in the rest of society a certain degree of civilization continues to prevail. This requires both rigid separations and carefully staged passages between the different emotional and interactional domains. As a consequence, the transition to a more flexible, more varied repertoire of relational and emotional modes, as Norbert Elias observed it in the long run of the western European civilizing process he studied, is suspended or even reversed under these conditions.

Thoroughly compartmentalized societies will develop quite strong but also quite rigid types of social control and self-control. Elaborate codes of conduct and expression may be maintained to the smallest detail, until one steps over the threshold and into the compartment of barbarity, where all cruelty and wildness are allowed, up to the moment that one again leaves this reservation and resumes one's controlled demeanor, *as if nothing had ever happened:* that is compartmentalized behavior.

The "regression in the service of the regime" is the very opposite of what Norbert Elias calls "the controlled decontrolling of emotional controls."[25] In the former, it is the regime that is in control and the individual who "lets go" within the imposed restraints; in the latter, it is the individual who intentionally "lets go" of certain controls and maintains others. What occurred in Nazi Germany, Elias considers "a collapse of civilization": a barbarizing or decivilizing process.[26] But this characterization, however striking, is not enough. It signals what disappeared; it does not specify the transformations of civilized behavior and the limitations imposed on it. Nor does it show how enclaves of barbarism are contained and restrained by the surrounding society. What has occurred is not so much the overall collapse of civilization as its rigidification and ritualization in society at large and its abolition in local enclaves of barbarism. Only thorough compartmentalization at all levels can maintain society in this precarious mode.

The perpetrators, too, are frequently closed off from the rest of society. They form part of secretive and exclusive units, in remote or isolated surroundings. They are often sworn to secrecy. Quite often, outside information does not reach them, as all communication with the world beyond the killing sites is censored and outsiders are prevented from contacting them.[27]

For a better understanding, more must also be known about the transitions, the recurrent *rites de passage* from "civil" to "brutal" conduct. How, after a day's work, the guard gets ready to leave and go home (washes up, changes clothes, combs his hair, puts on a different face, remains silent about it at home, denies everything, lies about it, or, maybe, recounts the day's events in vivid, lurid detail). Is there a distinct threshold to cross, a precise time schedule and calendar to adhere to, or do the guards and killers simply slip in and out of their roles in haphazard, irregular fashion?[28] Are the venues hidden, inaccessible, isolated by deserts, swamps, woods, screened off by walls and fences, or rather visible to passersby, who may even enter and watch at will, or, in extreme cases, join the carnage?[29] When there are no specially constructed extermination camps, in most instances by far the killers take their victims on a short march or ride, away from inhabited areas to a somewhat secluded killing site, out of the sight of bystanders who do not make a special effort to come and watch. This spatial separation, most likely, also marks the distinction between those who are to be killed and those who are left behind to be spared, as well as between those who are killers and those who do not kill (and are not killed).[30] Thus, the Khmer Rouge killed camp inmates in full view of the other detainees: "They just killed in public. For example, when somebody found a snail during work, and tried to eat it, when the Khmer Rouge leader saw him, he would come over and kill that person. He didn't bring him somewhere else, he just killed immediately, in front of all people."[31] But in other instances, the victims were herded in trucks to be executed in the forest, often at night.[32] "Angkar [the Party] always said we should not go there. They said the forest was haunted, the ghosts would scare us with strange noises." These actually were the screams of people being murdered.[33]

How do the guards, the torturers, the militiamen think about themselves? We almost always get to know them in a defensive stance, forced to speak before their judges. Little do we know about them when they were in full action, on the offensive, when they had to prove precisely the opposite: their zeal and zest and gusto, their conviction, loyalty, and commitment to the task. But again, how during one phase do they think of themselves in the other phase: are they "a different person," "do they turn off all emotions," "try not to think," or are they proud and pleased with themselves in their other capacity? All of these questions concern the nature of mental and social compartmentalization. They are discussed in more detail in chapter 8.

Compartmentalization need not be so extreme. It may occur under comparatively innocuous conditions. Thus, in contemporary consumer societies, butchery is equally relegated to special compartments: not only slaughterhouses but also agro-industrial pig and chicken farms are hidden from the public's view, and again, once out of sight, they are effectively out of mind. Even while enjoying their meat, consumers somehow manage to forget that they are actually eating the remnants of a living being and to ignore how it was raised, slaughtered, and carved up, even though they know it all very well.

In most societies prostitution is effectively shielded from the rest of social life: there are spatial enclosures, "zones of tolerance," "red light districts," "closed houses"; there are temporal separations ("darkness," "girls of the night"), and both the prostitutes and their clients usually succeed in slipping in and out of these reservations without being noticed. Similar observations can be made about prisons, insanity wards, and social theorist Michel Foucault's other favorite haunts.

The spatial isolation and social exclusion of a designated kind of people also occurs in the "ghettoization" of American inner cities, as French sociologist Loïc Wacquant has described it.[34] What adds much interest to his detailed account is Wacquant's explicit analysis in terms of "decivilization": as the state withdraws from the inner city areas, chains of interdependence break down, self-restraints disintegrate, "depacification" proceeds as violence proliferates without the police bothering to intervene, social differentiation is reversed, and only informal economic activities remain. . . . Islands of "decivilization" have emerged in the very midst of a relatively civilized society that continues without bothering much about these enclaves. Outside these "ghettos" life proceeds "as usual."[35] Wacquant stresses the necessary disidentification that keeps the "underclass" as a separate category outside the bounds of normal and moral citizenship. What he describes is in fact a situation of effective compartmentalization that maintains the precarious separation of "civilized" and "decivilized" spheres but remains very far removed from actual annihilation.

What matters here is how these pockets of decivilization are effectively shielded from the surrounding society, warded away from consciousness, exempted from affective or moral identification. No doubt, there already is an onset of brutalization under such conditions of de facto apartheid. The transition from indifferent neglect to actual extermination would, however, require many, most momentous and most unlikely, further steps.

Central to Elias's ideas on the civilizing process in its advanced phase is the notion that minimal standards of civilized behavior are maintained under all circumstances and more or less equally with respect to everyone. There is an implicit assumption of minimal equality, of some measure of equal treatment and equal esteem. Such a modicum of equality means that people identify with all others in their society as beings that are more or less the same as they themselves are.[36] It implies, moreover, a degree of equality before the law, and even some equalization in living standards. When one category of people is excluded from this minimum equality, the civilizing process may take a different turn and proceed along a different track. It takes a radical and annihilationist regime to complete the shift toward extreme compartmentalization.

The advanced stages of compartmentalization are increasingly incompatible with a free press and free association, or with legal guarantees such as freedom of movement or freedom of speech— all of which by their very nature tend to transgress, to transcend, the very borders that are essential to maintain compartments. Unless, of course, the excluded population is exempted from these rights and there is a silent consensus among all others to ignore whatever is done to it (somewhat like the situation that prevailed in the slaveholding society of the antebellum American South or in the early twentieth century on the plantations of the Netherlands Indies under Dutch colonial rule). Under those conditions the privileged group will enjoy a circumscribed freedom of the press and of association, without ever transgressing the limits that uphold the separation from the excluded group. Even a rather generous welfare state could exist in a compartmentalized society, pried loose from its universalist, egalitarian foundations, if only the targeted victims remain excluded from its benefits (somewhat like the welfare policies that prevailed in Nazi Germany).

A considerable degree of societal compartmentalization is a necessary condition for mass annihilation to occur, but it is not sufficient. There have been societies that were highly compartmentalized over long periods of time, and yet no large-scale killings occurred there. Slave societies are an example, precisely because the potential target population was of economic value to the dominant population. It happens occasionally, in brief spasms of small-scale collective violence, such as street riots, that victims are attacked randomly, or according to ad hoc grievances, but in longer lasting episodes of violence, on a larger scale, the targets have been defined beforehand according to long-standing criteria. Members of the attacking group have increasingly disidentified from their targets, and relations between them have become more and more compartmentalized.

An aggressive regime cannot conjure up a target group out of nothing, even if it wanted to. In all societies there are potential fault lines, and not all of those have been activated at any given time and place. As Michael Mann has accentuated, class tensions are almost omnipresent, and ethnic strains occur practically everywhere. At some point political entrepreneurs may try to fathom popular feeling to see which dimensions of latent conflict promise to bring the greatest support, in Mann's terms: "ethnicity trumps class," or the reverse.[37]

A radical regime must work with the vocabulary and the imagery that is dormant or vivid in the public's collective memory. Once it has selected its theme, the regime can exploit it to the full in order to sow hatred against the corresponding target group. It can build on existing compartmentalization to extend and intensify it to the most extreme level. As one group is set against another, the target group takes shape ever more clearly, and so does the group of the "regime's people." The threat from one side may prompt the other side to close ranks and prepare for conflict, which will induce the former side to do likewise. Fanaticization and radicalization acquire a momentum of their own. But the more unequal the relations of power between the regime's people and the target group, the smaller the opportunities for the targeted people to organize and defend themselves. Even if the target group is hardly a match for the regime and its supporters, the regime will try to convince its people that the target group is indeed an imminent threat, either because it is supported by outside powers or because it is part of a worldwide conspiracy or because it possesses secret resources, miracle weapons, or supernatural powers. The regime's activists sow among their own people not only hatred but also fear of a group that at face value is the weaker party by far. Fear much more than hatred legitimates aggression against an opponent, depicted not as a victim but as a menace. The perpetrators eagerly present themselves as their victims' victims.

The regime builds on existing conditions of compartmentalization and by its own efforts intensifies and extends the process. As it succeeds in isolating the target group, in vilifying and demonizing it, in society at large a social dialectic of threat and fear adds to the process with a dynamics of its own. People demand protection from the very threat that the regime has so successfully conjured up; they demand radical measures against the evildoers that the regime has so effectively designated. In the process, they increasingly become the "regime's people." Many among them help the official propaganda along by telling horror stories of their own or by provoking clashes with people from the target group that in turn enhance the feelings of hostility and contempt. All the while, opposing ideas and conflicting information coming from the domestic opposition, or from sources abroad, must be locked out and repressed: another aspect of the closure that comes with compartmentalization.

Although the radical policies of an annihilationist regime rarely follow from a rational, maximizing, informed, and planned project, there are great advantages in store for its leaders and supporters. For every official demoted, each job lost, every business transferred, or any house abandoned by the target people, there are regime protégés to profit from the occasion. Taxes can be levied on the target group collectively, its members can be chased off their fields and out of their homes, their churches and temples may be plundered—all to the benefit of the regime and its people.

In the case of the Turkish genocide, for example: "Liquidating the Armenians *in toto,* at least across Eastern Anatolia, provided the state with free unfettered access to substantial land, property and capital, which could then be redistributed or directly utilized for its own *dirigiste* purposes as a short-cut to state-led capital accumulation."[38]

The humiliation of the target group, moreover, cheers and uplifts the people of the regime. No matter how lowly, poor and ignorant, ugly and insignificant any one of them may seem, each one is better than the best of the contemptible and despicable target people. That in itself may prove a great consolation. The clarity, simplicity, and completeness of a worldview that explains all evil as the work of the target group can provide its adherents with the sense that the world is intelligible after all, that there is a moral direction to their life and that there are ways to bring about a better society now.

Strong disidentification *from* the others brings about more intense identification *with* one's own people. The ranks are closed and people feel more strongly the loyalty to their own kind and to the regime. Apparently, such togetherness in times of need and crisis satisfies a deeply felt urge. Quite often when people much later reminisce about that trying period, they remember it fondly and with keen nostalgia as somehow "warmer," "more generous," "more united" than the "cold and egotistical present"; in short, as the "good old days."[39]

Annihilationists, too, are often idealists, ready to sacrifice countless lives to achieve a better world. The task ahead of them may be bloody and harsh, but it is necessary. Almost without exception, regimes that engage in mass annihilation contend that their society stands at a turning point of history. *"It's now or never"*: now is the time to act, to act radically and decisively, to change the course of events once and for all. Destiny calls. The unique moment has arrived when a small but determined band can change the fate of society for good. This is the instantaneous view of history: the reduction of historical time to an instant, and one of instant change.

The radicals are ready to bring about the end of history. After one more, momentous effort by a heroic vanguard, history will come to a standstill in an ideal world. In many instances that visionary future is a return to an idealized, a mythical past. But in order to achieve that great task, one grand transformation is still required: the elimination of all those people who stand in the way of the ideal society. That is only a small price to pay (by the others, moreover) in order to realize an everlasting utopia.

This dichotomous view of the world, the mentality of "us" against "them" easily slides into a magical vision: the others are unclean, impure; they may contaminate and pollute us. The bour-

geois may infect the sober proletarian with their greed, material-
ism, and petty vices. They have their ways to seduce an innocent
mind. People of a different and therefore inferior race can contaminate us with their lust, laziness, and rapacity. Worse, licentiousness
and miscegenation will result in an impure breed of degenerate
mongrels.

In the twentieth century, magical thinking often took on the
disguise of scientific discourse, be it pseudo-Darwinian theories
of the unending battle between the races for living space and survival or a pseudo-Marxist brand of total and relentless war between
the possessed and the dispossessed classes. The historian Jacques
Sémelin especially stresses the predominance of a magical preoccupation with purity and radical purification through the destruction
of the unclean: "It combines hard-headed calculation and human
folly into delusional rationality [*rationalité délirante*]."[40]

THE FOUR MODES OF MASS ANNIHILATION

So far, I have made a series of general observations on regimes
that are moving toward mass annihilation or actually committing
it. None of them fits every single case, but all apply in varying degrees to most or almost all instances. Here we can now differentiate
among four modes of mass annihilation: conquerors' frenzy, rule by
terror, losers' triumph, and the rage of the crowds (megapogroms).

Three of the four modes concern instances that directly involve
the regime. The first, *conquerors' frenzy,* refers to mass annihilation in the wake of conquest and occupation. The second, *rule by
terror,* denotes the mass violence employed by more or less established regimes to implement their policies. The third mode, *losers'
victory,* concerns the mass violence committed by regimes in the
face of imminent defeat. The fourth mode, the *megapogrom,* concerns the mass violence perpetrated by armed gangs and popular
crowds across a territory without direct (but always with indirect)

involvement of the regime. Some cases may be assigned to more than one category, and some evolve over time from one category into another.

The first mode of mass annihilation, *conquerors' frenzy*, often occurs in the wake of victory and conquest, as a continuation of the armed struggle, with the same means but against different people: against those who can no longer threaten the killers or defend themselves against them. Many mass killings perpetrated by colonial armies on the move against an indigenous population fit this pattern of a victors' frenzy. The military command hopes to terrorize the conquered population into submission. It wants to chase the inhabitants from their houses and off their fields, so that colonizers from the victorious nation or its local allies can take over. But less "rational" and "calculated" motives are also in play. The soldiers faced fierce resistance, and their fear has now turned into rage and thirst for revenge. Usually, they are keen to avail themselves of the victors' privileges: rape and robbery. All too often, they will burn, torture, loot, and kill the defenseless and the defeated, just because they can, without risk to themselves, with impunity.

Randall Collins has called a similar killing spree at the small group level a "forward panic": "It is the ease of beating a long-sought enemy that makes for the transformation of tension/fear into the frenzied attack of forward panic. All the more so, when the enemy turns out not to be there at all, but only some helpless victims who are associated with the enemy side."[41] Although Collins mainly discusses small-scale, transient explosions of violence, he does apply his notion of forward panic to mass killings that continue over longer periods, such as ethnic riots and the Japanese Rape of Nanking.[42] The Dutch sociologist J. A. A. van Doorn and his coauthor W. J. Hendrix note that this *derailment of violence* by military units operating in unfamiliar terrain, among an alien and hostile population, occurs frequently, almost as an occupational hazard. The army command and field officers should be prepared for the eventuality and try to prevent and control it.[43]

Military units on a killing spree may act under orders from the regime in the home country. Their instructions may also have come independently from the military campaign headquarters, unknown to the authorities back home or against their express policy. The orders may even have been given by officers in the field on their own initiative. As the higher echelons of the command chain would rather not be responsible for an overt breach of treaties and customs on the conduct of war, sometimes a little innuendo from above suffices to insinuate to lower-ranking officers that a blind eye will be turned to the escapades of their troops.

Whatever the case, conquering campaigns far from home at the very least presuppose a state that can send armies abroad and supply them there, keeping them in effective fighting shape. The regime is always implicated in the events occurring in the war zone. The politicians may plead ignorance or an incapacity to prevent the misdeeds. Usually they are quite effective in covering up, minimizing, and denying the events in cahoots with the military headquarters and the field commanders.

The context of a conquering or occupying army in foreign, often faraway lands already assures a high degree of compartmentalization. Geographic distance is the natural physical separator for the regime's population, ignorance the psychic isolator between the public at home and the defeated people overseas. The colonial army consists of specialists in violence, military personnel—sometimes hardened professionals, at other times uncomfortable but mostly compliant conscripts. War against indigenous armies, between more or less symmetric parties, often prepares the ground for a subsequent massacre between unequal parties: a well-armed and well-organized, victorious military, on the one hand and, on the other, defeated and disarmed, disorganized and dispirited fighters or, by the same token, a civilian population lacking arms or organization, defenseless against the conquerors' rage.

The invading and the indigenous people hardly identify with one another; they regard each other as alien, most dissimilar, often as hardly human. The killing sites are far beyond the perception of the public in the home country, which is most often kept ignorant of what its remote military are up to and usually prefers not to uncover the sordid details. The distance from the war theater helps the home audience to keep its emotional and moral distance from the misdeeds, if they become known. The higher echelons invariably will advance arguments (if they need to argue their case) about the atrocities the enemy perpetrated first, the need to break the resistance of the local population and its support for the fighters on its side, the incapacity of the locals to understand reasonable argument, and the necessity to make them feel who's in charge—the list goes on.

For the perpetrators there is much to be gained from these murderous forays: the satisfaction that comes with revenge for their own hardships, anxiety, pain, and loss. There also is the raw pleasure of seeing people in fright, in awe, supplicating, begging to be spared, the glee in destroying houses and fields, churches, anything built up and cherished by the hated enemies, the excitement, rush of power, and satisfaction that comes with rape after long periods of frustration, and the triumphant sensation of killing a helpless alien in cold blood.

All the while, probably many perpetrators may well feel and think the opposite at the same time. "Deep down" they know they are committing evil. But that may be "too deep down," ignored for the time being, during their episode of elation and frenzy. Moreover, all too often, the victims are not considered as human beings: they are either so low or so evil as to be beneath any protection by ethical prescript. All the other comrades in arms are doing the same thing anyway, and didn't the commanding officer himself let them do it? No one in the outside world will ever find out. That is a quite realistic assessment (these observations anticipate the discussion of mental and social compartmentalization in chapter 8).

The second mode of mass annihilation, *rule by terror*, occurs in societies in which the regime is well established and in control of its army, police, secret service, and system of prison camps. Under those conditions, repression and extermination are the province of professionals, of specialists in surveillance, intelligence, investigation, interrogation, condemnation, deportation, detention, exploitation, and extermination. Such terror regimes may last for decennia, deporting, detaining, and killing millions, tens of millions of people. They usually emerge in the aftermath of war, civil war, revolution, or a coup. The memory, anticipation, and imagery of war are never far away, even during long periods of external peace. The domestic opposition is portrayed as a fifth column, an interior enemy, an irreconcilable and mortally dangerous foe. The conflict is depicted not just as political but as the decisive battle in the war throughout the ages between the indigenous and the alien races or as the final confrontation in the perennial war between the property-less and the propertied classes. The alleged opponents must be incapacitated at all costs. In extreme cases, the regime rounds up whomever it mistrusts, to jail them or deport them to remote camps, where they may be worked to death or killed outright. It is not always clear what unleashes these campaigns of terror, but in many cases factional rivalry within the regime is externalized by campaigns against a part of the population that is somehow seen to be linked to one or the other faction. After a while the terror campaign runs its course and is followed by a relatively quiet interlude before the next wave occurs.

The two most baffling examples of government by terror in the twentieth century are the two "dekamegamurderers" in Rudolph

Rummel's survey, the Soviet Union and Communist China, which each killed more than ten million domestic, civilian victims. North Korea to this very day terrorizes its population with the deliberate use of starvation in its vast penal system and through extreme scarcity with recurrent periods of famine in the country at large.[44]

A third mode of mass extermination occurs when the regime faces imminent defeat while it continues or even initiates a campaign of extermination against a defenseless target group within its own sphere of power. More often than not, this last-ditch annihilation drive receives priority over fighting the external enemy. If the regime must fall, at least it will have realized its historic mission of destroying the despised race, the detested class. This is the *"triumph of the losers."* From a psychological perspective it is a manner of "turning passive into active": since the regime is bound to lose the war, it chooses to fight another battle, which it can still win, even if that weakens the war effort against its military opponent. The regime is out to destroy a target population that cannot fight back. This course of action is as destructive as it is autodestructive. In terms of military strategy, it seems entirely irrational, but in terms of the regime's worldview, it may appear ineluctable.

In order to realize a losers' triumph, too, compartmentalization may require a sustained effort by the regime. It may build on an available vocabulary of discrimination between the regime's population and the target group, strengthening identifications among the former and disidentifications from the latter. It will have to enact exclusionary legislation, compel the media to concur in its propaganda, exclude the target group from institutions such as schools and hospitals, bar them from all or most employment, discourage encounters between its people and members of the target group, assign the latter separate living areas and facilities, and so on. These efforts presuppose a state capable of enforcing its policies throughout society, using its intelligence services, police force, tax inspectors, school administrators, censors, and domesticated media. However, almost by definition, the regimes that turn passive into active, just when they are fatally threatened by outside forces, will continue for a few more years at most, but not for generations, as have some terror regimes.

Nazi Germany is the paramount example of a regime that, once it started the war against the Soviet Union, set out to exterminate all Jews behind the Eastern Front in the manner of an extreme conquerors' frenzy. But once it became clear that Hitler would lose his war on the two battle fronts, he concentrated more and more on the one campaign he could win: the annihilation of the Jews of Europe. There are many more, albeit quite different, instances of annihilation in the mode of the losers' triumph.

Finally, there is a fourth form of mass annihilation that occurs more or less independently of the central government or its military command: when crowds or gangs—almost invariably incited by local politicians and firebrands—attack a target group. Usually they proceed without much planning, organization, or equipment. At the local level it looks like a pogrom or a deadly ethnic riot.[45] But these apparently improvised, spontaneous mob killings are part of a much larger sequence of events that involve millions of people on the move: a *megapogrom*.

Typically, target groups are attacked by mobs who plunder them, chase them from their homes, and kill them en masse, quite often after having raped many of the women. If the role of the local notables is hard to establish, since they tend to hide their part in the events, links with regional authorities and the central regime are even more difficult to trace. But quite often the ethnic cleansing that goes on at the grassroots level well serves the purpose of high-level officials and politicians who much prefer a more homogeneous nation and see the dirty work of deportation and extermination being taken out of their hands by rabble-rousers with covert support from local politicians, gang leaders, or police. The two largest megapogroms of the twentieth century occurred at the end of World War II in eastern and central Europe, mainly directed against civilians of German nationality or extraction, and, during the time of the Partition of 1947, in India and Pakistan, aimed at Muslims, Hindus, and Sikhs who happened to live among a majority of the other faith.

Compartmentalization is a feature of all instances of mass annihilation, but in varying degrees. It is carried furthest at all levels when an established regime resorts to rule by terror. The entire propaganda apparatus of the state and its complete repressive machinery can be mobilized to isolate the targeted groups in every sense and to have its specialized personnel destroy them in secluded compartments of murder. Compartmentalization is much less elaborate in societies where megapogroms occur. The regime remains at some distance of the killings, and mobs seem to assemble spontaneously to murder their targeted victims out in the open, in a brief period of bloody frenzy. But even then, the lines of identification and disidentification have long since been drawn, and the crowds create their own transient compartments of bloodshed. These four modes of mass annihilation are next illustrated in a case-by-case discussion of instances mass annihilation during the twentieth century.

CHAPTER 7

The Four Modes of Mass Annihilation
Case Histories

I NSTANCES OF MASS ANNIHILATION, NO matter how destructive,
occur in a social figuration of two human groups colliding in
an extremely asymmetric balance of power. But this tragic collision is the result of prior social developments that have shaped
the constellation in which killers and victims now find themselves.
Each historical case is different, and each is complex. General explanations, though necessary for an understanding of mass annihilation, are not sufficient. A better insight requires a discussion of
specific histories, even if they must remain very brief.

Conquerors' Frenzy

Victorious armies operate far from the home front in a temporary moral void, where anything can happen. And it often does
happen. They confront defeated enemies and a defenseless population. The troops have been brutalized by battle, and often they
have endured a period of intense fighting with all the anxiety and
rage that evoked. Now is the time to get back at these aliens, with
whom they seem to have nothing in common.

Imperialist Mass Annihilation

Throughout the ages, it was the common practice for conquering armies to indiscriminately kill defeated enemies and unarmed civilians. The conquerors boasted of the bloodbath they had
brought about, and the chroniclers exaggerated the numbers to
glorify their victorious heroes. Only in recent times has the gloat-
ing over the murdered masses abated.

The extermination of the aboriginal inhabitants of South
America by the Spanish conquistadores even now, more than five
centuries later, remains a prime example of wanton and wholesale
destruction of human lives by a conquering army that encountered
beings whom it considered wholly alien. The American Indians
literally lived in a different world from the Spanish, and the army
operated in a compartment entirely separate from the home society. Nevertheless, Dominican monks did try to alarm the king of
Spain about the mass murder perpetrated in his newly conquered
overseas territories.

The massacres that went with colonial conquest were mostly
ignored by the public in the home country, and they are largely
glossed over to this very day. One of the bloodiest wars the Dutch
ever fought was the succession of campaigns to subdue the rebellious warriors of Aceh that lasted from 1873 until 1913. This war
cost the lives of a thousand soldiers of the Netherlands Indian
Army, killed twenty thousand of the twenty-five thousand forced
laborers the Dutch brought along, and took the lives of anywhere
between fifty thousand and a hundred thousand people of Aceh,
fighters and noncombatants: three hundred to four hundred villages were burned during a single campaign. And yet, that war has
been almost entirely forgotten; there are only two books about its
history.[1] Historian Henk Schulte Nordholt argues that "colonial
expansion created a state of violence which is only marginally recognized in Dutch history books. It is a misconception to argue that

such violence was only a temporary situation. . . . It continued to resonate in the memories of the people until the end of the colonial period."[2] For all those years, the colonizers denied or ignored the violence of colonization.

Two other major instances of colonial mass murder occurred at the beginning of the twentieth century: by Belgian soldiers (and their vassals) in the Congo Free State and by German troops against the Hereros of South-West Africa (present-day Namibia).

The Congo Free State (1887–1908) was nothing less than a private venture of King Leopold II of Belgium. It was the scene of unparalleled savagery on the part of the Belgian invaders and traders, their local mercenaries and handpicked "chiefs." Historian Hendrik Wesseling writes: "The Free State itself became an exploitation company. The state lived off the revenues paid in kind, especially ivory and rubber, and the indigenous people were forced to supply these products. The consequences were disastrous. . . . This policy of exploitation was implemented with exceptional severity. The population was put under pressure in all manner of ways. People were threatened, intimidated, robbed, beaten, raped, maimed and murdered, all in order to bring in the highest possible yields."[3] The huge mortality was due in part to starvation and epidemics that resulted from so many people being uprooted and fleeing the king's soldiers. In part, it was due to deliberate punitive expeditions against any village that did not deliver enough rubber on time.

Many were killed by Europeans and their local helpers. Congolese villagers were forced to collect rubber, and those who did not meet their quota were routinely killed on the spot, their right hand chopped off and smoked as proof that bullets had been well spent. Others were whipped, maimed, and tortured.[4] Even more were chased from their villages and hunting grounds and perished from starvation; others died from mistreatment and exhaustion as compulsory bearers for military and merchant expeditions or as forced laborers. The upheaval also resulted in the rampant spread of contagious disease (especially sleeping sickness) that took millions of lives. "According to the most authoritative estimates, the population of the Congo was halved in the years between 1880 to 1920, dropping from 20 million to 10 million."[5]

Over time, the murderous exploitation became routinized and turned into a permanent rule by terror. The king's representatives set up elaborate schemes to regulate the exaction and taxation of the indigenous population; they sent out inspectors and tax collectors and kept records of the tribute in rubber they extorted and of the executions they had ordered.

The bloodshed and abuse finally caused such international outcry, especially in Great Britain, that, in 1908, the king was forced to transfer his personal empire to the Belgian state. He took every precaution that as little as possible would transpire at the time or for posterity. Leopold II was never held to account and died in office undisturbed two years later. It took a century or more before professional historians squarely confronted the facts of the mass annihilation in the Congo Free State.[6]

Belgian forgetfulness of mass annihilation in the Congo, like the Dutch oblivion of the mass violence in Aceh in the last quarter of the nineteenth century, fits a pattern of collective repression of colonial extermination among the former colonizers.

During the same period, in 1904, the German army under Lieutenant-General Adrian Dietrich Lothar von Trotha initiated what he called a "total war" against rebellious Herero warriors in South-West Africa, driving them and their families into the desert, where they would succumb from thirst and hunger without any chance of flight or surrender. The extermination of the Hereros was a deliberate exercise in genocide, even though the word did not then exist. It was a systematic campaign by troops with an overwhelming advantage in arms and equipment to wipe out an entire nation as punishment for its insurgency against the German settlers who were occupying Herero land. Lothar von Trotha carried out with zest and pride an old-fashioned and unashamed mass murder that was also in many respects a prelude to the methods of the Nazi regime. Quite a few veterans of the campaign against the Hereros and the Nama of Namibia later became active in the Freikorps and the Nazi Party in the 1920s and 1930s.[7]

Germany and Belgium were latecomers to overseas imperialism and had to catch up fast to secure their territories against the inroads of other European powers. Both the Congo and South-West Africa are clear instances of the aftermath of conquest, when the occupying troops have the field almost entirely to themselves. The Congolese were too numerous, maybe, to kill them all, and they could be of economic use as rubber collectors. The Hereros apparently did not appear exploitable in one way or another and were eliminated.

The autocratic and expansionist czarist regime in Russia became outright democidal during World War I. It deported some two hundred thousand indigenous Germans to the eastern territories, killing maybe half of them in the process. Armenian volunteers in the Russian army massacred untold Turkish Kurds in revenge for the wholesale extermination of Armenians by Kurdish militia at the command of the Turkish regime. Russian troops killed maybe half a million nomads in Central Asia. The Russian treatment of prisoners of war was especially gruesome and may have resulted in some four hundred thousand dead. Rudolph Rummel, who collected these figures for the years 1900–1917, reaches a total of well over a million, not counting the casualties of—more or less symmetric—regular warfare and rebellion. However, Rummel cautions that these statistics are even more uncertain than those for other "democidal" episodes, and for that caveat he can be taken at his word.[8]

By the end of the nineteenth century, Japan had embarked on an expansionist course. It fought the First Sino-Japanese War against the Qing dynasty over Formosa (Taiwan), from 1894 to 1895, and, after its victory, began a war against Russia over Manchuria from 1904 to 1905.

In 1937, it started the Second Sino-Japanese War, which was to last until 1945. Both Nationalist and Communist Chinese fought the Japanese invaders. In the early phase of the war, the Japanese took Shanghai and marched on to Nanking (Nanjing), at the time the capital of China. From November 1937 on, as they advanced on the city and finally took it, Japanese troops killed some three hundred thousand disarmed or unarmed Chinese in the span of three months: a massacre that became known as the Rape of Nanking.[9] It was in fact only one episode, albeit the bloodiest, in a chain of mass murders the Japanese perpetrated during their victorious onslaught into the Chinese heartland. One reason the killings, once begun, did not stop was that the Japanese wanted to hide their crimes and would not let any potential witness escape alive.[10] Randolph Rummel arrives at an overall estimate of three million noncombatant Chinese civilians and disarmed soldiers killed during the Japanese invasion and occupation.[11]

Settlers' Massacres

Imperialist campaigns were fought far away from home, against people considered wholly different and inferior and rightly perceived as defenseless. The setting was already thoroughly compartmentalized, and no further effort was required to separate the minds and shield the killing spaces from a critical outsider's view. This killers' isolation and the confidence in their impunity explain by themselves much of the extreme destruction that went on time and again.

The ethnic cleansing by "settler societies" represents a special case of violence by colonial conquerors. The colonizers occupied and cultivated the land and formed a new society, often governed by principles that resembled those prevailing in the mother country: "settler democracies." The United States, Australia, New Zealand, and Tasmania are cases in point.[12] The settlers and the natives "clashed over a monopolistic economic resource, land, and most settlers did not need native labor to work it. . . . The settlers could eliminate the out-group with little military or moral risk to themselves."[13] And they did. Still, the settlers were not as alien to the native peoples as the soldiers of a conquering army would have been. They traded and sometimes worked with native people, they negotiated with them over land rights, and at times they lived side by side with them and sometimes married indigenous partners. But there came a point at which they felt they needed ideological arguments to recompartmentalize a society in which settlers and native people had started to intermingle. They found their reasons in new ideas borrowed from a Darwinian discourse on the struggle for survival between races that were believed to be unbridgeably different and implacably hostile. The settler societies varied widely as to the democratic quality of their institutions. But most of the killing occurred in the frontier zones where free elections and the rule of law hardly mattered.[14]

One should grant Michael Mann, who coined the phrase "the dark side of democracy," that the authoritarian and restricted democracies of the late nineteenth and early twentieth centuries remained strikingly unaffected by the havoc wreaked in their name by armies that the regime had expedited to conquer and subdue peoples mostly unknown, at best considered alien and primitive. The democratic institutions of these societies may not often have actively instigated these remote massacres, and they may at times even have been ignorant of what happened so far away, but apparently, rarely did they put much in the way of the settlers' murderous zeal. Rather, these exclusive democracies turned out to be quite compatible with mass murder, as long as it occurred somewhere in the periphery, to "primitive aliens," to those who remained radically excluded from the citizens' circle of identification.

Massacres in the Mexican Revolution

During the revolutionary period in Mexico, between 1910 and 1920, 2 million or more people perished, partly in more or less equally matched military encounters that amounted to a civil war, and partly in massacres of unarmed citizens that were clear instances of mass annihilation. For example: "For more than half of 1912, General Juvencio Robles sowed terror in the state and introduced a scorched-earth policy: there were mass shootings; whole villages were sacked or burned down; and any peasant suspected of helping the rebels was tortured along with his family."[15] The best estimates put the total number of casualties, the total "demographic cost," at approximately 2.1 million people.[16] It appears impossible, on the basis of the available data, to estimate the proportion of unarmed and unorganized victims among the casualties of la Violencia. However, the revolutionary armies and the government's troops were not all that numerous; all in all they may have numbered no more than 150,000. Therefore, even allowing for some succession in the military ranks, their casualties from more or less symmetric warfare can hardly have outnumbered 100,000. The remaining 2 million must have been victims of asymmetric violence by the warring armies against unarmed and unorganized people. This is all the more plausible since the insurgent troops were accompanied by throngs of women with their children who could go nowhere else for food and protection.

Nazi Mass Extermination Behind the Eastern Front

The most devastating instance of conquerors' frenzy occurred no doubt during the Nazi victories in the first phase of World War II, initially with some self-restriction in the West but with quickly increasing savagery in eastern Poland, Czechoslovakia, and the Soviet Union.

As Christopher Browning writes: "It is my conclusion that victory euphoria in mid-July [1941] marked not only the conclusion of the decision-making process leading to the mass murder of the Soviet Jews but also the point at which Hitler inaugurated the decision-making process that led to the extension of the Final Solution to European Jewry."[17] Behind the Eastern Front, the SS and the Einsatzgruppen (execution squads), with much help from the regular Wehrmacht, rounded up all the Jews they could lay their hands on, marched them to a nearby clearing in the woods, made them dig their own graves, forced them to line up at the edge of the trench, and shot them at close range. Partisans and people's commissars were lucky to be executed on the spot. Some 1.5 million people were killed in this manner between June 1941 and the end of 1942.[18] But the onward march of the Nazi armies had already begun to stall in October 1941 and was stopped in its tracks with the eventual defeat at the Battle of Stalingrad in January 1943. Hitler must have made the final decision to completely exterminate the Jews of Europe sometime in the early autumn of 1941.[19] By January 1942 at the Wannsee Conference the legal and bureaucratic details were worked out and systematic planning began. By that time, the heady rush of inexorable victory had subsided. The army command realized that the battle against the Soviet Union would not soon be won and that it might well be lost. The United States entered the war on December 8, 1941, and this, too, spelled an uphill battle in the west and the possibility of outright defeat. But these adversities by no means persuaded the Nazi leadership to alter its course and suspend its campaign to exterminate all the Jews of Europe. On the contrary: as the prospect of defeat loomed ever larger, an unparalleled annihilation machinery was set up, a chain of extermination camps in the eastern part of occupied Poland. If Hitler could not succeed in creating a vast German Lebensraum in the east, where Slavs were to be expelled or used as slave labor on the estates of the Aryan Herrenvolk, at least he could realize that other grand historic vision, the Final Solution to the problem of the *Ewige Jude* (eternal Jew), even if it would divert precious resources from the war effort on the Eastern Front. The Holocaust began as an episode of victors' frenzy on an unparalleled scale, but as the odds of war turned, the annihilation of the Jews of Europe was continued with renewed zeal and with different techniques as a losers' triumph.[20] "By the terms of the German plans, the invasion of the Soviet Union was an utter fiasco."[21] But the Holocaust was "the war that Hitler won."[22]

RULE BY TERROR

Rule by terror is launched by established regimes and is carried out by specialists in violence from the military, the police, and the party's ranks. "Death squads generally operate in the context of state terrorism, i.e., the regular use of violence, particularly homicide, by state agents against political opponents for the primary purpose of intimidation."[23]

The Stalinist and Maoist episodes of terror and mass killings have much in common. The Soviet Union as well as the People's Republic of China emerged from the devastations of war, revolution, and civil war. Both regimes engaged in "classicide." In Michael Mann's terms, "class trumped ethnicity." The class struggle also served to overcome ethnic divisions in these multinational empires. Stalin's and Mao's regimes carried on a class struggle from the left against the landed kulaks and the bourgeoisie. In both cases domestic target groups were annihilated. This is in marked contrast to the German, Japanese, and colonial annihilation campaigns that were aimed at foreign peoples.

The Soviet Union

Czarist Russia carried on continual and murderous colonial campaigns in central Asia throughout the nineteenth century and made millions of victims among the local population, most likely in the manner of a victors' frenzy. Cohort after cohort of veterans must have returned home marked by the experience.

During World War I, Russia lost more soldiers (1.7 million) than any other Allied power. The succeeding civil war against the assembled interior opposition and the Western intervention armies once again cost up to a million lives in armed battle, from disease, executions, and pogroms.

Once Lenin's regime had established its dominance over the entire Soviet territory, a period of relative domestic peace ensued. It was then that successive waves of police repression and persecution set in. Stalin's Great Purge came in the years 1937–1938, during a period of most uneasy and precarious peace. A vast system of prisons and camps was put into place to stifle any opposition; it lasted until Stalin's death in 1953.

From the time it had established its power base, the Soviet regime ruled by terror. One purge followed another, one category of people after another being designated as the target of a new purification campaign. After achieving firm control, the Soviet regime it oversaw the detection, the persecution, the deportation and internment, and the final destruction of its victims. At least a million people were arrested, shot on the spot, or interrogated, tortured, given a mock trial, and executed. Millions were deported as slave laborers in the camps of the Gulag. When inmates were exhausted and could no longer cope, they were released to die at home. The

Stalin regime deported entire nations to break any capacity of resistance and prevent the possibility of collaboration with a potential foreign enemy. The first ethnic victims were the Cossacks, who were deported en masse to the Donets Basin. "Out of a population of 3 million, 300,000–500,000 were killed or deported in 1919 and 1920."[24] By the late 1930s ethnic Finns, Poles, and Germans were removed from their homelands in the west and forcibly moved to Central Asia, whereas ethnic Koreans and Chinese were resettled in Kazakhstan. To nip any "national" resistance in the bud, in 1944 the Chechens and Ingush, who had long resisted Moscow, were expelled in a surprise action that forcibly deported half a million people to Kazakhstan and Kirghizia. More than 100,000 perished as a result. A similar fate befell the Crimean Tatars. Their homeland had been occupied from 1941 until 1944 by the Nazis (who also had intended to expel them and turn their land into a settlement and holiday area). Immediately after the Soviets reconquered the Crimea, all Tatars, 190,000 of them, were driven out and transported to Kazakhstan. From the late 1930s on, under the threat of war, the struggle against the "class enemies" had increasingly evolved into a campaign of ethnic cleansings.[25]

The total number of casualties of terror and famine until the collapse of the Soviet Union in the years 1989–1991 were once estimated at fifty million. After the archives were made accessible, scholars came up with much lower figures (that are still stunning). Recent sources mention a total death toll of some twenty million.[26]

This mass annihilation was the work of specialists: secret police, interrogators, prosecutors, lawyers and judges, spies, camp guards, and so on. Once the whole machinery was put into place, the regime could precisely determine the number of arrests, select the persuasions, occupations, ethnic groupings, or regions whose turn had come for special treatment. It could carefully calibrate the visibility of the repression and the information it wanted to get out to the public. On the one hand, people should not know too much, so that they could not pin the blame on any particular section of the government or the party. On the other hand, the regime wanted its citizens to know that anyone could be arrested anytime so as to maintain the entire population in a state of paralyzing terror. Nevertheless, the whole, huge operation was quite chaotic. Mistakes were made, and quite likely people were often arrested more or less randomly, in order to fill quotas. The confusion may not have been intentional, but it certainly added to people's insecurity and anxiety. Everyone had to try and figure out why an arrest was made, what the detainee could possibly have done wrong, what the regime's rules and intentions might be this time. Many people became their own detectives, constantly watching themselves for anything that might possibly be interpreted as a telltale sign of opposition or even silent dissent. As it was everyone's task to inform on everyone else, neighbors on neighbors, colleagues at work on each other, and even schoolchildren on their parents, no one could be completely trusted, and even intimate conversations had to be guarded. At the lower echelons petty officials acted on their own initiative, eager to advance in the hierarchy and fearing arrest themselves. In the process, countless citizens were mobilized to denounce, round up, expel, and execute whomever the regime had set its sight on. Thus purges that started as bureaucratic and professional campaigns at the very pinnacle of the regime were complemented by more or less "spontaneous" actions by members of the party, the police, and the youth movement at the grassroots level, where perpetrators and victims were much less clearly compartmentalized.

Target groups were effectively isolated from the regime's people: "The Soviet Union was both a repressive and a tutelary state. To enact its dual mission, it categorized all of its citizens along the lines of class, nationality, and politics."[27] But this vast effort at the compartmentalization of so many socioeconomic, political, and increasingly ethnic target groups required an enormous bureaucratic and policing effort on the part of the Soviet state. Because individuals are not that easily classified, new distinctions had to be applied forever. "Bourgeois elements" or "rich kulaks" or "counter-revolutionary intellectuals and agitators" were separated, fired or dispossessed, arrested, deported, and exploited as slave labor in the camps, starved and abandoned to cold and disease. The target groups of Communist regimes kept changing with every new campaign. Communist party activists and officials were persecuted even more often than plain citizens. With each purge a new category of "conspirators," "spies," and "traitors" was weeded out and usually liquidated. The successive purges culminated in the Great Terror of 1936–1938, at the initiative of Stalin himself and his coterie.

Under the Stalinist regime, severe food shortages were a recurrent phenomenon, because of forced collectivization, inadequate storage facilities, insufficient means of transport, and inefficient distribution for lack of a market mechanism. Although such periods of scarcity created untold numbers of victims, that may not have been the intention, but rather a side effect of Soviet agricultural policies that the regime was willing to accept as the price of progress toward a communist society.

The greatest famine, which occurred in Ukraine in 1932–1934, took more than three million lives.[28] Stalin and his entourage stand accused of having immeasurably aggravated the results of forced collectivization by requisitioning the grain that the peasants needed for food and seeding, preventing them from moving elsewhere, wherever they could have found food, and letting them starve all across the countryside under the most desperate conditions, which finally led to rampant cannibalism. Apart from pure malice, Stalin's intention was most likely to eliminate the peasants who still worked their own land instead of joining the collective farms, as well as to fatally weaken any nationalist strivings among Ukrainians, who, he feared, might make common cause with Poland on the other side of the border.[29]

As Nicholas Werth points out, whereas the Armenian genocide and the Holocaust were completed within a year, the more varied and complex crimes of the Stalin regime were carried out over a long period and therefore never had the same impact on the conscience and memory of the outside world.

China

In China, after the uprising of 1911, the Nationalist regime terrorized the population for thirty years, killing millions. The Communist guerrillas who fought them made fewer victims, but still in the order of magnitude of a million.[30] The struggle against the Japanese invaders before and during World War II took many millions of casualties among Chinese soldiers and citizens. So much warfare and massacre must have brutalized and decivilized Chinese society. This may help to explain the campaigns of mass terror against unarmed citizens that became a signature trait of both the Soviet and the Chinese Communist regimes once they had conquered state power, just as the mass killing in the trenches of World War I may have left many veterans emotionally and morally desensitized and thus more inclined to inflict violence.

The Communists under the leadership of Mao Zedong took power in 1949. At that time, the Cold War had already thoroughly alienated the Soviet Union from its wartime allies in the West. China, through its proxy North Korea, soon became embroiled in the Korean War (1950–1953), where it faced the United States. By the 1960s, China's relations with the Soviet Union had disintegrated into open hostility, and tensions also had increased with its southern neighbor India.

Like the Soviets, after taking power the Chinese started a campaign to collectivize agriculture and industrialize production. From the outset, Maoist terror differed little from Stalinist rule by terror, and the Chinese may well have taken their cue from the Soviets. In 1958, Mao unleashed the Great Leap Forward, a campaign of forced industrialization and accelerated collectivization in the countryside. Famine soon racked rural China, especially in the south.[31] Party activists and local officials, were charged with requisitioning rice, grain, and other food stocks from rural peasants. The government's harvest statistics were wildly inflated, so peasants had to deliver quantities that were equally blown up, impossible to supply without giving up the food stock for their own use and the seed grains for the following year's harvest. But this was what they were forced to do, at gunpoint if necessary. The famine was entirely created by the regime's policies—its stubborn insistence on quotas based on official but faked statistics and a merciless requisitioning system that harshly punished for criminal neglect not only every official who did not collect as much as he had been told to but every peasant who did not surrender the required quantity of rice or wheat. In the three years of famine that resulted, tens of millions died of hunger.[32]

The Chinese Communist leadership had closely studied the policies of the Soviet regime, so it must have been aware of the earlier disastrous campaign in the Ukraine and its catastrophic results. In other words, Mao and his coterie must have known beforehand what would follow from the Great Leap Forward.

No one was ever held accountable for these deaths.[33] And although the consequences caused severe scarcities elsewhere, the policy of forced requisition and resulting mass starvation remained largely invisible outside the most affected areas in China.

In China, also, the Communist regime built a huge system of forced labor camps fed by a vast flow of denunciations from ordinary citizens and by arrests, interrogations, torture, fake trials, and rote verdicts by the secret police and a strictly controlled judiciary. Moreover, as in the Soviet Union, millions of Chinese were shot because of their "class background," their political convictions, on a whim, or for a trifle.

Unique to Mao's China was the Cultural Revolution, which began in 1966 and brought a decade of sometimes carnivalesque, mostly murderous upheaval, encouraged or condoned by Mao and his faction in the Communist Party. What made this episode unique was the mass participation of China's youth, who formed the Red Guards, groups that lacked formal ties to the party apparatus, the police, the army, or the bureaucracy. Since there was little or no organization or plan, almost anyone who somehow displayed bourgeois aberrations, such as reading books, looking "middle class," or simply keeping at a distance from Mao's devoted and fanatic rabble-rousers, could suddenly be picked out as a "bad element," with the wrong "bloodline" (family background) and as a member of a "bad class." Because people could never be sure that the roving student gangs would not suddenly turn them into the object of ridicule, humiliation, maltreatment, or worse, many tried to demonstrate their loyalty by denouncing bourgeois and antirevolutionary practices, joining in the chants, and participating in attacks on shops, offices, and passersby. Even the Red Guards themselves had to outdo their peers in revolutionary enthusiasm, theatrics, and outright cruelty so as not to be attacked. Young people from educated or propertied families were among the most extreme followers, as they tried to save their skin by even more radical behavior.[34] The police and military were under orders not to act against the Red Guards. But the mobs did depend for protection on local bosses who recruited their own gangs to fight rival groups of Red Guards. At times the guards would murder almost at random, fearful that otherwise survivors might denounce them or band together and turn against them. In those years probably a million or more people were killed by roaming bands of revolutionary "students";

others died as a result of expulsion from their jobs and homes, from deportation to the remote countryside, and by suicide.[35]

In rural communities, the local party cadres usually initiated the killings to demonstrate their loyalty, impress the villagers with their power, and despoil the victims. In these years, almost the only chance for advancement and for permission to leave one's village in hopes of finding a better life in the city was to become a cadre member; few positions were available, and officials were eager to distinguish themselves in carrying out the party line and even anticipating it. The actual executions were staged with much ceremony and theatrics, as public events. "The killers were individuals with questionable reputations. . . . Ruthlessness and cruelty became their human capital to raise their status," writes historian Yang Su, who adds: "To be associated with the state in a village under Mao's regime was to finally enter the mainstream of the community."[36]

By early 1969, the mayhem began to subside, but it continued in one form or another until Mao's death in 1976. Mao Zedong had unleashed the Cultural Revolution to forestall a coup by his rivals, and he exploited the rampant chaos to purge the party and army ranks from any elements that might oppose him. In this way, Mao hoped to create a grassroots movement that would make him entirely independent of the established state and military apparatus.

The massive violence under terror regimes occurs mostly under conditions of advanced compartmentalization at all levels. Under Communist rule by terror the target groups were fuzzy and might change any moment, so that anyone should feel threatened all the time. But the actual elimination of targeted people was the work of professionals controlled by bureaucratic organizations, operating largely out of public sight, in isolated interrogation centers, prisons, and camps. Even when entire ethnic communities were deported, they were quickly surrounded, rounded up, and packed in cattle wagons to be transported to some remote region. And the regions where peasants were robbed of their grain stock and left to starve were quite effectively closed off, both to prevent them from leaving to forage and beg in adjacent areas and to ensure that the outside world would not find out what was going on.

The Cultural Revolution was different. In urban areas, it was a free-for-all, especially for young students who might take on just anyone and turned their attacks into public performances that by-standers were forced to watch. In these respects it resembled another mode of mass annihilation, the megapogrom: outbursts of improvised, local mob violence coordinated all across the country. The "precipitating events" that synchronized and coordinated the mayhem were Mao's very public announcements and interventions. In this instance the actors were not professionals. The police and the military were told to stay out of the fray and leave the streets to the motley bands of Red Guards. Impunity seemed guaranteed even for the worst offenders, and this worked as a further stimulus for wanton violence.

For Mao, apparently, even rule by terror was not enough. He resented the limitations that a huge, repressive machinery imposes also on the man at the very top, and he feared that opposing factions might exploit the resources of the army and state bureaucracy to undermine his control of the apparatus. Mao opted for anarchistic tyranny.

Under the rule by terror, Communist annihilation campaigns were aimed at the domestic population; they targeted the land-owning farmers, ethnic minorities, small businesspeople, profes-sionals, artists, and intellectuals, and, most of all, the ranks of the party cadre, forever suspected of dissidence. Time and again, the threat of the class enemy was invoked, not in the avatar of armed opponents, but in the guise of devious, scheming, secret operators, possibly aided by equally shady foreign forces: not outright resis-tance but "sabotage," "espionage," and "secret propaganda" were the crimes of which the opponents of the regime were accused. The campaign targeted the enemy within, who stood accused of infiltrating the ranks of the loyal adherents of the regime, infesting their innermost thoughts and feelings. War it was, but an imaginary war against a mostly imaginary opponent and nonetheless murderous for it in reality.

Except during the Cultural Revolution, the Communist regime left the actual implementation of its rule by terror to specialized government personnel: regular, special, and secret police, the military, and party officials. In this respect the Communist system resembled Nazi Germany: within Germany, the Nazi regime functioned with rule by terror.

In these three totalitarian systems the actual work was done by paid employees of the state, and the local population was kept at some distance. This greatly facilitated the compartmentalization of the elimination campaigns. People might be arrested at home or in the street, preferably in the wee hours of the morning, causing at most a brief disturbance that could have upset neighbors or passersby, and then they would be taken away to enclosed prisons and remote camps, out of the public's sight. Only the regime and its servants, police and guards, knew at firsthand what was going on, and they were sworn to secrecy. And yet, something about the prisoners' fate had to transpire to the outside world and added to the overall atmosphere of fear: "The early German concentration camps (mostly for political opponents and ordinary criminals) were located in cities and the inmates were often released after some weeks or months (and severe mistreatment), partly as a warning to the rest of the population."[37] In 1933, the SS took over the camps and turned them into thoroughly secluded locations where prisoners were worked to death or murdered instantly. By that time, most of the German population had submitted to the regime, which now waged all-out war against the Jews, the Communists, and the remaining small minorities who persisted in their opposition: the disappearance of their relatives and comrades was not lost on them and added to their terror.

North Korea

In the sixty years of its existence, the Democratic People's Republic of Korea has maintained a regime of utter terror, so effectively and with such complete closure, that very little is known about everyday repression in Korean society or its vast system of prisons and camps, still in place to this day. The country suffers regular and serious food shortages. The mid-1990s was one such period of famine. In those years, peasants were not allowed to leave their village in search of food. Those who did lost all protection and often were detained in institutions where there was no food at all. Between 1994 and 2000, of an overall population of some 25 million, between 600,000 and 1.1 million people died of hunger.[38] On average, North Korean boys at age seven were found to be almost eight inches shorter than their South Korean counterparts.[39]

The Korean regime is thought to have deliberately allowed these famines to occur in order to exterminate suspect target groups, just as happened in Ukraine under the Stalinist regime of the 1930s and in Maoist China between 1958 and 1962. The absence of markets under the Communist system was the main cause of the permanent food shortages. Enforced requisitioning of food stock held by the peasants prevented them from sowing for the next season and in the worst years led to mass starvation in the countryside. Although the Korean government has repeatedly used threats of armed aggression to extort aid from the West, in the 1990s famine, at least 30 percent of the donated food went to the military and other favorites of the regime, which spent its scarce foreign currency to buy forty

MIG-21 jet fighters.[40] In recent years, the emergence of a web of smugglers and black marketeers, silently condoned by the regime, has somewhat improved circumstances.

As for the system of prison camps, for the years after 1953, when the regime was founded, the average number of inmates of the North Korean concentration camps has been estimated at two hundred thousand or more. Apart from the extreme hardship of forced labor, cold, and inadequate facilities, the prisoners suffered from imposed starvation, being fed just enough not to die of hunger. During these years, between one million and two million people are estimated to have died from executions and "penal starvation" alone.

The policy of penal starvation is a deliberate method of exterminating political opponents and other offenders. Concerning the mass famines, if the regime's intent to exterminate the less favored sections of the population through starvation cannot now be proven, the food shortages were, at the very least, a result of "reckless" policy, in express disregard of the foreseeable risks that the official measures entailed.[41]

North Korea is the only instance of a regime that continues its annihilationist policies toward its own population up to this very moment. Over all those years, mass starvation has served the regime to uphold its rule by terror.[42]

Under the Communist terror regimes, as in Nazi Germany, notwithstanding the total control of all media, the secrecy surrounding the camps or execution sites, and the penalties on spreading rumors, most citizens had a fair inkling of what happened, without exactly knowing how many people were taken away, and where to, what was to happen to them, and for which reasons exactly. This kept them in a constant state of fear and permanently insecure about the rules. "This public terror always worked in two directions, targeted both at the victim and at everybody else simultaneously[, in] a 'dual strategy of publicity and secrecy.'"[43] It seemed better to err on the side of caution, and so people policed themselves and one another, often more strictly than the authorities could. Since most people by far kept their doubts and disbelief to themselves, many thought they were the only one with misgivings about the regime, creating a constellation of multiple ignorance, a "spiral of silence."[44] By the same token, few people knew enough to be in a position where they could have given precise testimony or make pointed accusations against the authorities, should the occasion have ever arisen.[45]

The Indonesian Mass Killings of 1965

On September 30, 1965, President Sukarno of Indonesia was ousted in a complicated coup that resulted in a military junta taking power under General Suharto.[46] Almost immediately there followed a tidal wave of murders carried out by special army units and "black-shirted" Muslim gangs. The army encouraged, even ordered, the annihilation of Communists. It apparently promptly got its way, as loose local bands of "Muslim students" rounded up and murdered anyone they suspected of belonging to the Communist Party and its auxiliary organizations. Other gangs used the occasion to go after Chinese shopkeepers and traders or to settle scores with personal enemies. Once again, the expectation of impunity raised by the army greatly facilitated the annihilation of up to a million people in the space of three months.

At the time of the coup, Indonesia was engaged in minor border skirmishes with Malaysia on the borders of Sarawak (present-day Borneo). More important, the takeover occurred at the height of the Cold War, at a time of particular tension with Communist China. Yet the period could hardly be considered a time of war or even of acute threat of war. There is evidence that the American embassy sympathized (at the very least) with the putschists in the army and furnished them with lists of Communists to be eliminated. The Communist Party of Indonesia (PKI) had a mass following and was well organized. It had been holding demonstrations and agitating for land reform. This elicited the hatred of the mainly Muslim peasants in Java and the Hindu peasants in Bali. The Communists also had openly mocked and ridiculed religious tradition, and that may have been what most incensed the religious peasantry.

With hindsight, it now appears that there was no serious threat of a Communist takeover, as the generals alleged in order to justify their putsch. It is unclear whether the military themselves believed such danger existed.[47] In fact, the Communists turned out to be entirely unprepared for the massacres that followed, and they put up surprisingly little resistance.

Since the Nationalist regime remained in power until Suharto's abdication three decades later, in 1998, and the successor regimes has hesitated to initiate judicial proceedings against the perpetrators in the powerful armed forces, no one has been punished for the vast destruction of human life, and no judicial evidence has become available. But in the half-century that has since passed, scholars and activists have succeeded in reconstructing at least part of the events.[48]

Once the army let it be known not only that it was engaged in annihilating the Communists but that it actually encouraged citizen bands to join in the carnage, it was the cue for local notables and Muslim "student" bands to kill whomever they wanted. "The massacres occurred because of the convergence of deep communal hatreds, on the one hand, and state directed violence, on the other. The state utilized and directed the spontaneity of those hatreds."[49] The military units that had committed the coup now initiated rule by terror in a manner that left much to the collaboration of local vigilante groups: "But many people, too, were killed in wild orgies with mobs at their heels. Whole villages, children included, turned

out against some Communists, chasing them across fields and finally stoning and slashing them to death."[50] The "countercoup"
that followed on the assassination of six army generals had been
relatively bloodless, and apparently there was not much armed resistance to the new leader, Suharto. But there was the specter of
the Communists, organized in a tightly run party and mobilized by
mass organizations of peasants and farmhands, workers, women,
students, and other marginal groups. In the larger Asian context of
the 1960s, with China's example in particular, and with collectivist
agitation at home, the threat must have seemed quite real to many
right-wing officers and small Muslim farmers. However, a leftist
insurrection in Indonesia nowhere materialized. What occurred
seemed more like a preemptive counterrevolution. The military
putsch that was presented as the last chance to prevent a Communist takeover led to a bloodbath that may well have been much
worse than what even a revolution might have brought about.

As long as the archives remain closed and no perpetrators have
been tried, not much can be said about the regime's motives and
the intentions. It clearly was neither a case of conquest nor one of a
last massacre under the imminent threat of defeat. The Indonesian
army opted for *rule by terror*, and this was its campaign of intimidation against those who wanted to change the prevailing relations
of property and power, who agitated for land reform and workers'
rights, and who might have wanted to limit the army's economic
and political clout. As the campaign got under way, it received
massive help (maybe even unexpectedly) from gangs of Muslims
who came from the ranks of the small landholding peasantry. In
that respect the episode displayed some elements of a *megapogrom:*
"Sometimes villages were specifically assigned to purge themselves of their Communists. Then took place communal executions
as the village gathered its Communists together and clubbed or
knifed them to death. Sometimes the army handed back to a village

Communist Party members it had already arrested. The village as a whole was instructed to execute them. . . . And in several instances, whole villages with Communist affiliations were wiped out by neighboring non-Communist villages."[51] The extermination of the Communists was motivated not just in terms of self-interest by landed peasants who felt that their holdings were threatened, it was also justified as a religious mission: "The taste of mortal combat against a surprisingly ill-prepared enemy was an experience which galvanized many of the youthful Muslim participants, committing them to an absolute, religiously sanctioned crusade of extermination of their enemies. Many who were there today proudly speak of their deeds. Others who now have troubled feelings about what was done, nevertheless felt swept along by the collective spirit at the time."[52]

In Bali, killings started only after the paratroopers under the command of the notorious commander Sarwo Edhy had landed on the island. The Balinese Hindu peasant bands turned out to be as fanatical as Javanese Muslims: "The Balinese, however, exceeded their instructors, turning on PKI members and those associated with them with a chilling ferocity."[53] Most of the time, the Muslim militias drove the Communists to another village, along with their families, to prevent future revenge, and there killed them all, out of sight of their neighbors. But sometimes even such minimal seclusion was abandoned, and villagers were forced to murder their own Communist neighbors.[54] The military did round up their victims and herded them into warehouses, where they were then gunned down. It suited the villagers to pretend they had not heard what went on behind those walls so that they could feign ignorance.[55]

The Indonesian army, after its successful countercoup against the Sukarno regime, had little reason to fear defeat or even stubborn resistance, and yet it instigated and carried out one of the worst annihilation campaigns of the twentieth century in which countless peasants and students eagerly participated. In this instance, too, the villagers joined in gangs that killed together, in an atmosphere of collective, theatrical excitement. In this respect, the episode had some traits of a megapogrom. But Suharto's New Order regime had a large part in the killings, and the annihilation campaign established for many years to come its rule by terror, with much help from local vigilante groups.

The Mass Killings of Native Peoples in Guatemala

In Guatemala, indigenous Indian peoples and government troops had clashed on and off since the 1960s.[56] Mayas from various lineages resisted the ongoing expropriation of their plots in the highlands, which compelled them to seek work as plantation laborers under dire conditions. They rebelled with renewed élan in the early 1980s. The reaction to this insurrection was swift and deadly. Government forces began an antiguerrilla war against the rebel ranks, which counted a few thousand fighters at most. The bloodshed was greatly acerbated after General Efraín Ríos Montt seized power in March 1982. His military dictatorship organized an all-out extermination campaign. Routinely, soldiers would enter a village, destroy the crops in the fields, burn down the huts, and drive the inhabitants into the church. There they would decapitate the local priest and the elders, taking their heads with them to set an example for other villages. Next, they would set fire to the church, machine-gunning down those who tried to flee.[57] All Indians—women, children, even babies in the womb—were treated as potential insurgents and killed en masse, often after having been raped or tortured. Up to a million of approximately four million people of Mayan Ixil extraction were forcibly drafted into militias and compelled to fight the guerrillas.

This was a successful effort to suppress local peasant rebellions by an established government employing unrestrained violence against its own citizens: "In the Guatemalan case, however, genocide was not a result of state decomposition but rather state consolidation, the first step of the military's plan of national stability and return to constitutional rule. And it certainly was not the result of Washington's negligence but rather a direct consequence of its intervention."[58] It was a clear instance of rule by terror.

During the sixteen months of the Montt regime, countless Native Americans were murdered without any semblance of legal justification or due process. Almost a million Mayans were expelled from their lands, and many succumbed as a result.[59]

At the time, almost complete silence prevailed about the annihilation campaign, at home due to vigorous censorship, abroad due to general indifference and self-censorship in many American media, which helped cover up the active complicity of the US government and its CIA "assets" in the field. Even today, the genocidal campaign in Guatemala is rarely mentioned in scholarly literature. Notwithstanding the assiduous attempts to have the perpetrators and the instigators prosecuted, almost complete impunity has prevailed to this day. In January 2013 a Guatemalan judge ordered Montt to stand trial.[60] His subsequent conviction was overturned by a higher court, but legal proceedings against Montt continue.

Losers' Triumph: Turning Passive into Active

That conquerors in the rush of victory commit plunder, rape, and mass murder is a familiar theme from history. Many established regimes are known to have resorted to rule by terror. There are, however, also regimes that have carried through campaigns of mass annihilation against a domestic target group at a time of imminent defeat. This is counterintuitive: such destructive potential would be put to better use by deploying it against an external enemy about to get the upper hand.

This particular mode of mass annihilation may occur in times of war against an armed and organized foreign enemy when an unarmed and unorganized group within the regime's sphere of power has been identified as the target people. The target group is suspected of secretly collaborating with the enemy, operating as a fifth column and recruiting spies and saboteurs. At some point, the struggle against the target group comes to seem even more urgent than the battle against the approaching foreign enemy. Or rather, fighting the target group is the true historical mission of the regime, as important, if not more so, than waging the ongoing war: "Rwanda's Hutu Power Regime was sapping its frontline military effort in favor of completing the genocide, just as the Germans had done in the final months of World War II."[61]

At the point where the regime no longer trusts that it can win the war, it may turn in full force against the target group. In psychological terms, it starts a fight that it can win, precisely because it is bound to lose the war: the regime is "turning passive into active."[62]

This mechanism may well explain major aspects of the genocide that the Turks committed against the Armenians during their long retreat in World War I; the Holocaust that the Germans carried out against the Jews with redoubled effort as their armies were forced to retire and finally collapsed on all fronts during World War II; the extermination of the "new people" by the Cambodian Khmer Rouge as a Vietnamese invasion was about to be launched; the massive extermination of Bangladeshis by the (West) Pakistani army on the eve of the secession of East Pakistan; the Serbian drive against Bosnian Muslims when the Serbs had to surrender what was left of the Yugoslav federation; and, most telling of all, the Hutu Power genocide of the Tutsi people in Rwanda while the Tutsi Rwandan Patriotic Front advanced from the northern border toward the capital, Kigali. In all these instances, the regime that could not win on the battlefield could nevertheless destroy an unarmed target group: that is the losers' victory.

In all these instances, the war was already lost and many in the regime's inner circle knew it. And yet, precious resources were deployed to annihilate an enemy that was not even fighting back. It is tempting in these cases to decide with hindsight that the regime's leadership should have known at the time that events would take the course that we now know they did and that it was bound to lose the conflict. Back then, the leaders might still have continued to hope for victory against their own better judgment. However that may be, in each case the regime turned against the target group at a time when doing so clearly deflected resources from the war effort. It opted for destruction of the target population and so helped to bring about its own destruction. At face value, the choice is perverse. But in the perspective of the regime's vision of history it is intelligible. Radical, revolutionary regimes see themselves engaged in a battle of life and death against evil forces that have forever oppressed or menaced their people.[63] Their moment is a unique turning point in the history of that perennial struggle. This time is different. And it is now or never.

The Turkish Extermination of the Armenians

During a good part of the nineteenth century, the Ottoman Empire had been in decline, torn by recurrent rebellion, especially in its European provinces, and under constant pressure from the Western powers. Just before the turn of the century, under the reign of Sultan Abdul Hamid II, hundreds of local massacres of Armenians occurred. The death toll may have been around a quarter of million, and maybe "one million were pillaged and plundered."[64] After the Young Turk revolution of 1908, a more liberal regime was elected. It antagonized Islamist rebels who vented their rage, once again, in a series of pogroms against the Armenians. On the eve of World War I, the Greek population on the Aegean coast of Turkey became the target of bloody attacks by regular army units and nationalist militias, aimed at driving them from Turkish soil.[65] Strong protests from the Western powers temporarily ended this mass expulsion. But after the war started, the deportations resumed. The massacres of Armenians and the forced ouster of the Greeks had foreshadowed the policy of Islamization and Turkification that was soon to be implemented.

The Ottoman Empire entered the war on November 11, 1914, on the side of the Central Powers (the German Reich, the Austro-Hungarian Empire, and Bulgaria), fighting the Allied forces of Britain, France, and Russia (and, in the final stage, the United States). At the outset of the war, the Ottoman regime hoped to compensate for the loss of almost the entire Balkan region in preceding years with conquests in Central Asia and the Middle East. Earlier expulsions of the Turkish population from these lands also demanded revenge. The future empire was meant not only to unite Turkish-speaking nations to the east but also to comprise Muslim nations to Turkey's south. The new Islamic realm would no longer accommodate other faiths as the old empire had done: Greeks and Armenians, Christian peoples, were now considered alien elements that would only erode the unity of the nation.

However, the war took a different course, and the odds of holding on to the Middle Eastern parts of the empire, let alone of conquering new territories in that region, quickly receded with the adversities on the battlefield. As the prospects of Islamic expansion receded, the Young Turk regime became increasingly nationalistic and now aimed to create a Greater Turkish nation. The Armenians literally stood in the way of this grand project, since their territory lay on the route toward the Turkic-speaking peoples in Turkmenistan, Kazakhstan, Uzbekistan, and Kirgizstan (as they are now called).

The campaign to eradicate the Armenians began in earnest by the end of December 1914, after the catastrophic failure of a reckless offensive by the Turkish army under the command of Enver

Pasha against the Russian troops near the northeastern border, a region where many Armenians lived. The Armenian recruits in the Turkish army were disarmed, condemned to forced labor, and succumbed en masse. Turkish paramilitary units attacked Armenian villages, burning, looting, and murdering on a large scale and with impunity.

Historian Uğur Üngör has provided a detailed account of the extermination of Armenian communities, half a year later, in the southeastern province of Diyarbakir, when armed bands were wreaking havoc all over eastern Turkey.[66] The course of events depended heavily on the provincial governor and the local mayor, who interpreted the orders from Istanbul with more or less destructive zeal. Nomadic Kurdish bands were often called in to attack the Armenian citizens. Only a year later, it was the turn of the Islamic Kurds to be rounded up and deported, many of them to be resettled in Armenian villages that had by now been deserted and razed to the ground.[67]

The total death toll of the Turkish annihilation of the Armenians amounts to well over a million casualties.[68] Their extermination was the task of the so-called Special Organization, manned by ex-convicts and under the direct command of the Ottoman General Headquarters. Frequently local mobs were mobilized and willingly participated in the massacres. Sometimes, the victims who had taken refuge in the local church or had been herded in there were massacred on the spot; sometimes, too, they were taken away, hands bound, to be shot some distance from the village.[69] Otherwise, "the perpetrators mostly used daggers, swords, scimitars, bayonets, axes, saws and cudgels." Back in the villages, women, children, and the elderly were killed in "massive drowning operations" and "systematically burned alive in haylofts, stables, and large caves."[70]

Apparently, the killing compartments were manned not only by military men, organized specialists in violence, but also by "spontaneous volunteers," not so much selected as self-selected. The massacres were hardly hidden from view; anyone who wanted to could witness them. In these respects, the genocidal episodes were not thoroughly compartmentalized. Even a hundred years after the fact, Turkey officially persists in denying that the mass extermination of the Armenians was a genocide in the sense of the UN treaty.[71]

Once it had become clear that the Ottoman Empire could not be saved, the regime of radical nationalists decided to abandon their idea of a multiethnic society. Having failed to realize a multiethnic but solely Muslim realm, the Young Turks now aimed for a homogeneous Turkish nation-state.[72] As Üngör points out, the Young Turks had narrowed their circle of identification, rather than widening it, a pattern that corresponds to the collapse of the multiethnic empire.[73] They now disidentified from the non-Turkic, non-Muslim peoples that remained within their borders, beginning with the Armenians, of distinct religion and ethnicity.[74] Accusing them of supporting the Russian cause and fighting on Russia's side, the Young Turk regime in May 1915 initiated its final annihilation campaign. The deportation and extermination of its minorities of course did nothing to alter Turkey's disastrous course of defeat after defeat that culminated in the humiliating armistice ending World War I. As it had begun to realize that it could not fulfill its war objectives abroad, the Young Turk regime "turned its aggression inward," against its own citizens, and destroyed the Armenian community, in a final triumph of the loser.

Nazi Germany (bis): The Final Solution

The Nazi regime throughout its twelve-year existence ruled by terror at home, but it killed mostly abroad: initially, in the east, in a conquerors' frenzy and in its final phase in the mode of a losers' triumph. If ever there was a regime that turned its aggression outward, in conquest, oppression, exploitation, and extermination, it was Hitler's Third Reich. The overwhelming majority, more than 95 percent, of the people it killed had lived outside Germany's borders, most of them by far in those parts of central and eastern Europe that historian Timothy Snyder has called "the Bloodlands."

The attack of the German armies on September 1, 1939, led to a series of quick and almost effortless victories, first in the east, in Poland, followed by harsh occupation and an unrestricted victors' frenzy, and next to an equally sweeping conquest on the Western Front and a more moderate occupation regime. When the Nazi troops overwhelmed the Soviet Union, in June 1941, they quickly turned their untrammeled, murderous wrath against all "Jews" and "Bolsheviks" they could lay their hands on.

By the end of 1941, the United States had entered the war and fortunes on the battlefield in the east had changed. It became increasingly clear that the Allied powers might well gain the upper hand before too long. From early 1942 on, the Nazi regime began to plan the systematic extermination of the Jews of Europe, no longer more or less openly (albeit in remote areas) by execution squads, but in secluded extermination camps where the Jews would be assembled and either immediately killed in gas chambers or first worked to near death and then gassed, their corpses burned in crematoria installed for the purpose. This was an industrial machinery to kill human beings and dispose of their remains. No such installations had ever been designed, constructed, and actually operated. The Nazi officials in charge thought this procedure would spare the sensitivities of the men charged with the mass extermination, would allow the killings to be handled more discreetly, and most of all, would work much faster, destroying when necessary tens of thousands of "bodies" every day. Trains would not only bring in the eastern Jews but now also the Jews from France, Holland, and Belgium. Hundreds of thousands of Romas and Sinti were to be processed in the same manner.[75]

In this phase, the annihilation proceeded no longer in the open air, at the outskirts of rural villages, as it had occurred behind the Eastern Front.[76] The extermination took place in secluded camps, surrounded by fences, located in inaccessible areas. No outsiders were allowed to enter, not even to come near. The gas chambers and crematoria were walled in and camouflaged, sometimes with flower beds. Violent excesses could erupt anywhere, but for torture and executions the SS preferred special locations where it could exercise its métier without onlookers.

Although the final solution proceeded under extreme compartmentalization, everyone in a wide perimeter must have known. The smoke and smell of burning corpses could not be ignored for hundreds of yards away from the camps. Those who lived in the vicinity had to close their windows against the stench and to clean away the soot from the panes. Nor could they avoid the sight of burning chimneys or passing cattle trains, and many caught a glimpse of what went on inside if they approached the fence. It was strictly forbidden to mention the subject and "spread rumors": one precept they adhered to until long after the war.

The closer the specter of defeat came, the more fanatical Hitler and his entourage became about the scheme to exterminate all racially impure elements within their reach: the notions of Lebensraum and Endlösing, Hitler's twin obsessions, had evolved and radicalized under the spur of victory and opportunity. In defeat the evolution was over. "Henceforth Hitler would cling grimly to the scheme that had been definitively shaped in the fall of 1941."[77] Six weeks after the United States had joined the war, with the invasion of the Soviet Union stalled, Hitler convened the Wannsee Conference to implement his decision to exterminate *all* the Jews of Europe.[78] With this renewed commitment, Hitler regained the initiative that had now escaped him on the battlefield, writes the historian Philippe Burrin in *Hitler and the Jews*.[79] In other words, Hitler turned passive into active.

"The concentration camps did not fade away as the Nazi regime headed for total defeat. On the contrary: the closer the camp system came to collapse, the bigger it became,"[80] writes Nikolaus Wachsmann. And Daniel Goldhagen paints a stark picture of this self-destructive destruction: "To the very end the ordinary Germans who perpetrated the Holocaust willfully, faithfully and zealously slaughtered Jews. They did so even when they were risking their own capture. They did so even when they had received a command from no less a personage than Himmler that they desist from killing."[81]

If nothing else, the Final Solution was to be the one great accomplishment of the Thousand-Year Reich, which would forever alter the course of history and once and for all end the eternal struggle between the Jew and the Aryan. In this *Götterdämmerung*, the twilight of the gods, Hitler would secure his claim to immortality.[82] And he did.

Pakistan's Mass Murder in Bangladesh

Following the Partition of India and Pakistan in 1947, Pakistan consisted of two parts: in the northwest of the former British India the Urdu-speaking West Pakistan, in the northeast the Bengali-speaking East Pakistan. Almost a thousand miles of Indian territory separated the two wings of Pakistan. From the beginning, the western part dominated the eastern wing in almost every respect, causing resentment among the Bengali Pakistanis. When in the elections of 1970 the Awami League won 160 out of East Pakistan's 162 seats, it also obtained a majority in the all-Pakistani legislature and soon demanded de facto autonomy for the eastern part, to be called Bangladesh.[83] Huge demonstrations ensued in East Pakistan. The popular clamor for secession kept growing. When the Pakistani high command realized that the separatist movement in the east could not be stopped by political means or military threats, it decided to launch a massive military operation. This brought the risk of an invasion from the Indian south, which would be hard to ward off, considering the logistics of waging war at such great distance from the main base in West Pakistan. The Pakistani army consisted mostly of West Pakistanis, and only a small contingent was stationed in East Pakistan. Nevertheless, in March 1971 the Pakistani regime deployed its troops in an offensive that soon turned into an annihilation campaign against the civil population of Bangladesh. The military attacked demonstrating students and teachers, causing more than 35,000 casualties in a matter of days. Bengali police and border patrol units tried to fight off the Pakistani army without much success.

The West Pakistani army went after all able-bodied young men and systematically eliminated all Bangladeshis of Hindu origin. The killing squads especially targeted professionals and intellectuals. The army had intended to eliminate the intelligentsia, in hopes of so weakening the insurgent nation that it could never again become a threat and maybe one day might even be reconquered. But the looming presence of India across the Bangladeshi borders made that an unlikely prospect.

The killings on the eve of the secession of East Pakistan were most often initiated and carried out by elements within the (West) Pakistani army, but as the upheaval spread, all sorts of local scores were settled: an unknown number of the Bihari minority in Bangladesh, who had come from West Pakistan and now in great numbers made common cause with their former home country, were killed by Bengalis.[84] Pakistani and Bangladeshi Muslims attacked Bangladeshi Hindus, killing them on the spot or expelling them across the border with India. All in all, some ten million Bengalis fled to neighboring India. In the absence of solid data, it is a reasonable guess that between one million and three million people were killed in the nine months before the Indian army intervened and routed the West Pakistanis.[85]

Bangladeshi militias participated in these killings, as did "civilians." Because local government was in disarray, the rioters counted on impunity. Almost no one was punished for the murders. The Pakistani military, responsible for the greatest part of the killings by far, got away scot-free.[86] This had been agreed in the cease-fire agreements that ended the intervention of India in Bangladesh, ensured the retreat of the Pakistani army and formalized the secession and independence of Bangladesh.[87] Pakistan lost Bangladesh for good, but it had had its losers' triumph.

The Khmer Rouge and Mass Extermination in Cambodia

The worst democide of the twentieth century, in terms of the proportion of the population killed for every year of the regime's brief span in power, 1975–1979, was the mass extermination carried out by the Khmer Rouge in Cambodia. More than a million people out of a population of a little more than seven million were systematically exterminated by Pol Pot's revolutionary fighters: "class enemies," ethnic minorities, and indigenous Vietnamese. Pol Pot wanted to completely erase Cambodia's past and start anew with a pure, agrarian Communist society, untainted by any trace of bourgeois or capitalist tendencies. His clique wanted to outdo even the Chinese radicalism of the Cultural Revolution. Anyone who had been classified as "new people"—that is, anyone living in the cities, anyone with an education, anyone with "soft hands"—was deported to the countryside, locked up in a labor camp, and forced to work the land on a starvation diet, to the point of exhaustion. The slightest lapse—eating a potato from the field instead of handing it over—was a reason to be marched off to the nearest grove and be clobbered to death.[88]

Pol Pot and his tightly knit coterie from the outset intended to purify the entire population: anyone with "a Vietnamese mind in a Khmer body" had to be killed; the Cham, a Muslim people, were to be eradicated; any person who had been in contact with Americans or with Westerners in general was a "rotten apple" that should be discarded; all landowners and businesspeople were slated for liquidation; and, of course, the slightest show of disrespect or dissent was met with execution on the spot. In the selection for the movement's higher ranks, next to doctrinal orthodoxy, correct class origins and ethnic (Khmer) purity came to count for more and more. The bloodiest purges were reserved for the Khmer Rouge cadres themselves.

The small Communist vanguard under Pol Pot quickly gained adherents after the Americans began to bomb the Cambodian border zones in 1969 in order to prevent Vietnamese fighters from seeking refuge there. By 1973, all of Cambodia had come under American attack from the air. The total civilian death toll reached 150,000 victims.[89] More bombs fell on Cambodia in those years than on Japan in World War II. Desperate and enraged peasants joined the ranks of the Khmer Rouge by the thousands. The Khmer Rouge cadres radicalized even further.

With its ranks much increased, the Khmer Rouge slowly fought their way toward the capital, Phnom Penh, cleansing the countryside of all untoward elements it happened to encounter. On April 17, 1975, the government of Marshal Lon Nol surrendered and the Khmer Rouge took over Phnom Penh. The evacuation of the city began right away: all "new people" were rounded up and forced to march in endless columns to destinations in the countryside, where they were put to work in order to unlearn their urban ways and become like the "old" or "base" people: the peasants. Cambodia became one huge slave-labor camp. No one among the "new people" was exempt, not even children, the elderly, the handicapped, or the mentally disturbed. Rations were at starvation level. Someone who stealthily devoured a snail could be executed on the spot.

In the meantime, the purification of Democratic Kampuchea, as it was now called, continued unabated. "In the Cambodian countryside from 1975 to 1979, the CPK's [Communist Party of Kampuchea] extreme revolution caused the deaths of approximately 1.7 million people from overwork, diseases, starvation and, in some 500,000 cases, by outright murder of political and ethnic 'enemies.'"[90] The total population of Cambodia in 1975 numbered between 7 and 7.5 million people.[91] The Pol Pot regime used its Khmer Rouge recruits to expel, deport, starve, exploit, and kill its victims; civilian gangs and mobs had no part in it. Anyone could face death from one moment to another, but the killers belonged to a distinct compartment, the army. The actual executions took place at some distance from the workers in the field, usually out of sight: "Executions usually occurred at night in the jungle, a place that is associated with the amoral, uncivilized and disordered in Cambodian culture."[92]

Among the many enigmatic aspects of the Khmer Rouge regime was the extermination of the Vietnamese minority and anyone sympathizing with Vietnam. This was bound to anger neighboring Vietnam. The regime's continuous cross-border raids to reclaim disputed territory were even more provocative. In the last days of 1978, the Vietnamese counterattacked and rapidly gained ground, taking Phnom Penh on January 7, 1979.

The Pol Pot regime was brought to an end by the Vietnamese invasion with support from Khmer Rouge dissidents. However, the new government and its successor regimes were loath to upset the precarious balance of power in the country and never tried to prosecute the genocidal Khmer Rouge leaders or their henchmen. Only in recent years have some perpetrators been brought to trial; so far only one has been convicted.[93]

Strictly speaking, the Cambodian democide was not a genocide, since it persecuted and exterminated people in the first place because of their class origin and political background. It was not without foresight that the Soviet Union and China in 1948 had excluded "classicides" and "politicides" from the definition of *geno-cide* in the UN convention.

There is no way to reconcile the annihilationist policy of the Khmer Rouge with any rational conception of decision making. It was not only utterly destructive but also self-destructive.[94] In this case, too, the most plausible explanation is that the regime leadership, faced with impending collapse, "turned passive into active" and chose to fight on the one front where it could score a victory: against unarmed and unorganized people. Like other genocidal regimes on the edge of defeat, the Khmer Rouge leaders were obsessed by the idea that they were living and acting at a unique turning point in history. Time and again with their provocations they risked a confrontation with Vietnam.[95] Yet they made little effort to prepare for war with the Vietnamese. Instead, they turned their murderous rage against the "new people" of the cities. To Pol Pot and his comrades this was the first and last chance to forge a pure proletariat, a pure Khmer nation, just as for all the losing regimes it had been their one and unique opportunity to forge an untainted Turkish nation out of the Ottoman hodgepodge, to eliminate forever the Jewish race from the face of the earth, to terminate once and for all every trace of bourgeois hegemony in Cambodia, to definitively destroy an autonomous Bengali nation, or to liberate the Hutus from the century-long oppression by the Tutsi, or, as we will see next, to permanently secure a pure ethnic nation for the Serbs. As Jacques Sémelin has expressed it: purify and destroy.[96] Even if that must be the loser's only victory.

The Collapse of Yugoslavia

The campaigns of the Serbs and their Bosnian Serb allies in the early 1990s display elements of both conqueror's frenzy and losers' triumph. The worst massacres occurred each time the Serb units succeeded in invading Muslim territory. But the Serbian regime early in the war had abandoned all hope of reuniting the former socialist republics that once constituted the Yugoslav federation. The murderous campaigns, by the Serb ("Yugoslav") army and the Serb militias, and their genocidal excesses even more so, only alienated still further the peoples who had already seceded from the Socialist Federal Republic of Yugoslavia. The massacres further persuaded the nations that had not yet broken away to resist with all their might what increasingly looked like bloody usurpation by the Serbs.

This was the fourth wave of ethnic slaughter between Serbs and Croats (and Bosnians) in eighty years: during World War I; under Nazi occupation; in the aftermath of World War II under Tito; and again after the decomposition of Yugoslavia. Yet the various segments of the Yugoslav population do not differ in origin. There are no clearly distinctive physical traits. Linguistically, the different versions of Serbo-Croatian—Serb, Croatian, and Bosnian—are nearly identical and very similar to Macedonian and Slovenian. The Serbs use the Cyrillic alphabet, most other groups the Latin alphabet. The majority of Serbs belong to the Eastern Orthodox Church; most Croats are Roman Catholics. The same applies to the Bosnian Serbs and Croats, respectively. The third party in Bosnia consists mainly of Muslims. Serbs and Croats blamed Muslims for having abandoned their Christian faith under Ottoman rule for opportunistic reasons. In Yugoslavia, however, this one dimension of distinction, religion, was not all that salient. Under Communism, the churches had steadily lost influence, and after the collapse of Yugoslavia, the new ethnic leaders initially did not stress faith very much.

For many centuries the Yugoslav region was a frontier area between the Ottoman and the Habsburg Empires, with Russia always present in the east.[97] It was the area where Islam and Christianity faced each other. For a thousand years, moreover, Roman Catholics and Eastern Orthodox Christians had been divided by the "great schism" that continued to separate Serbs and Croats.[98]

The roots of the resentment between Croats and Serbs likely date back to the foundation of the kingdom of Yugoslavia in 1918: Serbs occupied most elite positions in the government, court, and army, and many Croats and Slovenes felt that they had been annexed by Serbia rather than united as equal partners into the new monarchy.

After the invasion of Yugoslavia by the Axis powers in April 1941, the Nazis murdered more than half a million Jews, "Gypsies," and other "enemies," with help from their Hungarian vassals. In Croatia, they installed the fascist puppet regime of Ante Pavelić, which turned its Catholic Ustaša militias against Romas and Jews, as well as against the Orthodox Christian Serbs, killing about half a million people with the full knowledge and complicity of the Roman Catholic hierarchy: "It was genocide pure and simple."[99] At the same time, royalist Serb Chetniks, under Dragoljub "Draža" Mihailović, and Serb Communists led by Josip Broz Tito, fought the Ustaše and one another with equal fanaticism. The Italian and German occupation authorities aided and abetted both the Chetnik and Ustaša terror, since it spared them the dirty work of having to root out partisan fighters and other "undesirable elements" themselves. Tito, although of Croat and Slovene parentage, had sided with the Serbs against the mainly Croat army of Mihailović and after the war remained sympathetic to the Serb side, even as he became the leader of the newly united Yugoslav federal republic.

Tito's rule brought no end to the bloodshed. Already in the last phase of the war his partisans had started to purify their own ranks of non-Communists and to liquidate "class enemies and prisoners" of war in the areas under their control. The number of their victims may have run in the hundreds of thousands.[100] As the war came to an end, Tito consolidated his rule by expelling, jailing, or outright murdering "renegades," "anticommunists," "collaborators," Ustaše, Chetniks, and ethnic Germans. When the rupture with Stalin came in 1948, the Tito regime turned against the "Cominformists." Nevertheless, the ethnic and religious tensions that had erupted so murderously during the war years seem to have gradually subsided, and—on the surface—the different groupings mingled peacefully under Tito's rule.

When the federation began to fall apart in the early 1990s, in part as a reaction to resurgent Serb nationalism, Slovenia and, later, Croatia opted for secession. Germany and Austria were among the first to recognize the new countries.[101] The Serbs reacted furiously against this dismemberment of the republic. They tried to regain some of the lost ground and at least hold on to Bosnia. Another round of ethnic killings ensued, once more pitching the Serbs against Croatians and against Croat or Muslim Bosnians.[102] Although the Serbs invoked the memory of the Battle of Kosovo in 1389, the bloodshed is better understood against the background of the much more recent carnage of World War II and its aftermath. The politicians and commanders who now called the shots were the children and grandchildren of the generation that had lived through the bloodiest and most fearful epoch of Yugoslav history. Many among them may well have been traumatized by their elders' and their own childhood experiences.[103]

Hardly had they assumed power in 1990 when the Croats under Franjo Tuđman declared independence and adopted the symbols of the former fascist Ustaša regime. On their part, the Serbs led by Slobodan Milošević set out to restore the position of dominance they had held under Tito, with a vengeance. The governments of the respective successor states organized their own armies and militias to expel minorities from the territories they had claimed.

The nadir came in July 1995, with the massacre of some eight thousand Bosnian Muslim men by Bosnian Serb troops under Ratko Mladić after the Dutch UN battalion had abandoned its advanced position in Srebrenica, which had provided some protection to the Bosnian Muslims assembled there.[104] In the end, the total casualties of the violence during the 1990s in the former Yugoslavia came to three hundred thousand dead. Two-thirds of these victims were civilians or prisoners of war. More than four million people had been expelled from their homes.[105]

In the massacres that followed the collapse of Yugoslavia, civilians died by the thousands and tens of thousands, but civilian perpetrators had a much less active part in the events than, for example, in Rwanda or Indonesia. The killings were the province of specialists and were mostly carried out where witnesses were few, out of sight of the international news media. In this respect, mass annihilation in Yugoslavia was much more compartmentalized than in similar episodes in other countries.

The Serbs under Milošević considered themselves the defenders of the old Yugoslavia, and they controlled the remains of the old Yugoslav army and its auxiliary militias. In the end, all other successor republics chose independence and the Serbs were left with no more than a rump Serbia. Maybe the Bosnian Serbs had operated under the illusion that they could hold on to all of Bosnia (or at least divide the spoils with the Croats). Most of the ethnic cleansing on the part of the Serbs was indeed a last attempt to create a homogeneous Orthodox, Serbian land in the face of the dismantlement of the former Yugoslavia and the expulsion of the Serbs from the other successor republics.

It now appears that Serbia engaged in a rather desperate attempt to expel or annihilate all non-Serb groupings in the territories it could grab or hold on to, even as it had to abandon the rest of Yugoslavia and face interventions by the United Nations and, finally, punitive bombings by NATO aircraft: another case of triumph of the losers. Under the conditions of dispersed and intermittent battles, the Serbian cleansing forays provided ample excuse for the Croats or the Bosnian Muslims to engage in their own campaigns of ethnic purification and wanton murder by their military units and militias. "Essentially," writes political scientist Mary Kaldor, "the war was not directed against opposing sides, but against civilian populations."[106] All sides used militias, manned by criminals and a minority of nationalist fanatics, who would terrorize the local inhabitants, executing the leaders and intellectuals, robbing and killing those they believed to be wealthy, raping and maiming the women, so as to chase out the remaining population in an ethnic cleansing of the area. The paramilitary bands made secret deals with the militias on the other side to divide the most lucrative spoils.[107]

In this complicated, three-cornered, volatile civil war, armed groups in a successful advance would kill to terrorize and cleanse the hostile population of the newly acquired territory in a brief conquerors' frenzy, only to be forced out in the next confrontation and retreat with equally murderous zeal, killing whomever remained at their mercy out of spite and revenge, in a loser's triumph.

The long shadow of the horrors of World War II greatly exacerbated the old divisions between the religious and "ethnic" groups that had survived from the Ottoman period. Under Tito, however, these ethnic resentments were played down, on the face of it quite successfully. Yet once Yugoslavia disintegrated, the Serb and Croat appeals to ethnic loyalties turned out to be quite effective. Since overall government protection had disintegrated, any call for ethnic mobilization on the one side forced people on the other side to seek safety among "their" ethnic group even if they had not bothered much about such bonds before then.[108] At such moments, the memories of what went on half a century earlier were suddenly resuscitated.

Tito's reign can be seen as an attempt to replace ethnic politics with class politics. In that sense, indeed, the violence of the 1990s was "a return of the repressed." Under Communism the compartmentalization of Yugoslavian society diminished considerably, and by design. The dissolution of Tito's Yugoslavia led to a "recompartmentalization": a renewed division along ethnic lines, an increasing spatial and social separation, increasing mutual disidentification, a decline of interaction among groups, and the gradual dissolution of mixed friendships, even marriages. The breakup of Yugoslavia was in great part the result of deliberate political and military initiatives, but it could not have occurred if the "ethnoreligious" dividing lines had not existed before and had lain dormant in a kind of hibernation under Tito's republic to be reactivated after the end of his reign.

If, under conditions of increasing anomie, one witnesses others banding together as "Serbs," one better find shelter with kindred "anti-Serbs," even if they have to be reinvented in the process as Bosnian Muslims or Bosnian Croats. But such labels can be invoked effectively only if they are elements of a collectively constructed past. Once the dialectics of identifications and disidentifications is in full play, fantasies mutually exacerbate one another. At this point, activists will resort to violence for their own purposes: to oust members of the opposite group from rewarding positions, to take over their houses, shops, jobs, and land. This is the "rational choice" aspect of the spiraling violence. Rape is an essential, symbolic and sexual, part of this expropriation. All these violent acts will vindicate the worst fears of the other group and prompt it to respond in kind. Every incident is magnified and resounds in the fantasies of the parties concerned. In that sense, compartmentalization breeds compartmentalization.

The presence of distrusted neighbor states and the threat of armed invasion reinforced and accelerated the process. Every outside intervention that should have pacified the warring factions was perceived as an act of aggression by at least one of them. This compelled outside forces either to stay out of the fray entirely or move in with massive force and subdue the entire population with military means. If no external power is willing and able to accomplish this feat, only the lack of resources or the fatigue of battle can end the fighting.

The genocide of Tutsis by the Hutu Power movement in Rwanda in 1995 was discussed in chapter 5. It is a clear case of a losers' triumph by a regime that chose to exterminate a domestic minority in the face of imminent defeat at the hands of an invading army: an exemplary instance of self-destructive destruction.

MEGAPOGROMS

The fourth mode of mass annihilation is best called a *megapogrom*. In this instance, the role of the central state is much less visible. The initiators are local notables, politicians, gangsters, clerics. The perpetrators are not in the service of the regime, and they, too, are local men. Because there is little organization and minimal logistic support, the killing episodes in any given location last only a few days or weeks at most. What turns these pogroms into instances of mass annihilation is that they occur more or less simultaneously in dozens of locations, apparently spontaneously and without visible coordination.

Megapogroms are concatenated local riots, synchronized by a major crisis on a supralocal, national, or even supranational level. In the absence of coordinated leadership and mutual communication, an event perceived by all, and perceived by everyone to be perceived by all, functions instead as a central coordination mechanism and thus as a "precipitant" of mob initiatives.[109] But this presupposes that they interpret the precipitating event in a similar manner and that, again, everyone assumes that all their peers interpret it in that way. In other words, it requires widely shared cultural understandings among the potential rioters and, in a different vein, also among the potential targets.

The most glaring instances of such megapogroms in the twentieth century were the massive expulsion and mass murder of Germans in eastern and central Europe at the end of World War II and its aftermath and the massive expulsion and mass murder of Muslims, Sikhs, and Hindus during the period of the Partition of the South Asian subcontinent into India and Pakistan.

Mass Expulsion and Mass Murder After the German Defeat in Central Europe

Many millions of German-speaking inhabitants of Middle Europe became the helpless targets of local mobs and armed groups. Polish and Czechoslovakian Nationalists and Communists were in agreement on one point: after the war all Germans were to be expelled from their territories. Their politicians in exile in Moscow and London, the army command, and the partisan militias were all of the same opinion. Even Winston Churchill and Joseph Stalin agreed on this: there had to be "an orderly and humane" displacement of Germans. It did not matter how Germans had arrived on Polish or Czechoslovakian soil or whether they had lived there for six centuries or six years, as peasants or as SS men: they all had to go. The first motive may have been revenge; the other was a desire to create an ethnically homogeneous nation. To reinforce their claims on German territories in the west, the Czechs, and the Poles in compensation for parts of Ukraine that were to be annexed by the Soviet Union, wanted to clear their new territories of all German-speaking dwellers. Speaking German had become the telltale and easily verified criterion of German background (which also happened to single out the remaining German- or Yiddish-speaking Jews).

As soon as the German troops withdrew and the Soviet soldiers were approaching, the Germans who had remained behind lost all protection. The Nazi regime had made no preparations whatsoever for a mass return of Germans from central Europe to the old Reich. Any anticipation of defeat had been considered defeatist and treasonous, and now the refugees were abandoned to their quite foreseeable fate. Poles and Czechs knew that their military and political leaders wanted the ouster of the Germans and that the Allies supported the expulsions.[110]

The Czech and Polish authorities certainly were implicated in the mob violence, although the full extent of their complicity remains unclear. The newly established regimes at the very least condoned most of the expulsions and massacres because they served their designs.[111]

Poles and Czechs took revenge on a grand scale. Some twelve million Germans were expelled or forced to flee from eastern and central Europe to what remained of Germany.[112] Many were stuck without food or shelter in the biting cold of the final winter of war. Countless others were killed by Polish and Czech mobs.

All sorts of armed groups, police squads, resistance groups, regular army units, and local gangs initiated or assisted the attacks on German homes, hospitals, churches. The perpetrators trusted that they would not be punished no matter how outrageous their deeds. Indeed, they were proved to be right. The provisional authorities, even if they had the means to stop the atrocities, turned a blind eye.

Tens of thousands, more likely hundreds of thousands, of Germans were humiliated, beaten, robbed, plundered, and killed in every imaginable or unimaginable way. Those who could still walk were chased away on death marches toward Germany. Others were packed into boxcars that sometimes stood still on the tracks for days as the refugees were once more robbed by marauding gangs and succumbed in great numbers from hunger and thirst, cold and exhaustion. Once they arrived on German soil the refugees were not welcome, certainly not as long as Hitler was alive. After the surrender, the Allied occupation forces took charge, but they lacked the means to absorb the millions of Displaced Persons in a country that had been heavily bombed by the Allies and exhausted by Hitler's wars.

While Germany collapsed under the onslaught of the Red Army, the advancing Soviets sent German civilians and prisoners of war to camps in the east. Two hundred thousand civilians and 363,000 prisoners of war died there. A roughly equal number of war prisoners succumbed on their way to the camps.[113] All in all, possibly a million German civilians perished in the six months before and two years after Germany's final defeat.[114]

The Germans in Middle Europe were the victims now. Many Volksdeutsche had enthusiastically supported the Nazis, welcomed their invasion, and profited from it. About half a million Germans had arrived with the occupying forces as functionaries of the Nazi regime or as privileged settlers on requisitioned estates. They had been part of an occupation that had exterminated millions of Jews and millions of Slavs, bent on the annihilation of European Jewry, the partial annihilation of the Slavs, and the enslavement of those who remained. The Nazis had wanted to demolish the economic infrastructure of the lands conquered in the east and put in place a feudal agrarian society to be ruled by the Aryan Herrenvolk.

In their rage, the Poles and Czechs did not discriminate between the worst perpetrators or profiteers of the Nazi occupation and the rest of the Germans who might or might not have reaped some advantages from the occupation. In the mayhem, many rioters were eager to appropriate whatever German possessions they could lay hands on and to take over the homes and shops of the Germans who were now under attack. Behind the seething lust or revenge often hid practical calculations.[115]

The extreme viciousness of the attacks also had a theatrical quality: the atrocities often occurred in public, before an eager audience. Germans were made to wear armbands with Nazi emblems; swastikas were inscribed or carved on their skin; they were not allowed to walk the curb, forbidden to use public spaces, forced to beat each other, or to dance in the midst of a crowd, in an almost ritual reversal of roles. The former masters were now ostentatiously turned into the lowest of the low. The erstwhile executioners had become the victims, and the former victims now acted out their newly won mastery. The violence had a carnivalesque quality: what had been forbidden for so long now could be openly expressed. The cruelties were often conspicuously obscene, so as to display the total domination of the newly liberated. The crowd felt free to enhance the thrill of cruelty with a tinge of sexual excitement, the most taboo mixture of all. Yet of course it was not a carnival but a real atrocity. Nor was it a temporary reversal of roles for the duration of the feast. This time it spelled a historical transformation that would not soon be turned back.

Historian Karl Schlögel has remarked that it is difficult to discuss a crime that is overshadowed by another crime.[116] Indeed, the expulsion and murder of Germans in Poland, Czechoslovakia, and other countries can only be understood against the background of what Germans had wreaked in the years before.

In almost all locations, the pogroms subsided after a few days or weeks, and a more selective but not necessarily more humane treatment of Germans ensued. Many were locked up in prisons and camps under horrendous conditions and released only after months or years. Pogroms against Germans would break out again whenever there was the expectation that German territories would be ceded to Poland or Czechoslovakia: it appeared politically expedient to have them cleansed of their German inhabitants beforehand. There were always some rabble-rousers who anticipated that under the circumstances they could act with impunity and who would assemble a crowd to attack the few remaining Germans.

More than anything else the Nazi occupation had separated the Germans and the other inhabitants of Poland, Czechoslovakia, and the other countries of central and eastern Europe. The compartmentalization of different ethnic groups (*Rassenscheidung*) had been the first article of Nazi faith and its highest priority of policy. When the German armies left, the crowds acted along the lines of distinction the Nazis had drawn, albeit this time in a rough and ready manner, without the legalistic and bureaucratic pretense the Nazis had insisted on.

In these megapogroms, the separation between professional specialists of violence—police, militias, the military—and the rest of the population was not as neat as in other modes of mass violence. Resistance fighters or regular army units often were among the first to attack German homes, though in a rather haphazard and chaotic way. Crowds quickly gathered and joined in the violence. It was indeed a free-for-all. The presence of uniformed men added to the sense of safety and impunity for the civilians in the mob.

The megapogroms did not need authorities to order the violence. The mob attacks were not the result of obedience to superiors. They were an instance of private initiative and collective action. There was, therefore, a strong element of self-selection among the perpetrators. It is hard to assess the force of group loyalty and peer pressure to join. But the mobs were ephemeral, local, and impulsive. Those who did not want to be part of the action could stay away from it. Quite likely, many people did.

In this case, the authority-obedience paradigm does not apply. Peer loyalty and mutual imitation certainly played their part. The political and military situation was one of transition and great uncertainty, the local context was chaotic, and yet the emotional constellation was highly structured: "The hated and all-powerful enemies are now helpless, we who have been their powerless, frightened and humiliated victims can finally do unto them what they did unto us, and, no matter what we do, we will not be punished by the new authorities." Everyone involved knew that everyone else felt and thought the same: a case of reciprocal knowledge.

Amid high-spirited moral discourse sometimes the simple truth is lost: that it is shameful to lose. The Czechs and the Poles (and the other nations of Europe once vanquished by the Nazis) had been defeated, they had been unable to defend themselves, and they had not been capable of liberating themselves. Even the shame about defeat is in itself shameful, as one is supposed to bear loss with dignity.

The orgy of cruelty that occurred at the end of the war in Poland and Czechoslovakia (and in other countries, too, although on a smaller scale) may be connected to this hidden shame. In the simplest terms: the defeated of yesterday are losers no more; they are today's victors. Not only the perpetrators of the humiliation, but also those who were party to it, must be obliterated to put an end to shame. That is why it may not have mattered what individual Germans had actually done; what mattered was that all Germans had witnessed the humiliation, and therefore their memory—that is, their person—had to be destroyed.

Communal Massacres in India and Pakistan
After Independence and Partition

Only two years later, as the aftershocks of the expulsion of the Germans from central Europe still reverberated, in 1947, another displacement of populations on a similar scale took place on the South Asian subcontinent. British India was about to become independent, but it would be split: Pakistan in two parts, in the northwest and northeast, would become a Muslim homeland. Indians would be free to choose whether they wanted to move to where a majority would share their religion: Muslims to the new Pakistan,

Hindus to the new India, Sikhs to the Punjab in the new India. The new India would remain a multireligious society with a preponderance of Hindus.

What had been intended as a peaceful exchange of Muslims from India to Pakistan and Hindus in the opposite direction quickly turned into a vortex of bloody communal riots and a tidal wave of desperate refugees.[117] Muslims fled toward the north, Hindus left Pakistan, and Sikhs came from everywhere to the part of the Punjab that was assigned to the new India and where they hoped to create a Sikh state.

A year before independence, while the final compromise was still in the making, bloody battles broke out between Hindus and Muslims in Calcutta. The confrontations were much more violent than prior communal riots. This may have sounded the alarm for many minority groups across the country and triggered many local ethnic riots. Immediately upon the news that the independence covenant had been signed, on August 14 and 15, 1947, communal riots broke out across the subcontinent. Muslim mobs attacked Hindus in Pakistan, and Hindu mobs attacked Muslims throughout India.

The governing Congress Party, led by Jawaharlal Nehru and Mahatma Gandhi, may have been sincerely committed to religious pluralism, but the loosely organized Hindu nationalists certainly were not, and they counted numerous fanatics in their ranks. The founding formula of the new Dominion of Pakistan was Islam, although its founder and first governor, Muhammad Ali Jinnah, had intended to maintain the Hindu presence in the new country, reckoning that Hindus had much to contribute to the budding Pakistani economy and could one day be of use as hostages against India.[118]

Neither government explicitly encouraged communal violence, and neither government proposed compulsory migration, but implicitly, and more explicitly at the lower levels, there were signals that violence might at the very least be condoned.[119] As in the case of the Germans in Europe, there was a "precipitant," in this instance a very clear signal at a precise moment: the signing of the independence treaty. Riots broke out immediately after. Each riot acted as an alarm signal for the other party to close its ranks and seek means to defend itself. It also sent a message of legitimation to those bands of religious zealots who were waiting to attack minority believers in their area. Under the circumstances, as the message spread, violence anywhere quickly begat violence elsewhere.

The regular army was not involved in India. The police in most cases stood by idly and sometimes joined the crowd. Once the mob was in motion, the patterns were frighteningly similar to those in central Europe. Local thugs, politicians, clergymen, and party militias took the lead, and once a mob had gathered, they marched to the quarter where the adherents of the other faith lived. There they would taunt and mock them, shout insults, throw stones, attack passersby, break windows, and overturn carts. By then, the time had come to grab the women, plunder the homes and burn them down, beat up anyone they happened to lay hands on, and torture whomever caught their eye. If the victims tried to defend themselves, that was one more proof that they were the aggressors and that they therefore deserved to be taught a lesson.

Once fires raged and blood began to flow, the excitement grew and anything became possible if a bold rioter would be the first to try it. As long as the authorities did not send in the police or the army, things would only get worse. In most cases local officials did not interfere. The news of atrocities committed in Pakistan against Hindus or in India against Muslims merely justified and aggravated the violence of the other party, if it still needed encouragement.

Pakistani Hindus and Indian Muslims tried to flee and were chased out of their villages. They formed long columns of miserable and exhausted refugees, carrying their children and what little else they had with them. They were loaded onto trains, which again became the target of plunderers and bullies, and were made to wait for days on end on the tracks, because of the general chaos of the railroads or out of indifference and pure malice. Once they were on the move, the refugees became the helpless victims of preying robbers, looters, rapists, and murderers. A favored ploy was to ambush trains transporting evacuees of the other faith and massacre every one of them. All in all, maybe a million died from all sorts of causes: exhaustion, disease, starvation, arson, assault, and outright murder.

The megapogrom on the Indian subcontinent was globally symmetric: what Muslims did unto Hindus in one place on the subcontinent, Hindus did unto Muslims elsewhere. But in every location, the violence was extremely asymmetric: one predominant religious group attacking a defenseless religious minority in the vicinity. The Sikhs were attacked by and attacked both Hindus and Muslims.

The megapogrom in central Europe, on the contrary, was globally *and* locally asymmetric: Czechs, Poles, and other recently liberated peoples attacked the Germans in their midst, who recently had become the defenseless party. But over time, there was a certain reciprocity. The Germans had been the first to commit massive atrocities, and now the time for revenge had come: the symmetry operated across time, like a pendulum. But on the Indian subcontinent as in Middle Europe, one party's atrocities served to legitimize and propel the other side's outrages.

The European and the Indian megapogroms were not carried out by distinct violence specialists alone; many rioters were civilians without experience with deadly violence. Both in India and in Europe there was loot for the taking, there were abandoned homes and fields to occupy. In quite a few communities, the religious target group was a wealthy trading minority who now could be dispossessed and expelled from their property. Or it consisted of business rivals who could now be eliminated by other means than economic competition alone. But such material considerations, important as they were, do not explain the "excess violence," the seemingly senseless infliction of pain and death.

As in Europe, the riots in India were the result, not of people's obedience to authority, but more likely of peer pressure, imitation, and, once they got under way, a growing excitement of being part of a crowd that could commit whatever misdeed someone could think of. The excitement, too, fed upon itself.

Relations between the religious communities were different from one village to the other. In most places, the believers of different faiths had easily intermingled outside the home. Elsewhere, there had been long-standing enmities and mutual avoidance. It may be that independence itself radically transformed intergroup relations, as suddenly the third party, the British colonizer, withdrew. This left the Muslims and Hindus to their own devices in dealing with each other without the colonial authority as a common enemy to unite against and as an umpire to separate them whenever they clashed.

In one respect, Muslim-Hindu or, rather, Pakistani-Indian relations were not symmetric. The Muslims under Muhammad Ali Jinnah opted for separation and secession, whereas the Congress Party had wanted to maintain the unity of colonial India after independence. Part of Jinnah's Muslim League wanted to drive out all Hindus from Pakistan to create the homogeneous Islamic state they had long envisaged. The Hindu nationalists mirrored the Muslim League in this respect, but at the time, the Congress Party was in power in India, and it continued its pluralist program.

By the second half of 1946, "there was a transition from the 'consensual' traditional communal riot to the 'genocidal' violence which marked subsequent communal conflagrations. Violence not only became more intense, but it became more organised."[120] All in all, the Partition violence forced some fifteen million people to

leave their homes and seek a safer haven under the direst circumstances: "the largest migration in the twentieth century" may have
cost from half a million to a million lives.[121]

Ethnic violence is contagious and compelling. Conflict, even
violent conflict along religious lines, was of course not without
precedent in India. On the contrary, probably everyone remembered prior clashes, even if they had occurred long ago and far
away. Such collective memories made threats all the more credible
and effective. Wherever people had lived for many years at peace in
mixed communities, suspicion and fear now surged under the impact of rumors that violence might be imminent. A minor incident
was enough to destroy the last shred of mutual confidence. On the
news of one such provocation elsewhere in the country, neighbors
began to organize along lines of creed, and this was sufficient to
convince their neighbors of the other faith that the time had also
come for them to close ranks. The better armed and organized and
more numerous side set out to teach the other group a lesson they
would not soon forget, finding justification in similar massacres committed in other parts of the land by crowds of the opposite faith.

From that moment on, collisions became harder and harder to
avoid. A small incident could explode into a major conflagration.
Each turn of events confirmed people in their worst expectations,
prompting them to act accordingly and to bring about the other
group's worst expectations. And so on.

Even at the time of Partition, it was evident that local politicians collaborated with local thugs to initiate pogroms: the gangs
were rewarded with the booty of plunder and the heady pleasures
of "recreational violence."[122] The gang leaders established their
reputation as strongmen in the community and would "bask in the
consuming gratification that killing an enemy can provide."[123] The
political bosses could rid themselves of competing local manipula-

tors and buy the loyalty of their supporters by granting them the possessions of the ousted enemies.

What was less visible and remains unclear today is the part played by state and national politicians in condoning and encouraging the violence: "The accepted view until the 1980s was that the violence was the result of a 'temporary madness' which had little to do with politics or modernity. Rather, violence was considered a throwback to medieval barbarity. The whole thrust of modern scholarship, in contrast, has been to question these assumptions."[124] Recent research has established a pattern of large-scale and effective organization behind the "spontaneous mob attacks": police complicity and the stubborn inaction of state authorities to prosecute the perpetrators.[125]

Local ethnic and religious riots seemingly erupt "spontaneously," but usually there are initiators, local bosses, thugs, politicos. In contemporary South Asia, quite often such riots occur on the eve of elections as a way to ensure that voters on one's own side will continue to vote along ethnic lines. As a result, usually, voters on the other side, having been under attack, will also close ranks in the elections. As such, ethnic riots perpetuate ethnic voting (and they are a clear example of Michael Mann's "dark side of democracy"). As a matter of fact, national elections synchronize local politics all over the country and increase political tension everywhere. They constitute the precipitating event. Whenever local governments condone the violence, major riots may still occur. Yet at present, state governments in India most often intervene and do not allow the expectation of impunity to take hold, thus removing a necessary condition for local pogroms. This is why megapogroms have not occurred again in central Europe or on the Indian subcontinent.

CHAPTER 8

Genocidal Perpetrators and the Compartmentalization of Personality

What stands out from these facts is the fragility of human compassion,
empathy, and moral emotions.
—Nico Frijda

WHEN A REGIME TURNS TO MASS EXTERMINATION, it must select the men to do the killing, provide them with the necessary tools, and find suitable sites for murder en masse. It is the regime that selects the killers, and it is the regime that creates the conditions for them to work under. Prevailing opinion has it that the genocidaires are just ordinary people who are brought to commit mass murder because of the situation they find themselves in, regardless of their personal makeup. In the starkest terms, what counts in the prevalent approach is "situation, not disposition." It is most plausible, indeed, that the actual situation strongly shapes people's actions. But there is more, much more, to it.

First of all, in a *macrosociological* perspective, transformations of society imbue people with shared memories, collective mentalities, and similar dispositions (which all still differ considerably from one person to the next). At the next level, in a *mesosociological* perspective, the regime puts in place the institutions it needs to realize its policies and all the while actively tries to shape people's mentality and dispositions through education and propaganda. On a third level, in the *microsociological* perspective, people function within the context of these institutions, such as schools and hospitals, prisons or camps, in situations that strongly influence their behavior. And last, in a *psychosociological* perspective, individual people act with and against other people according to their particular dispositions and their specific "definition of the situation." An attempt to understand genocidal episodes and the perpetrators that take part in them should take into account all four of these levels and their interactions.

In the preceding chapter, about genocidal episodes, the macrosociological level of societal transformations and the mesosociological level of regime interventions served to clarify those events. Those accounts now form the background for a discussion of perpetrators with their particular dispositions in a genocidal situation.

Perhaps the most common notion in the human sciences is that people must be understood in terms of the specific situation they find themselves in *and* in terms of their particular personal disposition as it was shaped by their genetic makeup, their early childhood, and their subsequent life course in the context of the society they are part of. Strangely enough, this maxim is generally ignored when it comes to the perpetrators of mass violence: "The obedience explanation is decontextualized: it needs to be accompanied by an account of the historical processes that generate a genocidal context in which orders for mass murder are given and obeyed."[1] The perpetrators are presented as if they have no past, not until they became mass murderers. At least in this respect they seem unique.

The fact that psychological tests so far have been unable to find much difference between those who refuse an order to inflict harm and those who comply does not mean that there are no such differences. It just means that test batteries can't find most of them. And it has not been tried very hard. Those who wish to argue against pure situationism in favor of an analysis in terms of both situation and disposition, as I do, must try to show differences in personality among perpetrators and also among most perpetrators and other people of their generation and nationality. That is not an easy task. But it is worth a try.

First of all, the opposition between situation and disposition is not as stark as it is made to appear in the literature on genocidal perpetrators. Historical processes over time transform the individual dispositions of those who live through them. Thus the collective experiences of war and its aftermath, of tyranny, economic depression, mass unemployment, poverty, pandemics, and famine, may profoundly and lastingly affect individual personalities.

In this respect, the insights of developmental psychologists can be especially germane. They study the small social figuration that is the nuclear family; their timescale spans the years of childhood. The body of knowledge about early development that they have assembled has been mostly ignored in the study of genocidal perpetrators. Of course, one should not conclude solely on the basis of observed adult behavior that there is a preexisting disposition to such behavior in the perpetrator of the act: a *vitium genocidale*, an inborn or inbred genocidal drive hidden deep inside the agent. That indeed would be "the fundamental attribution error" of inferring a disposition in the actor when we observe behavior that might be explained as well by the actual situation.[2] Moreover, such a genocidal disposition would still beg the question: Is everyone deep down disposed to kill en masse, but is this inclination dormant until it is awakened in a specific situation? If so, this brand of universal dispositional thinking would turn into a situationist view. In this perspective, after all, the actual context is the direct cause that latent murderous inclinations, shared by everyone, turn into de facto murderous behavior by some.[3]

The alternative assumption is that some people are *more disposed* to become mass killers than others. They might have lived in a society or under a regime that encourages aggression against outsider groups, and they might thus have come to share the cultural codes of their social environment. That would make an entire nation, or at least a particular generation within it, more prone to mass murder than other nations or age groups. This assumption also fits the macro- and mesosociological perspective. Alternatively, somebody's proclivity to kill en masse may be the result of genetic inheritance and lived experience that made this particular person especially inclined to participate in episodes of mass annihilation. This fits the psychosociological approach.

SHARED MEMORIES, COLLECTIVE MENTALITY, AND DECIVILIZATION

What kind of broad social transformations could have affected people's dispositions to make them more likely to obey someone in a position of authority who incites them to mass murder? The answer is transformations that strengthen the tendency to comply with orders, to remain loyal to one's peers, to overcome moral inhibitions against harming strangers, to break down inhibitions against violent behavior, to despise certain categories of "other" people, and to weaken empathy with the victims.

In fact, what is evoked here is what Norbert Elias calls the "decivilizing process." It is a reversal of the civilizing process that he traces from the late Middle Ages to the end of the nineteenth century in western Europe, especially France. Later in life (in 1989), in his book *The Germans*, Elias identified the social processes that over a century produced a personality type among the upper classes that in the end facilitated the *Regression zur Barbarei* (regression into barbarism) in Germany.[4] A key process was the recruitment and formation of students from an aristocratic background in the university fraternities. These *Burschenschaften*, with their aristocratic honor codes and dueling rituals, were closely connected to the officers' caste and permeated by a military mentality of unquestioning loyalty and hereditary leadership. In these circles especially, the failure to restore the legendary grandeur of Germany in times long gone by inspired increasing frustration and anger. The German nation was entitled to a leading position among the nations, and any means to achieve it seemed legitimate. World War I, fought to realize that vision, ended in catastrophe. Someone had to take the blame, but the military and aristocratic circles who had started and lost the war certainly were not going to accept responsibility for Germany's ruin. The military command maintained that there had been a *Dolchstoss im Rücken,* a stab in the back by the Social Democrats who had made peace prematurely. The radical nationalists accused international Jewry of conspiracy and treason against the Fatherland.

Daniel Goldhagen has traced the pervasiveness of anti-Semitism, and the emergence of a particularly murderous brand of it, in Germany: "Much *positive* evidence exists that antisemitism, albeit an antisemitism evolving in content with the changing times, continued to be an axiom of German culture throughout the nineteenth and twentieth centuries, and that its regnant version in Germany during its Nazi period was but a more accentuated, intensified, and elaborated form of an already broadly accepted basic model."[5] Goldhagen may have overstated his case, and sometimes buttressed it with inadequate arguments.[6] What matters here is his insistence that nations have a past, have gone through a collective experience, and that their history shapes a broadly shared *mentalité,* albeit to varying degrees and in different ways from one person to another. Yet, on the whole, in Nazi Germany, a mentality came to prevail that was quite compatible with annihilationist anti-Semitism.

This argument leads to the position taken by Harold Welzer, that "during the National Socialist era a large proportion of the Germans were committed to a moral code, which instead of condemning, actually demanded the degradation and persecution of other people, and which among other things prescribed that it was necessary and good to kill."[7] Since, in the National Socialist view, Jews were not just alien and inferior but the ultimate and total enemy of the German nation, it follows that they had to be exterminated. This was the ethos that the Nazi elite and its killers subscribed to. They did not have to overcome moral scruples or an aversion to kill, if such inhibitions functioned at all. On the contrary, their moral ethos incited them to mass murder. They did what they did because they believed it was necessary and justified.

In Goldhagen's and Welzer's view, the perpetrators were not so much "ordinary men" as "ordinary Germans." These ordinary Germans with their inexorable and murderous moral code were exceptional among the nations. A question remains: Was it not the same eliminationist anti-Semitism that drove so many willing collaborators and Jew hunters in quite a few other European countries during those years?

Welzer considers "wishful thinking" the notion that the Germans would have had to overcome their scruples before they engaged in genocide and argues that the Nazis' moral convictions never formed an obstacle for genocide but, on the contrary, that their moral code helped them to kill by the millions and feel righteous about it.

This is a forceful argument, but Welzer overshoots his mark. Even Nazi Germany was no monolith; the vast majority of its citizens had been brought up with Christian ethics and humanistic (even socialist) beliefs that were not entirely erased in one stroke as soon as Hitler came to power. In other words, the National Socialist worldview remained contested throughout, even among many "ordinary Germans." It required an enormous propagandistic effort and the total closure of the German public sphere to convert citizens to eliminationist anti-Semitism, and even then it met with limited success. The annihilationist project was kept secret until the very last. Only the inner Nazi elite seemed to have subscribed to it wholeheartedly. The rank-and-file perpetrators may have upheld the Nazi code of eliminationist anti-Semitism to a degree, when it both stoked their genocidal zeal and served them to justify their actions. By the same token, time and again they could not but recognize their victims as human beings. Welzer makes it appear as if most Germans had changed into zombies, entirely in the grip of the Nazi ideology, which transformed the perpetrators among them into killing automatons. It is an instance of what Paul Roth calls "cultural dope-ism."[8] It is an equally oversocialized conception of man that prompts Welzer to ignore the social and psychological contradictions that inhabit people and the social and mental maneuvers they use to deal with them.

There are many instances of mass annihilation in which anti-Semitism played no role at all. Radical Communism comes closest as an elaborate moral code with similar lethal potential. Extreme Turkish nationalism may have functioned in the same manner in Turkey during the campaign to annihilate the Armenians. Ethnic hatred against the Tutsis or radical nationalist hostility among Serbs, Croats, and Bosnians after the fall of Yugoslavia supplied the raw material for moral codes that worked to the same effect. But, on the other hand, the Indonesian army and its helpers in the 1965 killings or, for that matter, the Pakistani military in 1973 in Bangladesh did not subscribe to any comparable moral code and must have heeded rather lapidary precepts, such as the prevention of potential rebellion or the suppression of a secessionist movement.

Developments in society at large over a longer period of time shape the collective memories and the shared mentality of a nation. The wounds of war, the humiliations of defeat, the pervasive fear under tyranny, the pain of mass unemployment, and the penury of economic crisis constitute such formative experiences. These may be considered the *macrosociological* processes that make for a turn toward mass violence.

In reaction to these collective traumas, politicians, academics, writers, clerics (all of them "people of the word") will come up with explanations that exonerate the nation and its leaders and place the blame on "others," abroad or at home. "It's all the fault of someone else." When anger is displaced toward these outsiders, they become the target of collective hatred and contempt, and once the regime concurs in this campaign or initiates it, this target group will be blamed for—mostly or entirely—imaginary crimes. This is the stage of ideological compartmentalization. In this phase new ideas emerge and are assimilated by a good part of the regime's people. The target group should be made to pay for its misdeeds. It should be treated according to different rules than the regime's population. This is when radicalized gangs and bands of thugs may provoke street brawls, attack shops, and torch a church or a school.

GENOCIDAL SITUATIONS IN SOCIETAL CONTEXT

Scholars agree that the immediate social context in which perpetrators find themselves strongly shapes their actions. But what circumstances give rise to this genocidal situation?

Most of these have been discussed at some length above; here they are listed by way of a summary.

First of all, there are macrosociological conditions, the outcome of large-scale societal processes:

- Most important are *major upheavals* in the recent past, such as war, civil war, revolution, economic crisis, hyperinflation, or mass unemployment.
- Over time, large groups in society ("the regime's people") have come to share a *disidentification* from a particular group of people, who are singled out as the target group.
- The regime and the regime's people have gained control of the resources—the personnel, information, organization, and equipment—needed to kill members of the target group without running a similar risk themselves. A considerable *inequality*

of power prevails between the regime with its people and their target group.

Next are macrosociological conditions that apply when mass annihilation occurs. They strongly determine the "opportunity structure" for the regime.[9] Under these circumstances the regime can act to bring about a series of mesosociological conditions:

- The regime encourages further *compartmentalization* of society at all levels, creating an ever sharper separation between the regime's people and the target people.
- The regime's *propaganda* insistently dehumanizes and demonizes the target group.
- The target group is depicted as the (potential) *aggressor:* the regime's people are the ones being threatened, and they risk becoming the victim of the target group and its foreign patrons.
- According to the regime, the present moment is a decisive *turning point in history.* From now on everything will be different, if only the regime's people seize their chance to act together resolutely.
- The regime takes a long series of *institutional and legal measures* to keep separate the people of the regime and the people of the target group and drive them even further apart: inequality before the law, separate schools, hospitals, and neighborhoods, and all the other forms of legal and institutional compartmentalization that have been mentioned before and that have a psychological impact by further exacerbating the separation of minds.

These are some mesosociological conditions that in turn help shape the microsociological, genocidal situation:

- The situation is structured so that the perpetrators operate in tightly *coherent groups* in which *obedience* to superiors and *loyalty* to peers take precedence over everything else.
- No alternative information or contrary opinion reaches them in their genocidal compartment.
- The perpetrators often do not know beforehand what their task will entail.

- The perpetrators' actions are either not verbalized or spoken of in innocuous, veiled terms, *euphemisms*, such as the "final solution" for the extermination of millions of people.

- The instigators deceive the perpetrators about the evil nature and actions of the target group. Often, the perpetrators are initially aware of the deception but knowingly repeat the convenient untruths, until gradually through self-deception they themselves come to believe them.[10]

- The perpetrators are made to believe that they are fulfilling a difficult and exacting but *necessary task* for the survival of their own people.

- The perpetrators are confident that they can commit their acts with *impunity;* in many instances, they risk sanctions for refusing to harm the victims.

- The perpetrators are *rewarded* with food and money, booty, sexual opportunities, status, and promotion on the job.

- In many instances, the perpetrators are lavishly supplied with alcohol and act in a drunken haze.

- The perpetrators *blame the victims* for being filthy, sickly, cowardly, cringing, greedy, unreliable, corrupt, and selfish and for either stubbornly resisting or passively accepting their fate. As the victims are treated inhumanely, they increasingly lose their composure and self-control, coming to resemble more and more the stereotypes held by the perpetrators, who therefore feel more justified to treat them inhumanely. There is regression not only on the part of the perpetrators but also among the victims.[11]

- As the perpetrators grow accustomed to their task, one step leads to the next. As they go from bad to worse, they might as well commit one further outrage, since stopping at any point implies that the preceding steps were somehow wrong and that they are implicated in a crime.[12] In this *incremental* sequence, it seems as if there never is a definite choice, just a succession of minor adaptations: "We became more and more calm, more and more bloody."[13]

- The perpetrators often experience the heady excitement of feeling omnipotent, of having total power over their victims. (In fact, their power is entirely derived from their commanders' orders.)

- In many cases, the perpetrators go about their task as if it is
"*work*"—a scheduled and specified job that they must carry out
as well they can and bring to successful completion.[14] "They
had been given a task and, even if disgusting, the task would be
done, and as well as possible."[15]
- The perpetrators are together in the "flow"; they go with the
rhythm of the shared task; they march together, sing together,
kill together, and relax with one another after a job well done.[16]

These, and no doubt many more, "facilitating conditions" operate respectively at the level of society as a whole, at the level of
the regime, and at the level of the actual killing situation. Their
combined effect on the actions of the perpetrators is very strong,
and before Stanley Milgram published the outcomes of his experiments, their impact was greatly underestimated.

Once they have been recruited as guards and killers, the perpetrators are encouraged by their superiors and peers to murder their
victims, and they allow themselves to do so. It appears as if they have
no inhibitions left, no sense of a morality of their own. They are,
as Milgram once called it, in an "agentic state," in which they cannot but obey the authority placed above them.[17] They seem no longer to feel responsible for their acts and to have abandoned their
sense of an autonomous moral self, relinquishing all decisions to
a higher authority, and indulging in whatever barbaric act they are
told to perform, or not forbidden to carry out.[18] As long as they
serve their superiors and conform to their peers, the perpetrators
can and even must abandon their inhibitions and give their aggressive, destructive tendencies free rein. They do not need to think
or judge; they just must do as they are told. Even in their wildest
and most barbarian acts they are serving the regime. Indeed, their
barbarity benefits the regime, making sure that the program of extermination will be carried out precisely when, where, and how the
regime wants it to be accomplished. The perpetrators now are in an
advanced stage of regression in the service of the regime.

Yet the perpetrators are no blank automatons who begin to kill the moment they are put in a genocidal situation. Moreover, the actual "situation" cannot be neatly distinguished from the society in which it is embedded; macrosociological processes necessarily determine the microsociological aspects of the immediate context. Thus, widely held notions in mid-twentieth-century American society shaped what subjects in Philip Zimbardo's prison experiment expected a prison environment to be like and how "wardens" and "prisoners" were supposed to behave, just as such ideas determined the expectations of Milgram's subjects about "laboratory experiments" and "researchers in lab coats."

This leaves one question dangling overhead: why a third or more of the subjects in a Milgram experiment at some point refused to go along with the authority in charge. The experimental setup is the same for all; they share roughly the same "cultural" notions, which give meaning to the experimental setting. By the same token, one should ask why some people manage to stay out of the killing compartments entirely while others somehow end up there. And next one might ask why some of those who find themselves in a genocidal situation carry out their orders eagerly, some with indifference, and still others only with reluctance. These differences in behavior by people in the same situation can only be explained in terms of differences in their personal disposition.

PERPETRATORS AND OTHER ORDINARY PEOPLE: THE DIFFERENCES

No matter how deeply they may have regressed during the time they spent in the killing compartments, the perpetrators are not people without history. The genocidaires are overwhelmingly young and healthy men, and the great majority of them have a background in the military, the police, and the regime's militias.

Most of them by far sympathize with the regime, having joined the party or its auxiliary movements. They have been steeped in the official propaganda and learned to identify with their peers and disidentify from the target group, often with corresponding feelings of loyalty and loathing. Of course, quite a few were opportunists who were in it for the pay and the loot, but that should not have prevented them from molding their feelings and opinions after the pattern prescribed by the regime.

In a genocidal situation, moreover, certain personal characteristics make some people more suited than others as guards, interrogators, or executioners. They have their particular past, which shaped their memories, convictions, emotions, ideals. They had a particular childhood, they went to a certain school, made special friends, became part of a network of acquaintances, held a specific job (or never found one), in most cases married and became fathers. They went through their particular formative experiences. Their ideas, like most people's, may well have been confused, changing, contradictory. But they were neither blank slates nor of one cloth. In brief, even though they may have ignored it, even if they denied it, even if their environment denied it, the genocidaires, too, had an inner life of their own.

The circumstances for the recruitment differ very much from one genocidal episode to the next. In societies such as Nazi Germany, or the Soviet Union under Stalin, with complex government bureaucracies, with professional police, secret service, and armed forces, the genocidaires were selected largely from among these specialists in violence. People embarked on such careers in part through self-selection, in part through selection by the respective services. Under those conditions, recruits with certain personality characteristics were more likely to apply and more likely to be recruited for genocidal work: "A self-selection process for brutality appears to exist."[19] In the words of psychologist Ervin Staub:

> Many of the direct perpetrators are usually not simply forced or pressured by the authorities to obey. Instead, they *join* leaders and decision makers, or a movement that shapes and guides them to become perpetrators. Decision makers and perpetrators share a *cultural-societal tilt*. They are part of the same culture and experience the same life problems; they probably respond with similar needs and share the inclination for the same potentially destructive modes of their fulfillment. Many who become direct perpetrators voluntarily join the movement and enter roles that in the end lead them to perpetrate mass killing.[20]

Once selected, the recruits' personal predisposition played a role in how they coped with their tasks and in their career patterns. The SS employed common criminals as camp guards. There were a disproportionate number of "half-educated men" among the killers, who mobilized their limited knowledge to adopt elements from Nazi ideology for their own justification and often bitterly resented people who had superior qualifications.[21]

In predominantly agrarian societies, however, such as Cambodia, Indonesia, and Rwanda, it appears as if all young peasants were readily available for the job. It is unclear how they were rounded up and who, if anyone, refused or avoided the call. Sometimes the waverers or the objectors were punished, offered the choice to kill or be killed, on the spot. In other cases, those who objected were relieved from the task without any reprisals.

In Rwanda, for example, the Interahamwe militia consisted mostly of volunteers who were steeped in the Hutu Power ideology. But the ranks of these killer bands were reinforced by plain Hutu peasants. Much depended on the village mayor or the regional prefect, who might or might not use his authority to incite or even compel local Hutus to participate in the massacres. Much as the peasants had for generations been summoned for corvée duty, they now found themselves "working" to rob, rape, and kill Tutsis.[22] In other villages, young, poor, and mostly single young males banded together in excited gangs to attack the homes of "wealthy" Tutsi neighbors.

At times, testimonies or documents allow one to read between the lines who volunteered, who was forced to join, who was punished for refusing, and who got away with a refusal. Speaking of "ethnic riots," or pogroms, Donald Horowitz states: "What is more striking in ethnic violence is the participation of ordinary people, albeit, obviously, not all or most ordinary people. Some will surely resist the temptation. The frolicky atmosphere of brutal violence also indicates that riot participation will be strongly skewed towards those attracted to bullying and sadism, and certainly those local toughs who excel in violence are indispensable participants."[23]

One may speculate that under such conditions young men with an aversion to killing, and to killing en masse, managed, with some luck and guile, to keep away from the killing fields. But after the facts only the perpetrators were interrogated—that is, some of them. Those who maneuvered themselves away from the mayhem have remained unknown to posterity.

The genocidaires were a very diverse lot and no single characteristic differentiates them from the vast majority of people who never engaged in mass killing: "The men who performed the destructive work varied not only in their backgrounds but also in their psychological attributes."[24] A first clue comes from studies of the social origins of perpetrators: Where were they born and where did they grow up? What were their class backgrounds, religious affiliations, political persuasions, and educational and occupational careers? A few researchers have assembled sizable collections of genocidaires' biographies, again, mostly based on judicial documents.[25]

Michael Mann collected biographical notes on 1,581 Nazi perpetrators.[26] Their social and economic origins varied considerably, especially when not just the rank and file but also the higher echelons of command are taken into consideration.[27] But even then, and not surprisingly, militia members, the military, and the police were vastly overrepresented in genocidal circles: they are after all specialists in violence. Less obvious is Mann's finding that medical men and lawyers were also more numerous in the Nazi ranks of genocidal killers than might be expected.[28] Like military men, doctors and lawyers may be better trained than others to suspend their feelings at the sight of someone suffering. In Nazi Germany, they may also have been more exposed to ideological indoctrination. On the other hand, military and police codes of honor require that unarmed civilians be protected. The Hippocratic oath tells doctors *primum non nocere*, or "first of all, do no harm." Lawyers are bound to respect the rule of law and put their clients' interest first.

Some authors find that Lutherans or Catholics joined the ranks of the SS more frequently than other Germans, but on the whole religion does not seem to have been relevant either way. This fits the general pattern. In many instances of mass annihilation, religious identifications and disidentifications were the main separator between the regime's people and the target group, and at times they were a major justification for mass murder. In almost all cases there were clerics and believers who joined in instigating and perpetrating mass violence. Institutionalized religion rarely opposed it. Some religious people did risk their lives resisting the destruction and helping the victims. On balance, the kindest statement that can be made is that organized religion has seldom stood in the way of mass annihilation.[29]

Last, political persuasion was indeed crucial: a large percentage of the German genocidaires had enlisted in the Nazi Party. Quite a few of those were Nazis who had signed up before 1933.

Variables such as class, religion, income, education, and political conviction are indicative of one's general outlook on life, but they reveal anything about a person's emotional disposition only indirectly. Yet National Socialism was a highly aggressive persuasion, constantly inciting the populace to hatred of its enemies, evoking visions of relentless war and merciless destruction. It was also saturated with enthusiasm for *Volk und Vaterland*, for one's own people and one's own country. Initially, such ideals may well have appealed especially to people of a latent aggressive disposition, people who were ready to hate and relished scenes of destruction. These inclinations could very well go together with a willingness to make sacrifices in the struggle for the German nation and the Hitler state. They also easily combined with single-minded ambition, greed, and corruption (the latter two sternly condemned in official Nazi discourse).

John M. Steiner, a former concentration camp inmate who after the war attended SS gatherings and interviewed many SS men, administered the authoritarian personality test known as the California F-scale, developed by Theodor Adorno and colleagues in 1947, to two hundred former SS members and two hundred ex-Wehrmacht men. He found that the SS scored significantly higher than the Wehrmacht on this "F-scale" (the "F" stands for "fascist"). His SS informants also came disproportionately from "extremely authoritarian" families. On the whole, however, Steiner found too much variety among the SS men he studied to consider them as a clearly distinct group.

Steiner suggested that some people might be prone to violence without showing it, even without knowing it themselves; they would be "sleepers" who can be awakened once their potential is "unlocked" by the appropriate "key." But he immediately robs this notion of its specific explanatory potential by adding a situationist note: "In some way, all persons are sleepers in as much as they have a violent potential that under specific conditions can be triggered."[30]

Michael Mann concludes the analysis of his collection of perpetrators' biographies with the observation that "there were few banal, bureaucratic killers. . . . The vast majority of those involved in the actual killing knew what they were doing. Most thought there was good reason for it." And he adds: "What was modern about these killings was not so much bureaucracy as the role of mass movement. Those involved were not so much ordinary Germans as Germans who had become real Nazis."[31] Their biographical antecedents suggest certain personal dispositions, but no more than that.[32]

Reluctant, Indifferent, and Eager Perpetrators

In some cases, personal predisposition can hardly have played a role at all in the selection of genocidaires. Reserve Police Battalion 101, studied by both Christopher Browning and Daniel Goldhagen, represents an exceptional instance. Initially, the Einsatzkommandos charged with exterminating Jews, Soviet commissars, and partisans behind the Eastern Front were recruited from rank-and-file German police. However, by the summer of 1941, when the mass shootings in the east began, the former policemen who made up Battalion 101 had been dismissed and the ranks were now filled with civilians. These recruits were more or less randomly selected among men who had not yet been drafted for other uniformed units. Browning and Goldhagen differ on major points but are in complete agreement on this key issue: according to all criteria, Battalion 101 was a fair sample of those remaining German male adults who had not already been drafted in one of the multitude of armed and uniformed units of the Third Reich.[33] If they were not just "ordinary men" (Browning's title), they were indeed "ordinary Germans" (Goldhagen's subtitle).

At the outset, their commander, Major Wilhelm Trapp, gave the men of Battalion 101 a chance to withdraw from the task ahead.

Their decision would not be held against them, they were told, and indeed nothing happened to those who opted out. Famously, only a dozen out of five hundred men stepped forward and asked to be dismissed. Their comrades chided and scolded them, called them "weakling" and "shithead," . . . and left it at that. But what exactly did the men who refused say "no" to, and what was it that tacitly the other 98 percent of recruits had accepted?

They had not been prepared to enter village after village by surprise, rounding up the local Jews as the neighbors stood by and watched how the men, women, and children they had known all their lives were lined up and marched off. The recruits for Battalion 101 did not guess that they would soon be looting the victims' houses, ripping off their jewelry, and leaving the rest for the local peasants to steal from the corpses, once night came. They had not been told beforehand that soon they would be driving their victims on, with kicks and lashes, tearing babies from their mothers' arms, pulling toddlers away from her skirts, dragging parents away from their children, and jerking couples apart, beating the elderly to stand up as they stumbled. When they arrived at the killing site, a nearby grove or riverbank, the victims were made to take off all their clothes and wait. The men among them were forced to dig the trenches that were to serve as mass graves. Next, the victims were ordered to line up at the edge of the trench, one row at a time. The executioners of Battalion 101 had not imagined that they would shoot them from nearby with machine guns and pistols. When the bullets hit them in the back, the victims fell into the trench, on top of the bodies already shot. The men of Battalion 101 could not know that they would be splattered with the blood and the brains of the dying as they murdered them at gunpoint. The executioners had to finish off anybody who still seemed to be moving, all the while leaving many victims who had not yet died struggling under the weight of the next rows of corpses as they were being covered with quicklime and dirt. These ordinary recruits could not have dreamed that they would pick out a Jewish girl to have sex with for a few days, weeks, or even months and, after she became pregnant, ask a comrade to finish her off behind some nearby trees as they themselves were too sensitive for the job. They did not know yet that they were soon to drown all that guilty knowledge in bottle after bottle of schnapps for their minds to stay as numb by night as they had been by day. Yet these were the jobs they had been recruited for. No, they could not have known beforehand what they did not say "no" to at the time. But once they were at their task, they did as they were told. By all appearances, during their years as genocidaires, or after, few seem to have suffered more than transient discomfort.[34] But these appearances may yet turn out to be deceptive.

The wives and girlfriends of the executioners were not left in the dark, either. They were told what went on in letters home and saw their husbands and lovers at work with their own eyes when they came to visit the battalion on location. Although this mass extermination was an official secret, the SS of course knew, and SS men collaborated in the killings. The regular Wehrmacht soldiers on the Eastern Front were also aware of it. Many came to watch and sometimes to lend a hand.[35] At times entire army units joined in the extermination of the Jews behind the Eastern Front.

The record of Police Battalion 101 presents the strongest evidence available in the literature that more or less randomly selected men could almost all be made to perform these tasks, and for as long as it was required of them. What they had in common, apart from their compliance, was in the first place the "situation" in which they found themselves: one of obedience to authority and loyalty to their peers and of isolation in hostile terrain from all contrary influences.

In second place, many among them had seen combat during World War I, and all of them had lived through the aftermath of war, the hyperinflation, the period of crisis and unemployment, and then the first eight years of the Third Reich. The men of Battalion 101 shared this "cultural" background and the moral codes that came with it. That was their common macrosociological past.

During those eight years, the Nazi regime kept up an avalanche of racist and bellicose propaganda, but it also put in place employment and social policies that profited wage earners and the unemployed. It set up a huge military machine, which provided jobs in supply industries and in the ranks of the services themselves. And it organized hundreds of extermination squads, which had to be manned with many thousands of executioners. All this represented the institutional matrix that defined the opportunities and limitations for the recruits of Battalion 101 and their like. It defined their shared mesosociological background.

Most of the men had grown up under the authoritarian conditions that prevailed in German families at the time and had imbibed at home and in school the omnipresent anti-Semitism in all its shades up to the fanatical, "eliminationist" brand touted by the Nazis. No more can be said here about the psychosociological background of Battalion 101's executioners. Possibly the judicial records contain information about their childhood and adolescence, but they remain to be mined for these data.

Christopher Browning has stressed the situationist (that is, the microsociological) aspects. Daniel Goldhagen accentuated the "culturalist," or macrosociological, side. The members of Battalion 101 had lived through the same societal upheavals, shared the experiences under the Nazi regime, and now found themselves in the same situation: this shared background at all three—mutually complementing—levels helps to explain their similar behavior.

Even so, the men of Battalion 101 coped in quite different ways with the situation they found themselves in. They were not automatons, utterly transformed by the circumstances without a vestige of their own former selves. Most of them, after a few days or weeks, adapted to the situation. They did what their hand found to do, dispassionately to all outward appearance. Some tried to make the best of it, by avoiding the worst, doing what they were told to do, but all the while attempting to steer clear of the executions as best they could and refraining from beating, raping, and robbing their victims. They volunteered for other, less bloody jobs or, in some cases, requested a transfer. That did not make them into resistance fighters. They just tried to get by while saving as much of their self-respect as possible. They were the reluctant compliers, and they made up a sizable minority.

There also were the indifferent compliers. They just did their job and mishandled or plundered when the situation allowed or demanded it, killed without much ado when they had to. Milgram's impassive complier is a prime example from the laboratory.[36] Last, were the substantial minority of "executioners," the avid compliers. They typically went from bad to worse in a matter of a few weeks. They began to experience a strange elation at work, uncanny at first and faintly shameful, an excitement at the wailing and crying of the victims, the spasms and paroxysms of the dying, the ecstasy of being the one who imparts death without fear, without mercy, like a superhuman being. Sometimes they would commit acts of kindness, if refraining from cruelty can be called that. In these little tokens of mercy they could experience their power and their independence, their freedom not to hit, kick, and maim at one moment, and therefore their power at another moment to bully, humiliate, and torture above and beyond the call of duty. These margins of power and freedom within the overall order of compulsion were just that, marginal. For the victims these marginal acts might mean the difference between life and death.[37]

Even, or especially, the most brutal executioners time and again are reported to have bestowed small favors on their victims every once in a while. They did so because they could. This was what gave them their sense of power. Of course, once defeat at the hands of enemy forces seemed imminent, the perpetrators had good reasons to rein in their cruelty and allow their victims some privileges. In the near future, when the tables might well be turned on them, these prisoners might yet testify in their favor.

Is there a perpetrators' profile, a series of characteristics, that increases the probability that someone will be part of an execution squad and commit mass murder? That profile need not contain psychopathological traits in a psychiatric sense. It may be a matter of more perpetrators displaying more of some significant trait than the rest of the population. Or rather, as we shall see, less of the same.

PERPETRATORS AND OTHER ORDINARY PEOPLE: CONSCIENCE, AGENCY, EMPATHY

Mass murderers are best characterized by what they are not and what they have not or, rather, what they are less and what they have less, compared to other people living at the same time in the same society. First of all, it would be tempting to deny the mass murderers any conscience. But most of them clearly display a moral consciousness. They obeyed their superiors and were loyal to their comrades, often even when they had to make sacrifices in doing so. Their "superego functions" seem to have been for the larger part absorbed by this obedience toward their superiors and loyalty toward their peers. In addition, many may have been sincerely devoted to the great cause that their leaders and comrades also served. This is roughly what Welzer has called their "moral code." Although many readers may question a morality of unquestioning obedience and loyalty, undeniably these can be the dictates of a moral code, albeit of a particular kind. Many perpetrators, moreover, were intensely committed to their wife and children; this, too, suggests not only affective involvement but also moral conviction of a kind.

Obedience, loyalty, and often family fidelity were the ethical values many genocidaires lived by. There appears, however, a striking lack in this moral makeup: anyone who did not belong to the regime's people remained in effect outside the domain of the genocidaires' moral conscience. In terms of the "emotional triangle," their basic stance toward such an outsider was one of moral indifference.[38] The perpetrators hardly identified with them but, under the impact of the regime's propaganda, easily developed a strong, even extreme sense of disidentification toward the target people.

Judicial documents as sources for the reconstruction of genocidal psychology can make for distortions.[39] Obedience to "legal" orders from commanding officers was initially accepted as a legitimate defense in German trials of Nazi crimes, and the accused therefore tended to accentuate their readiness to comply with commands. Loyalty to comrades, although it may have been considered respectable, was not accepted as a defense in court.

On trial, the accused often tended to play down their indifference toward all strangers and their loathing of strangers considered enemies. Before their judges they generally did not want to appear strongly motivated. These sentiments were therefore underrepresented in the records. The judges may well have been sensitive to testimony about the defendant as a good family father. Therefore, such aspects of the defendants' moral conscience were stressed as positive character evidence. Browning supposes that perpetrators called as witnesses sometimes underplayed their own reluctance or resistance to kill en masse, so as not to make their comrades in the defendants' booth look worse by comparison.[40]

There is another striking feature in the judicial statements of the genocidaires, as well as in the biographies of the likes of Franz Stangl, Adolf Eichmann, Rudolf Höss, and Alfred Mengele. It appears as if somehow they never made a choice during their life under the Third Reich. It all just happened to them. A friendly superior proposed a new position, a colleague suggested another job, and off they went, into the Gestapo, the SS, or the ranks of the guards in the extermination camps: no questions asked, no doubts or qualms. It seems as if events occurred without anybody resisting them, but also without anyone desiring them. As they told it, there were no existential choices, no ethical dilemmas, just a succession of events, places, acquaintances, and jobs: "They had once and for all chosen for not choosing."[41]

In part, these are artifacts of the judicial sources. Many defendants must have thought that it would work to their advantage if they could convince their interrogators and, later on, the judges that they had never intended to kill and never wanted to be part of the killing machinery, that they just happened to get absorbed into it. Before their judges the accused also tried to appear less racist or anti-Semitic than they probably were. Likewise, they protested that they were never ardent Nazis (or Interahamwe, for that matter); they just received a membership card and raised their arm in salute when everyone else did, too. After all, they needed a job and they had a family to feed. There may well be some truth in this defense, varying from case to case. And there might be a grain of truth in their assertion that they just happened to be deployed as guards in the Nazi camps.

The eerie absence of any plan or choice, and therefore the lack of a sense of responsibility, as reflected in the records, may have been in part a distortion due to the defense strategy in court. But autobiographical accounts in general tend to be rather messy, often with little design and much coincidence. Even so, the life stories of genocidal perpetrators often stand out by their professed lack of plan, insight or decision, in one word: a lack of *agency*.[42]

During the hundreds of trials against camp guards, almost never did a defendant voice the conviction that the camps had been a necessary and beneficial institution and that he still stood behind the acts he committed at the time. The opposite occurred as seldom: only rarely did a defendant repent.[43]

There are in fact, instances of contrition: most cases that are known concern perpetrators on trial, especially in their last words before sentence is passed.[44] Such statements are particularly difficult to evaluate, as they may have been self-serving or sincere or even both at the same time.

There were some embarrassed mumblings, but hardly ever a full admission of guilt or an apology for crimes committed. Robert Jay Lifton extensively interviewed medical doctors who had worked in the Nazi extermination camps, and he notes "their virtually complete absence of moral confrontation, of acknowledgment of their own moments of evil or even of the degree to which they had become part of an evil project."[45]

Very few perpetrators ever uttered a word of commiseration with their victims. Some did complain about the hardship they themselves suffered while going through their murderous routines. One SS-Obersturmführer spoke of the shooting of Jewish children at the edge of a mass grave, already half full: "The wailing was indescribable. I shall never forget the scene throughout my life. I find it very hard to bear."[46] He did indeed register the suffering of his victims, but it was too hard on *him*. This provides the key to a third characteristic of genocidal perpetrators: they lacked any sense of empathy, let alone sympathy, with those they tortured and murdered. In other words, in the genocidal situation the killers disidentified from their victims to an extreme degree. They could undo any remaining sense of identification by denying all similarity with their targets, by degrading, dehumanizing, and demonizing them.

Repentance may be an emotion that is too hard to bear. After all, those who repent thereby admit that they did wrong and that therefore they were evil and maybe still are. But commiseration does not even demand that admission. It only presupposes the sense that the victim, too, was a human being, equally capable of feeling pain. Most perpetrators did not allow themselves to experience that sense of similarity, the empathy with the victim as a human being, and as a result, the vicarious experience of the other person's suffering. They could not afford to. Not during the genocidal episode, because it would have made their work impossible. And not after the fact, because it would have confronted them with their guilt. They had to think of their victims as subhuman, to hate and despise them and hold them in contempt.

Contempt—as Nico Frijda says—is a "cool emotion."[47] It reflects and reinforces the contemptuous person's superiority and the contemptible person's inferiority: their social inequality. To do its work, contempt must be displayed, to one's peers as well as to one's social inferiors. The lowly person may claim to be a person of equal worth, may insist on a common humanity, but the person who has the upper hand can afford to disregard these claims ostentatiously and with haughty disdain, thereby diminishing or destroying the other's social value. Frijda mentions that contemptuous persons feel free from the bounds of sympathy or morality that might constrain them in their actions toward those they hold in contempt. Hatred would allow them to do the same, but it is a "hot emotion," and it does not necessarily imply that the hated person is a social inferior. And Frijda adds: "Cruelty—a hot emotion—rests on interest in the victim's suffering and its results yield pleasure, satisfaction, or even joy."[48] All three emotions help the members of one group to disidentify from the other group and, in the process, through their shared hatred, contempt, or cruelty, to identify even more with one another.

MENTALIZATION AND DYSMENTALIZATION: EMPATHY AND THE LACK OF IT

There is near unanimity that the genocidal situation explains much of the genocidaires' demeanor and mentality. But during episodes of mass annihilation, some people stay far from the killing compartments, whereas others end up as mass murderers. That is partly a result of the macrosociological conditions that have helped to determine their position in society; it depends also on the mesosociological impact of social institutions and the regime on their life course and in part also on the psychosociological aspect: the disposition they acquired in the course of their life. And there is always an element of chance.

Once they did find themselves in the killing compartments, the microsociological impact of this shared situation strongly pressed them to turn into perpetrators. But even then, they might yet become indifferent, reluctant, or eager mass killers. These differences remain to be explained. The explanation must come from the divergent individual predispositions they acquired during their early childhood in the family and in their subsequent life course through the wider society.

What most distinguishes the perpetrators from other "ordinary" people is their apparent lack of compassion toward their victims. People can only feel compassion with the sufferings of others if they can at all imagine the feelings of another person, if they are capable of empathy with someone else.

There is by now a considerable literature on the emergence of empathy in early childhood. Building on a tradition established by Anna Freud, Melanie Klein, and Donald Winnicott, John Bowlby studied the relation between the infant and its mother. If the relationship is sufficiently secure and stable, the child develops a solid attachment to the "good enough" mother. This is indispensable for the emergence of a sense of an inner life as somehow distinct from outer reality. If all goes well, and it usually does, a small child learns to recognize its emotions as its own, distinct from the surrounding world, from its mother, and from other people. In other words, it acquires a mental life of its own. Subsequently, the young child learns to recognize the feelings of other people in its vicinity. That is how it develops its potential for empathy with others.

Peter Fonagy and his coauthors have called this learning process "mentalization," or "mentalizing."[49] Fonagy and his colleagues build forth on the work of the British psychologists of early childhood, combining it with recent results from cognitive psychology, neuropsychology, and evolutionary psychology. *Mentalization* is defined as "the mental process by which an individual implicitly and explicitly interprets the actions of himself and others as meaningful on the basis of intentional mental states such as personal desires, needs, feelings, beliefs and reasons."[50]

John Allen and Peter Fonagy point out that the potential to mentalize rests on inborn neuronal networks (among them quite likely the "mirror neurons").[51] The actual capacity to interpret one's own actions and those of others in terms of what goes on in the mind is acquired in early childhood in a sufficiently secure relation with the mother as she conveys to the child that she perceives its mental states as its own. The mother does so by mirroring (and often comically—and didactically—exaggerating) the affect she perceives in her baby through her empathy for the child: "Now you're angry, aren't you . . . !" or "Oh, don't you love those little kittens!"[52]

Mentalization has also been characterized as "mind mindedness," the opposite of "mind blindness." It entails an understanding of one's own mental states, and it is a necessary condition for the development of empathy (at a later stage of early childhood). Jon Allen writes: "Although empathy is but one facet of mentalizing, it might be the most important."[53]

Martin Hoffman has distinguished two aspects of empathy: "the cognitive awareness of another person's internal states" (knowing what the other feels) and "the vicarious affective response to another person" (feeling what the other feels). This composite empathy is the foundation for moral development. Moreover, it is what moves people to help others in need.[54]

A major, maybe the most important feature, of empathy is that it "entails awareness of emotional distress in others."[55] This, in most cases, evokes compassion. Compassionate people will be inclined to come to the aid of someone whom they see suffering.

Nico Frijda has introduced the notion of "action readiness" as an important feature of emotions in general.[56] Accordingly, when people feel, for example, compassion, they will be inclined to act on it, to comfort, succor, or protect someone who needs it.

That is precisely what genocidal perpetrators don't do. On the contrary, they inflict suffering, pitilessly, without mercy, and generally without remorse. We must therefore look into the absence, the deficiency, or the breakdown of compassion.

When the mother and child do not succeed in maintaining a secure relation, or when it is interrupted, in many instances the mentalizing process may never take off or it may break down prematurely. Under those conditions children may grow up with "zero degrees of empathy," as Simon Baron-Cohen has called it. In the normal distribution of empathy, these people are on the extreme left of the curve. They are usually diagnosed (if they ever come to the attention of a psychiatrist or psychologist) as "borderline," "narcissist," or "psychopath." People with a psychopathic personality disorder are willing to do "*whatever it takes* to satisfy their desires."[57]

Genocidaires at work in their killing compartment may often *look like* psychopaths, but before and after their genocidal episode, or outside the genocidal setting, they usually are quite capable of empathy and even compassion to those they consider close to them. In fact, people with "zero degrees of empathy" make up only a few percent of the general population, and most likely an only slightly larger fraction of the perpetrators.

If most people develop a capacity to empathize with others, to feel compassion with their distress and come to their aid in times of need, how is this apparent total lack of compassion among the perpetrators to be explained?

First of all, there may be significant cultural differences in the ways young children are raised, resulting in varying degrees of early mentalization from one setting to another. Family settings and educational patterns diverge among societies, religious communities, and social classes, and they change over generations. On the one hand, the mentalizing process seems so fundamental, so much an integral part of the universal mother-child dyad, that it appears impervious to cultural, class, religious, or national differences. If the mother herself has gone through successful mentalization in her early childhood, and if she and her child find themselves in a reasonably safe situation, they can now maintain an undisturbed bond. The child will learn to mentalize and develop a capacity for empathy and compassion for those in its immediate surroundings.

On the other hand, cultures or subcultures do differ in the way they allow mother and child to remain close, intimate, and finely attuned. Sometimes children are separated from their mothers at an early stage and entrusted to a wet nurse, a nursery, or an orphanage where they have insufficient opportunity to develop a "good enough" relation with their mother or another caretaker.

Much of what the infant has learned may also be unlearned at a later stage, when little boys must try to become men by suppressing their longings for affection or their inclination for tenderness and must learn to be hard and not depend on the love of women (but, rather, to seek the approval of men). As they grow up, they learn to reserve their empathy and compassion for their close comrades only, to deny their inner experiences and ignore the emotions of other people. In the words of Wouter Gomperts, who coined the concept, they are trained to "dysmentalize."[58]

Depending on the cultural or subcultural setting, the role of fathers in raising their children may vary considerably: they may be expected to complement mothers in being protective, supportive, and encouraging, or they are pressed by the prevailing norms to remain distant, aloof, forbidding, and authoritarian. Displays of attachment and empathy are condemned as soft and sentimental, and boys, in their turn, should learn to avoid them.

From early on children learn to distinguish among social categories as they are defined in the surrounding society. They learn to reserve their empathy for "their own people" and to be more reserved to outsiders, according to the prevailing circles of identification and disidentification.[59] Clearly, these collective identifications define the borders of individual empathy and compassion. Members of the other group do not deserve to be valued or respected; they are depicted as contemptible, suspect, threatening—the list goes on.

As children grow up, they are absorbed into larger institutions such as the school, the church, and—especially germane in this context—sometimes in a political mass movement. In these settings national, ethnic, religious, or political identifications are more strongly inculcated. The new lines of division may coincide with those that the parents taught them from early on, or they may be quite different: in that case these young people must resolve conflicts of loyalty and reconcile divergent sympathies. Most likely, social identifications acquired during childhood coexist uneasily with those learned later on, sometimes being relegated to different mental compartments. In strongly compartmentalized societies with intense antagonism between groups, young people may actually learn to overcome their empathy for outsiders. This is where the "fragility of compassion" shows and the "erosion of empathy" begins.[60]

People who are less inclined to empathize with others outside their immediate circle of identification are more likely to join the ranks of perpetrators than others. In times of upheaval, their usual, steady life course is interrupted and they are confronted with a sequence of incidents that prompt them to go either way. Through this succession of events even a small difference in the capacity to mentalize and empathize may result in very divergent itineraries. Like a vibrating sieve that in a sequence of slight tremors in the end separates the smaller from the larger pebbles, a succession of minor chance events may sort out the less compassionate for careers in the killing compartments while discarding those whose disposition makes them less suitable for the job. It appears as if personal choice plays no role in the process, and yet, at every turn there was a choice, at least with hindsight.

The strongest case against any form of selection of the perpetrators is that of Battalion 101, which indeed seems to have been recruited for the extermination squads randomly from somewhat older men, albeit in the extremely compartmentalized and indoctrinated society that was Nazi Germany in 1942. But the regime generally selected its killers from the ranks of the military, the police, and the criminal class—that is, among the specialists in violence. Most often these men at some point had opted for such a career, had been selected and trained to apply force with little compassion, and were deployed and promoted accordingly.

In less bureaucratized and professionalized settings, the perpetrators appear to be implicated in the killing more or less randomly. But there is more self-selection than meets the eye. Everyone in the crowd seems to have joined in the atrocities, but many or even most people stayed far from the scene. They have remained invisible, including to the investigators or researchers who long after the event attempt to reconstruct what occurred.

Finally, there is the discrepancy, noted earlier, between two widespread observations in social science. In peacetime, when people get into a quarrel, they are generally reluctant to actually engage in physical fighting. Moreover, there is abundant evidence that most soldiers, even under direct enemy fire, shoot in the air or do not even shoot at all, rather than aim and kill their opponents.[61] On the other hand, many people, once they find themselves in a genocidal situation, turn out to be reluctant, indifferent, or even willing executioners. The contradiction can be explained only by the processes of—often hidden—selection and self-selection, and by the erosion of empathy that occurs in the course of genocidal episodes.

DYSMENTALIZATION IN THE KILLING COMPARTMENTS

In the genocidal situation perpetrators are pressured to abandon whatever vestiges of empathy they still may hold for their victims. They follow a crash course in dysmentalization. The situation determines people's actions; their disposition may as well be ignored. The counterevidence is that some people do not comply, even under strong situational pressure. And those who do go along with the demands of obedience and solidarity, still do so reluctantly, indifferently, or eagerly. What explains these crucial individual differences in one and the same situation?

The answer is, the individual disposition to empathize. Here is the first possibility: When confronted with their victims, the executioners may feel as much compassion as anyone; they just will not show it, let alone act upon it, either out of fear or shame before their superiors and comrades or out of hatred and anger toward their victims. In other words, these genocidaires live with an inner conflict. This has been ascertained in some cases, and it may be true in most or even all instances, but evidence for such mental contradictions is hard to come by.[62]

The second option is that genocidaires may be as compassionate as the next person, but not when it comes to their enemies who happen to be their victims. This might be so because, somehow, they never learned to empathize with "unknown strangers," just their relatives, neighbors, colleagues, and acquaintances. This modality is not mentioned in the mentalization literature, which concentrates on therapy patients whose first interest is in themselves and in their immediate surroundings, rarely in the more remote circles of strangers or enemies. "Political" issues about their empathy for members of other national, ethnic, or religious groups are seldom raised. During a stint of collective reeducation or in a sustained campaign of hate propaganda, the genocidaires often learned to exclude the despised target group from their "circle of empathy." In his Posen speech before ninety-two SS officers on October 4, 1943, Heinrich Himmler explicitly mentioned the annihilation of the Jews of Europe and in that context held his killers to a strict and sharply restricted morality: "One ground rule applies for every SS man absolutely: we must be honest, decent, faithful, and loyal to those who are of our blood, and to no one else."

Third, it may be that on entering the killing compartment, the perpetrators who did feel compassion with the victims gradually lost it as the demands of the situation took over. There are indeed indications that many people are quite capable of curbing their empathy and can be trained to do so even more effectively. After all, much professional training involves the selective suspension of empathy in the appropriate situations and toward designated categories: lawyers, doctors, and soldiers all learn to suspend personal sympathies or antipathies for opponents, patients, or enemies.

Fourth, perhaps the genocidaires are as empathic as anyone, but not compassionate. They are well aware of other people's distress, yet this inspires them, not with compassion, but on the contrary with cruel excitement or with the pleasure of revenge. They like to see their victims suffer.[63] Before their interrogators and their judges, as well as in letters to their relatives, the perpetrators would most likely have covered up their sadistic excitement.[64] Such arousal may be much more common than the available data suggest, since it is often felt to be particularly shameful, more embarrassing apparently than murder "in cold blood." Another kind of pleasure in the victim's suffering can be called "retaliatory satisfaction," the contentment that the enemy's torment is his "just dessert." This is less shameful than sadistic excitement and does shine through at times in "ego documents," such as diaries, letters, and memoirs, written by the perpetrators. In fact, quite a few report that when they found it hard to continue killing they would try to think of what the enemy had done to their side.

Last, the genocidaires may indeed lack empathy, even with those closest to them. Their mentalization failed from the start. They are incapable of recognizing their own or someone else's emotions, and they have a tenuous sense of an inner life, both their own and that of others. For these individuals, emotions can only be overwhelming and essentially destructive or must be acted on immediately. Such mental states are described under the heading of "psychopathy" and "antisocial disorder." These terms, forever contested, usually refer to individuals who commit their misdeeds alone or with a few accomplices at most and without support from their wider environment. This is very different from the genocidaires, who are supported in every respect and by all means, if not actually pressed by their immediate environment ("the situation") to torture and kill. Even so, without much empirical underpinning, there is a broad consensus in the literature that only a small percentage (say, 5 percent) of genocidal perpetrators are indeed "psychopaths" or "sadists," no more than in the general population. Such deviants may make good murderers, but their antisocial tendencies make them less suitable as underlings and comrades in the socially dense milieu of execution squads and extermination camps.

The International Criminal Court for Yugoslavia convicted defendant Zoran Žigić to twenty-five years for atrocities committed, mostly while drunk, in the Serbian concentration camp Omarska. Žigić regularly visited Omarska, where the guards allowed him to abuse, torture, and kill inmates at will. Apart from Žigić, other outsiders could enter the camp to maltreat the prisoners for their own and the guards' entertainment, including an alcoholic drifter and a prostitute's young daughter.[65] What is at least as upsetting as the behavior of these miscreants is the guards' broad complicity.

All in all, the itinerary of dysmentalization fits the genocidaires best. It explains a strong attachment to close relatives, a remnant of early mentalization. It equally explains the "unquestioning" obedience to superiors and the "unconditional" loyalty to comrades: a superimposed form of primitive mentalization, or "emotional contagion." This is reminiscent of the recurrent fantasy of being absorbed in a perfect unity. Hans-Joachim Heuer writes that the perpetrators of the Gestapo, the Nazi secret police, were shackled with "symbiotic ties" to a "bureaucracy of comrades."[66] Dieter Pohl characterizes the perpetrators in these settings, where all inhibitions on wanton cruelty and murder have been lifted, as acting in a transient, quasi-delusional state; their moral conscience has been transferred to the commander and turned into a "superego in uniform."[67] For the elite fighting units, the platoon is one, it marches in step, its single goal is shared by all, and it confronts a common enemy who will spare none of them. Because obedience is unquestioning, it excludes any reflection, any distinction between the order and its execution, between the superior's desire and the inferior's act. That is the meaning of *Befehl ist Befehl* (Orders are orders). Loyalty is equally unconditional: an attack on a comrade is an attack on oneself and an attack on the unit as a whole. This may not correspond to the realities of an army platoon, but it does represent the shared fantasy of its members in a male-bonding, military subculture. Last, and most important, this itinerary of partial mentalization and subsequent dysmentalization can explain the often startling lack of empathy on the perpetrators' part for anyone outside these tight circles of mutual identification. That is indeed a collective *regression in the service of the regime.*

Many Nazi genocidaires apparently fared quite well after serving their stint as mass killers: they were often economically successful (in "aggressive trades," Steiner notes), they played a role in their community, and they are often reported to have been "loving spouses" and "devoted fathers," not only before, but also during and after the genocidal episode. All this suggests that they were mentally and socially well integrated.[68] This is all the more surprising, since they showed very few signs of intellectual or moral autonomy during their genocidal period. If and when, afterward, the political and moral tables were turned against them, they should have had a hard time in maintaining their self-image in a climate of accusations and reproach. They could, however, seek the company of like-minded veterans, "buddies" from their genocidal days, together denying what happened, ignoring outside accusations, insisting that they never knew the full extent of the killings, pointing out that they only followed orders and would have been punished for disobedience, and arguing that their enemies had committed crimes at least as bad as theirs.[69] They could present themselves as the potential or actual victims of their victims: either because the targets represented an acute menace to their country and way of life or because they, the executioners, suffered terribly from having had to carry out their gruesome task.[70] These arguments may be factually incorrect, dishonest in their distortion of facts and values, or willful lies. But they belong to a different order than the statements of a psychotic criminal who protests that God ordered him to do it, that the CIA wired his mind to control his thoughts and actions, or that voices told him to kill whoever crossed his path.

The observation that many genocidal perpetrators after their crimes lived ostensibly normal, even successful and apparently gratifying lives, is not in itself proof of "normalcy." One might have expected in "ordinary people" some stirrings of conscience, a few pangs of guilt, a modicum of shame, sorrow, and remorse. There is none of the kind.[71] Again and again, across cultures, there is a striking absence of visible signs of mourning, pity, guilt, or shame in the perpetrators.

In everyday life, the former perpetrators in most cases hid their past for good practical reasons, living as they did among fellow citizens that had turned hostile or at least weary of the killings. But among their peers, the murderers were sometimes boastful, even nostalgic for the "good old days."[72]

Many survivors of mass annihilation campaigns suffer the psychic consequences for the rest of their lives. Some of the bystanders remain traumatized for scores of years. A significant proportion of combat veterans develop "shell shock," as it was once called, or "post-traumatic stress syndrome." Not the genocidaires. Most of them did just fine, or so it seems. On the face of it, they appeared unscathed by their experience, untroubled by their past. There is an explanation for this equanimity: because they acted with all the support of the ruling regime and with the expectation of impunity against defenseless victims, they did not have to live continually with the fear of sudden, violent death as combat soldiers and as, of course, their victims had to. Murdering unarmed, unorganized, and unprotected people, even by the thousands, is a much safer task than fighting more or less equally equipped and organized troops, and Rwandese Interahamwe or German camp guards much preferred their killers' work to fighting the enemy on the battlefront.

On the other hand, John Steiner found, in 1975, that the combat veterans in his sample of SS men fared better after the war than those who had been camp guards or death squad members: the former fighters continued to value their SS identity, whereas the genocidal killers, "especially when the cause of National Socialism could no longer be upheld," lost this sense of a desirable identity.[73] In plain words: they felt ashamed.

Dan Bar-On, around 1986, approached fifty-six German clergymen, physicians, nurses, psychiatrists, and psychotherapists to ask them whether, in the years after the war, Holocaust perpetrators had ever "confessed" to them or otherwise sought help. He found only a single instance. Israel Charny mailed "hundreds of questionnaires" with the same inquiry to psychotherapists and psychiatrists all over Europe and received only one report, by hearsay.[74]

The one case reported to Bar-On concerned a perpetrator who told his confessor that in all the years since the war a pair of eyes had followed him. "These were the eyes of a six-year-old Jewish child who had come out of a bunker during the Warsaw ghetto uprising and had run over to him with a frightened look in her eyes and her arms held out to hug him." The commander had told him to stab her to death, and he did. The story conveys some idea of what kind of stories these were that were never told.[75]

It remains remarkable that apparently the former perpetrators did not avail themselves of the heavily shielded, institutionalized compartments of the confessional or the therapist's office and instead preferred to go it alone.[76] However, in postwar West Germany and in exile, former Nazis could congregate in shielded settings, such as the chapters of their "Mutual Help Organization," HIAG, or in veterans' clubs. There they could resume their former identity, be their "old selves" again, and among their old comrades reminisce with nostalgia. Such social compartments may have diminished the necessity for mental compartmentalization. Whether atrocities committed against defenseless civilians were flaunted as openly is doubtful.

In some instances, however, such as in post-apartheid South Africa, former killers did present the symptoms of post-traumatic stress disorder that are so familiar today from combat veterans and survivors of mass annihilation: "Like their surviving victims, many of the retired death squad operatives and soldiers suffer from post-traumatic stress disorder. In interviews, many of them say they experience feelings of waste; have insomnia or nightmares of swimming pools filed with blood; and engage in heavy drinking to combat their troubles."[77]

South Africa's Truth and Reconciliation Commission created a social compartment where the perpetrators could confess their deeds and repent and mourn them, while perpetrators from the other side did likewise. This social setting may have affected the individual management of memory and emotion by diminishing the need for individual compartmentalization. Feelings that were never openly expressed in other postgenocidal settings became manifest in this public context.

In Rwanda, after the victory of the RPF forces, more than one hundred thousand Rwandese were rounded up and jailed on suspicion of complicity in the genocide, many more than could be tried. The government shifted a great number of the suspects to the traditional village courts. In these *gaçaça* (literally, "soft grass") meetings the perpetrators could confess their crimes before the village community and be judged by their fellow citizens. According to Jean Hatzfeld, much depended on local circumstance.[78] Where Tutsi survivors were few, Tutsis were often jeered and threatened by their Hutu neighbors and the killers persisted in their denial; where there was a strong official presence and Hutu genocidaires risked a jail sentence, they tended to be more forthcoming and show repentance, all the while making sure that they would not own up to major crimes or implicate their comrades, who might yet take revenge on them. Depending on the setting, they hid or confessed their deeds, expressed varying degrees of contrition, whether sincere or not, and most likely managed their feelings in accordance with their social environment.

Where genocidal perpetrators have remained unpunished and were rarely or never made to account for their crimes in public, as in Indonesia in the half-century since the mass killings of 1965, or in Cambodia after the massacres of 1975–1979, the killers need not hide, not even dissimulate their satisfaction at having defeated "the enemy," even if that enemy consisted of hapless, helpless citizens. On the other hand, these circumstances left scarcely any room for the perpetrators to express or even experience their misgivings, shame, or remorse. Maybe the killers had been so brutalized that they never had such emotions, not even in retrospect. Perhaps the most shameful acts were "forgotten" and the more painful emotions denied, since they had no place in the social environment of the former killers. Where social repression stymies memory and emotion, mental compartmentalization takes over.

Former perpetrators hiding their emotions from everyone else may be hiding them from themselves in the first place. There is every reason to suspect that in many cases underneath the placid appearances psychic stress and unresolved conflict persist. Just as they did during their genocidal period, so afterward the perpetrators compartmentalized their murderous self from their civil self, but this time the concealed and accessible sides were reversed.

In Robert Jay Lifton's term, the genocidaires managed their psychological contradictions by "doubling": during and after the genocidal episode, the merciless killer was "not their real self." James Waller has argued that in the genocidal context, this divided self was only "an initial short-term adaptation to the perpetrators' own atrocities." In the course of time, the social forces at work in the immediate situation would fundamentally transform "the primary, and only, self" and diminish the need to compartmentalize: "Harming victims can become 'normal' behavior."[79]

During episodes of mass annihilation the perpetrators went in and out of the killing compartment, on furlough or every day. After a day's work, they returned home or to their barracks. Even while they were effectively locked into the genocidal setting, they did fantasize about a gentler, more loving life outside and after the genocidal episode. Volunteer member of an Einsatzkommando in eastern Poland Felix Landau writes in his diary on August 2, 1941: "Since I had twenty men shot for refusing to work, everything's been running smoothly. This evening four of the men are off to Radom. So that means a quick letter to my Trude. I also have to send the money, 180 RM, to my wife. . . . Will Trudchen be pleased? I also sent some toys to my wife for the children."[80]

Once the genocidal period is over and the perpetrators return to their more civil, civilian existence, the killing compartment is behind them once and for all. Now they can definitively relegate their murderous self to a separate and "closed" compartment of their mental and social existence. These compartments are not impermeable, neither socially nor mentally; memories do not "disappear"—the perpetrators just no longer think of them. Then, they were "another person." Now they are their old civilian selves again. This is rather different from the Freudian notion of "splitting of the ego." Lifton's "doubling" is "compartmentalizing light." The main point is that mental compartmentalization corresponds to social compartmentalization and that mental repression is congruent with social repression.

The difference between Waller's position and Lifton's position (or mine) is subtle. But there remains a significant distinction. Waller, and the situationists in general, limit their analysis to the features of the immediate social context. Some authors also take into account longer-term and broader social and societal developments (as does Harald Welzer, for example). But their "ordinary men" in the final analysis remain empty automatons, adapting mindlessly to the immediate situation. In my view, most perpetrators by far are indeed ordinary people: like everyone else, they have emotions, they construct meanings and justifications, no matter how hard they may deny it; they find ways to live with their inner conflicts, for example, by relegating each side to a different mental compartment.

Some insight in the former perpetrators' personality structure comes from their children. Quite a few of them sought professional help, and there now exists a small body of literature on their cases. In general, these children had a hard time growing up with fathers who had once been mass killers but to whom they could not help feeling devoted, as children are wont to. They grew up in a society that condemned (or whitewashed) the deeds of their fathers. Many of these children came to reject their parents' views and actions. More often than not, they felt ashamed of them. Yet they colluded with their parents in hiding, denying, minimizing, and glossing over their father's past while maintaining throughout childhood and adolescence a childlike loyalty to a father who was also dearly beloved.[81]

Often the part the father played in the mass killings remained a family secret, not entirely unknown, darkly hinted at, and covered up by silence and avoidance. In the memoirs of the perpetrators' children as they published them or as they were summarized and anonymized by their therapists, the fathers are often depicted as at times loving and caring but also and almost without exception as generally distant, rigid, harsh, cold, authoritarian, and disciplinarian, sometimes with a mean and cruel streak. However, these characteristics may have applied equally to many other fathers of that same generation and social status who were military men, policemen, or just conservative and especially strict yet entirely innocent of mass murder.

Nevertheless, after the defeat of the genocidal regime, most perpetrators' families survived as "families with a secret," as parents and children colluded to avoid mentioning, let alone discussing, the burdensome past.[82] There were sharp separations between "what was then" and "what is now," between the father as a former executioner and the father as a dedicated family man and breadwinner. Equally, a keen divide obtained between the family father at home, without a past, and the crony of his wartime buddies, fondly reminiscing about the good old days at the veterans' reunion.

CONCLUSION

People who are recruited as perpetrators for mass annihilation are socialized under much the same conditions as many or most of their contemporaries and fellow citizens. Once these recruits are induced into a genocidal situation, chances are that many will comply with the orders of their commanders and with the pressure of their peers and that they will murder en masse.

But some people are more likely than others to be recruited for the killing compartments. Even relatively small differences in personal makeup can result in very different life itineraries, especially in times of upheaval, since at each bifurcation they tend slightly to one direction rather than another. Young men with a restricted moral consciousness, a low sense of agency, and reduced empathy are more likely to end up as genocidaires than their opposites.

In some instances the recruits had little choice; in other cases they had every opportunity to remain far from the killings or could actively participate if they so wished. The much-discussed example of Police Battalion 101 was an exceptional instance of almost random recruitment, without express selection, and with at least one moment of opportunity to opt out. At the other extreme are the SS units that were selectively recruited from volunteers, or—in a very different context—the megapogroms where young men eagerly joined the killings often alongside professional specialists in violence from the police, militias, and army. Whenever there is an element of self-selection, personal predisposition is bound to play a part in either joining in the mass killing or staying away from them.

Inside the killing compartments, the context determines behavior, but not entirely. There are still different strategies of adaptation. Some perpetrators kill reluctantly, others indifferently, and some with eagerness: since the circumstances are more or less the same for all, the degree of compliance is a matter of personal disposition.

The perpetrators are not of one cloth, and none of them is of one piece. Their pregenocidal experiences were shaped by the regime, which had inculcated the population with an ideology that helped to prepare some to become mass killers. But the perpetrators also had been steeped in other moral codes: in familial, educational, and religious teachings that ruled out the extermination of defenseless victims. They were not completely devoid of a moral sense toward their victims; neither did they lack all empathy and compassion. After all, no matter how far they had been dehumanized, they were unmistakably human. It was hard mental work for them to ignore or deny that. At any moment the victim's humanity could hit the executioner. There was therefore always the potential for inner conflict. The perpetrators had to avoid such contradictions. They could do so only by trying to be less human themselves, by shutting off all stirrings of inopportune emotions.

On the basis of his lengthy, in-depth interviews with Nazi doctors in Auschwitz, Lifton concluded that they could do what they did because they disavowed their actions, ascribing them to another self. This Auschwitz self existed next to their original self, which remained unaffected by what they did there.[83] The perpetrators could mentally cope with the situation because they succeeded in "doubling," as Lifton calls it: they managed to live with two selves. "One self did not know what the other self did." The original self could disavow the other self, thus enabling it to commit whatever violent act without compromising the original self. In a completely compartmentalized society, mental compartmentalization becomes a necessity for psychological survival.[84] Franz Stangl, the former commandant of the Treblinka extermination camp, once he had been condemned and imprisoned, told Gita Sereny, his relentless interviewer: "That's what I'm to explain to you; the only way I could live was by compartmentalizing my thinking."[85] After seventy hours of questions and mostly evasive answers, Stangl finally owned up to "his guilt." He died the next day of heart failure.

Once the period of mass annihilation is over, the perpetrators must adapt again. From now on they must live in an environment that, at best, tries to repress whatever happened and, at worst—for them—remembers and condemns it. This time, it is their genocidal past that must be hidden and forgotten. In this phase, too, doubling helps them cope. They are back to their "original self." The mass murderer never was their "real self." It was all forced on them, they never had a choice, and, anyway, it never really happened, or if some of it did occur, it was very different from the exaggerated and distorted tales being told now. Once again, they succeed in compartmentalizing their past from their present, their genocidal self from their "recivilized" self. Except that this time, it is the other compartment that is hidden, denied, or forgotten.

It would be tempting to describe men such as Adolf Eichmann, Rudolf Höss, and Franz Stangl, or Khmer Rouge comrade Deuch or Serbian Bosnia's Ratko Mladić or the commander of the Ngoma camp in Rwanda, Ildephonse Hategekimana, as lacking any moral sense whatever.[86] But they may have felt loyal to their comrades and bound to obey their superiors. They may have believed that their murderous work would in the end benefit their country and their nation, their race or their class, the party or the movement: all of them goals "greater" than any single human being. Many of them may have been hypocrites and opportunists, masking greed, lust, and ambition under the guise of lofty ideals. But some, maybe even many, did believe they were serving higher values and were willing to make some sacrifice in the service of their commanders and for the sake of their peers.

It would be equally tempting to characterize them as men without a "heart," bereft of tender or caring emotions, incapable of loving another human being. But again, most of them married, founded a family, and cared for their wife and children, before, during, or after the genocidal episode. Moreover, some of them desperately needed the acceptance and the continued allegiance of their family, such as Stangl, in jail: "'They . . . they . . . my children believe in me,' he said again. 'My family stands by me.'"[87]

Many former genocidaires were valued by their friends, colleagues, and employers. At face value, they proved themselves capable of intense and lasting bonds with other people. And yet, this may all be the facade of good humor and fake geniality of a *faux bonhomme.* Closer scrutiny may reveal loveless, authoritarian, overbearing, and disciplinarian ways. Some of the rare published memoirs of perpetrators' children have hinted at that. What appeared an ordinary existence was no more than a case of "pseudo-normality," as psychoanalysts would call it.

Even the characteristics that are shared by quite a few perpetrators afterward may be in large part a result of their genocidal period, rather than the reflection of an underlying, prior disposition. The genocidaires could not be investigated before the genocidal episode, let alone when they were busy killing. Who they were can be reconstructed only after the fact. Judicial documents present a systematically distorted picture. Testimonies by camp inmates provide only a partial impression of the guards "at work," by observers who had every reason to stay out of their way as much as possible.

And yet, their restricted moral conscience, the absence of a sense of agency and design, and above all the compartmentalized empathy and utter lack of pity for anyone beyond their circle of identification all point to a mode of mental functioning characterized by stunted mentalization, or by "dysmentalization": a regression to a condition marked by (1) weakened superego functions, allowing only for compliance to authority figures and loyalty to immediate peers and close relatives; (2) a lowered sense of personal responsibility; and (3) an absence of empathy for anybody who is not very close. At the same time, many perpetrators succeeded in coping with their killing task by "doubling": functioning with an "original self" that remained more or less unaffected by the acts of their other, murderous self. After the genocidal episode they could return to their original self, try to forget about their destructive past, and, if ever they had to confront it again, they could always maintain that this self had not been their "real" self but a transient double that in their present state they could not really be held accountable for.

Such a regression can be functional in times of upheaval, danger, and uncertainty. It is a regression in the service of the regime. It suits those in command very well. And it very effectively serves their underlings.

CHAPTER 9

Conclusion

W**HY DO REGIMES RESORT TO MASS ANNIHILATION,** and why do people kill massively in their service? These are the questions I set out to answer in this book. And now is the place to assess how far and how well they have been answered.

Getting the question right already provides half the answer. Genocidal killers never operate in isolation or in tiny secluded groups, as homicidal criminals do. The genocidaires function in a social and physical setting that is not of their own making but was provided for them by the genocidal regime. They do their work in a highly supportive, even compelling environment. Not surprisingly, this genocidal *situation* offers a first explanation of the perpetrators' actions. Yet even though most contemporary scholars limit themselves to this immediate context, there is more to be said in explanation of genocidal behavior.

First of all, the setting of the mass killings was deliberately arranged by the *regime* in power, or at the very least, it knowingly allowed the local occasion for mass murder to occur.

The genocidaires, like their contemporaries and fellow nationals, lived through a particular period in the history of their *society* that helped to shape a collective mentality, shared "cultural codes" and opinions widely held. In these respects, they were similar to many or most of their compatriots but, like them, quite unlike the citizens of other nations that followed different trajectories.

And last, the perpetrators each had their particular congenital and social inheritance and their individual experiences, all of which contributed to form certain *individual dispositions* that made them less, or more, suitable for the mass murderers' trade. In brief, if we want to understand and even explain genocidal perpetrators, we must approach them on four levels at once: the societal, the institutional, the situational, and the personal, or the macrosociological, the mesosociological, the microsociological, and the psychosociological levels.

In social science, this fourfold approach is perfectly obvious: that is how social scientists operate. But that is not at all how the great majority of students of mass annihilation approach their subject. On the contrary, the consensus in the field holds that it is ordinary people who commit extraordinary evil. Neither the perpetrators' collective past nor their individual biography plays much of a part in this view; it is the immediate setting that brings these ordinary people to their extraordinary deeds: any one of us, under similar conditions, might well commit the same evil.

The idea that obedience to authority could bring people to commit the most outrageous crimes was already quite widespread in the 1950s: the Nazi mentality was routinely mocked with the ironic slogan *Befehl ist Befehl*, "Orders are orders." It was in this zeitgeist that Hannah Arendt wrote *Eichmann in Jerusalem: A Report on the Banality of Evil*, in which she portrayed one of the main organizers of the Holocaust as an utterly insignificant character, no more than a cog in the vast machinery of extermination. Even then, in 1961, there was plenty of evidence that Eichmann was the opposite, a fanatic, indefatigable Jew hunter, and all research since then has only confirmed this picture. Nevertheless, "the banality of evil" became a catchphrase in the popular discourse on genocide, and Eichmann became the embodiment of the faceless, thoughtless, deskbound murderer. If such a banal personality could have committed crimes of such magnitude, then just anybody might be capable of the same evil.

Not much later, Stanley Milgram staged a laboratory experiment in which voluntary subjects were instructed to give electrical shocks of increasing voltage to a "learner" each time he failed to reproduce certain word combinations he had tried to memorize. The student was an actor, and the shocks were fake. But the experiment and its numerous replications showed that a majority of subjects were willing to shock someone with a voltage that they may well have believed to be extremely painful and possibly lethal, just because the experimenter told them to. Still, a considerable minority, and under slightly different conditions a majority, refused to continue at some point.

The experiment does not warrant either the popular conclusion that in real life most people will comply with a genocidal dictatorship or its contrary, much less popular conclusion that a sizable minority would resist it in reality. It is hard to decide whether the subjects actually believed they were administering severe torture or even a death penalty to their subject or, rather, that they experienced the setup as a very serious game. Moreover, the difference between the compliers and the naysayers was never thoroughly explored by Milgram and his followers. But Milgram did establish that people are much more prone to obey a person of authority ordering them to harm someone else than just about anyone had expected before his experiments.

In 1992, Christopher Browning published an account of the Nazi execution squads in eastern Poland who rounded up Jews, marched them to a killing site, made them dig a mass grave, and executed them then and there by the tens of thousands. The book's title was *Ordinary Men,* and it mustered painstaking historical documentation in support of Arendt's philosophical speculation and Milgram's experimental evidence. Especially disconcerting was the fact that Browning's men had not been specially selected or trained for the task but more or less haphazardly recruited from those German males who had not yet been drafted for other uniformed units. In this case, the men were given at the outset a choice to withdraw from the mission without further consequences. Only a handful of the five hundred did so.

However, the others could not have imagined what it was they did not say "no" to. Once they found out, some tried to shirk their task as much they could, others complied more or less indifferently, and still others turned out to be "willing executioners" (in Daniel Goldhagen's words). But, it should be added, all of these men had lived through the dismal period after Germany's defeat in World War I, followed by hyperinflation, political chaos, economic crisis, and mass unemployment, and then had been exposed to the unrelenting intimidation and propaganda of the Nazi regime, and experienced the triumphant onset of World War II before they joined Reserve Police Battalion 101. If they were ordinary indeed, then they were—as Goldhagen's subtitle has it—"ordinary Germans" during an extraordinary period of German history.

If genocidal perpetrators are ordinary people, then, in a similar perspective, genocide must be an essential feature of the present times. Zygmunt Bauman, in *Modernity and the Holocaust*, considers mass annihilation an essential feature of the modern era, continuing an intellectual tradition that began with the reaction to the senseless mechanical and chemical slaughter of World War I.

In fact, the line of argument in terms of banality and modernity would make much more sense if applied to the battlefields of World War I or the mass bombings of civilians in World War II. Bauman mostly ignores the bloody "Holocaust by bullets" in the east and takes at face value the presentation of the camps as the epitome of dispassionate industrial extermination, whereas it was in fact a chaotic and boundless destruction of human beings. Nazism was at once reactionary *and* modernist, rationalist bureaucracy *and* bestial barbarism.

In *The Dark Side of Democracy*, Michael Mann discusses ethnic cleansing in the twentieth century. The worst instances of mass extermination occurred under totalitarian regimes that indeed had a populist side: National Socialism and the "people's democracies" of the Soviet Union and China. But democracies they certainly were not.

Mann does remind his readers of the uncomfortable fact that in many "settler democracies" colonists massacred the native dwellers of the lands they had recently conquered and occupied. One might add that imperialist democracies sent their armies to conquer faraway lands and allowed them to massacre the alien and exotic inhabitants. Also, in some democracies, India for example, politicians regularly foment ethnic ("communal") conflict in order to cement the ties of the ethnic group they rely on for electoral support. Mann also points out that when authoritarian regimes fall apart, politicians try to win over popular support by setting one class or ethnic group against the other. Yet annihilation on a mass scale occurs less on the dark side of democracy than on the hidden side of dictatorship.

Humans are the far descendants of a primate species, chimpanzees, in which violence by males, alone or in groups, is not exceptional. Nor is there much doubt that early hunter-gatherers fought other human beings frequently and with lethal result. To all appearances, throughout the ages males have been the more violent gender.

As human beings began to live together in larger, sedentary units, practicing agriculture, the scale of violence increased accordingly, but the frequency of violent incidents tended to diminish. Where warlords and their warriors succeeded in monopolizing the means of violence, violent individuals and cliques could be quite effectively subdued, while outside threats from competing warlords could be warded off more or less successfully. A spiral of domestic pacification and early state formation began when warlords imposed regular tribute on the peasantry with which they could pay their soldiers to come and collect the taxes that served to support even more soldiers who could be used for further exactions: the perfect cycle of the predatory state. Yet, as a result of this early monopolization of the means of violence, and routinization of tribute, people no longer needed to be prepared at all times for violent attacks, nor could they themselves anymore afford to attack others at their whim. The social regulation of the self-regulation of violent impulses became stricter, the individual controls more stable and stronger. Where the incidence of violence subsided, people could also better afford the risks of mutual collaboration and reap its benefits. The exercise of violence more and more became a matter for specialists, for the military, the police, and criminals.

These civilizing processes, as Norbert Elias has described them, occurred through fits and starts, reversals and deviations, reaching higher levels of internal pacification in some areas than in others. The formation of an advanced state apparatus also meant the accumulation of a huge capacity of destruction. In large-scale wars and mass exterminations this potential was realized: the barbaric counterpoint to the civilizing process.[1]

Human inclinations to violence were transformed in the course of the species' evolution, and the occasions for violence changed accordingly. In human history, there were not only wars between more or less symmetric parties but as many or more instances of mass annihilation in which one camp, much better equipped and organized, completely destroyed the other, which lacked arms and organization. Few of these massacres left any trace in human memory; literally no one survived to tell the story, and even if some people did, they lacked the means to document it and make it widely known. Victorious armies would kill their disarmed and fleeing enemies to the last man and rob or rape, enslave, or kill anyone else they happened upon. If chronicles of these feats have survived at all, they are full of glee and triumph, inflating the number of victims to add to the glory of the victors.

What is modern is not mass murder but rather the embarrassment about it. The past hundred years were as bloody as preceding periods. In the twentieth century, the number of casualties of asymmetric mass violence was in the order of magnitude of 100 million to 150 million. That is three to four times as much as the total number of combat dead in war—in symmetric conflict, that is. Yet it is not at all certain that more victims of mass violence fell in the past hundred years than in the century before, even when the civilian casualties of asymmetric violence "at a distance," by shelling and air raids, are included.

A survey of some twenty episodes of mass annihilation in the twentieth century conveys an impression of their incidence, diversity, and size. Except for the destruction wreaked by some established regimes that ruled by terror, they all occurred in the shadow or in the aftermath of war, civil war, revolution, or a coup. They never proceeded in dispassionate, calculated destruction. Without exception, these episodes were grisly, bloody, and wild.

All this violence served to annihilate the other group and to benefit one's own. Even if the enemies were unarmed and defenseless, they had to be destroyed once and for all, so that they would never constitute a threat. The world had to be purified, cleansed of the enemies' polluting presence: "purify and destroy," as Jacques Sémelin has summed it up. The more outrageous the atrocities committed, the more reason to kill whoever was still alive so that no one would survive to tell the story. Even babies and toddlers had to be destroyed, since one day as grownups they might take revenge.

But why did people who had never met one another, who mostly did not even know of each other's existence, come to have such strong emotions about one another, feelings of hatred for the others and of equally intense loyalty toward their own?

Hominids and their descendants, humans, have always lived in groups. All group formation implies inclusion of one's own and exclusion of the others as outsiders. People who feel they belong together develop a sense of mutual similarity in almost all respects that matter to them: in other words, they identify with one another. On the contrary, those who have been excluded from the group are felt to be different in almost every respect that matters: the group members *dis*identify from these outsiders.

Processes of identification and disidentification go together. As the scale of human group formation increases, the circles of identification and disidentification expand likewise. But the rhetoric of identification remains remarkably constant. Since the early survival bands of hunters and gatherers the metaphors of kinship were evoked to confirm mutual loyalties. To this day, metaphors of a fatherland, a mother tongue, children of one father, and brothers and sisters in the faith (or in arms) help to mobilize vicariously the strong feelings of kinship in cementing much larger social entities.

With the emergence of sedentary agriculture, people came to live next to one another, even if they were not related. It was there that another metaphor emerged, of neighbors. This, too, can instill feelings of loyalty among people even today. Kinship and proximity ("blood and soil") are the perennial common denominators of social bonding. The corresponding identifications and disidentifications expanded to encompass cities or regions and, at a later stage, entire nations. They may also comprise a race, an ethnic group, a class, a faith, always pitched against its despised complement: Herrenvolk versus Untermensch, natives against intruders, the proletariat against the bourgeoisie, true believers versus the infidels.

All these oppositions, no matter how strongly imposed and how intensely experienced, were the outcome of historical transformations. They were constructed and reconstructed over time. They may have lain dormant, mostly forgotten, and then were revived by resourceful and powerful manipulators of thought and sentiment. Most people hold various identifications and disidentifications that may well intersect or contradict one another. In times of upheaval, however, the regime imposes a single set of identifications and their complementary disidentifications at the exclusion of all others. The rise of the Hutu-Tutsi dichotomy as the overriding distinction between the citizens of twentieth-century Rwanda provides a case in point. The division was presented as perennial and encompassing. Although the terms had been around for centuries, their meaning had been transformed under first the German and then the Belgian occupation of Rwanda and, still later, under the impact of the propaganda by the Hutu Power movement. In spite of the ideological definition of Hutus and Tutsis as internally homogeneous and mutually exclusive entities, in daily life it was often unclear to which group a Rwandan was supposed to belong.

Strong and even lethal patterns of identification and disidentification may rest entirely on imaginary, often expressly fabricated differences and similarities among people. Genocidal regimes exist on fantasies of likeness and contrast, purity and impurity, superiority and inferiority, often fanatically held.

To transform society along the lines of the regime's genocidal vision, social life must be thoroughly compartmentalized at every level. Compartmentalization is the process through which people are ideologically separated in opposite categories, socially and spatially segregated, institutionally discriminated, and mentally isolated. It is a process that permeates the bureaucracy and the courts, the schools and hospitals, the spheres of work and leisure, the private sphere, intimate relations, and even personal thought and sentiment, creating at all these levels separate compartments for people belonging to the one and the other category. In due course, it strengthens the identifications among the regime's people and intensifies the disidentifications from the target people (and vice versa, as exclusion generally also leads to stronger mutual identification among the excluded).

All societies are compartmentalized to some degree. But genocidal regimes greatly intensify the separation of minds, people, and institutions. Even so, there are major differences in the degrees and the modes of compartmentalization in the diverse societies that have endured an episode of mass annihilation. Thus, German society under National Socialism was much more compartmentalized than mostly agrarian societies such as Indonesia or Rwanda, where Muslims and "Communists" or Tutsis and Hutus lived together in the villages, went to the same schools, carried on business together, and frequently intermarried across the dividing lines, and even so, Muslim and Hutu peasants in large numbers joined in the killings of their earmarked neighbors.

Four modes of mass violence can be distinguished, according to the social constellation that impels them and the degree of compartmentalization that prevails. In the *conquerors' frenzy* a victorious army massacres a remote and alien people with little interference from the public at home. This is what happened in many colonial expeditions and in the expansionist campaigns of imperial Japan in China and Nazi Germany in eastern Europe.

Rule by terror is imposed domestically by an established regime in an attempt to advance and safeguard its reforms. Usually the wave of mass murder and intimidation is unleashed by factional strife within the bosom of the regime. The campaign is carried out by professional forces—secret police, special military units, party militias—clearly distinct from the civilian population. The telltale examples are the Stalinist terror of the 1930s in the Soviet Union and Maoist terror in the 1950s and 1970s in China.

Some regimes, in the face of imminent defeat at the hands of an armed and organized enemy nevertheless continue and even intensify their campaign of extermination against their target people.

This is the *losers' triumph*. Even if the regime seems bound to lose and will most likely perish soon, it will have completed its great historical mission of exterminating once and for all its eternal, implacable enemies. In doing so, the regime turns passive into active and triumphs in defeat. Once it became clear that the Soviet Union could not be overrun and the tide had turned against it, Nazi Germany expanded and accelerated its efforts to annihilate all the Jews of Europe. Similarly autodestructive destruction was wreaked by the Young Turks upon the Armenians in the face of defeat in World War I, by the Hutu Power regime in Rwanda when the Tutsi army advanced from the north, and by the Khmer Rouge of Cambodia as they provoked an invasion by Vietnam.

Sometimes the role of the regime is much more remote and covert, as instant mobs with the support of irregular army units, militias, or criminal gangs rob, expel, rape, and murder the people of a target group in their home area. These local pogroms are concatenated into a genocidal *megapogrom* under the impact of events on a national or even continental scale, such as the collapse of Nazi Germany across Middle Europe in the winter of 1945 and the withdrawal of the British army from the Indian empire and the Partition of British India into Pakistan and India in 1947. There is less compartmentalization in such cases, and it seems as if people join the carnage more or less ad hoc, while the killing of the target group occurs openly and on the spot. Although the regime can deny direct involvement, the massive cleansing does serve its interests.

In these instances, tens of thousands, hundreds of thousands of perpetrators were implicated in the annihilation of hundreds of thousands, millions, even tens of millions of human beings. The killers and the victims seem mostly faceless, nameless, and speechless shadows in a fog of destruction.

Once the havoc subsided and in the rare instances that a successor regime allowed it, the survivors made every effort to revive the memory of the victims, establish their identities, reconstruct what happened to them, and commemorate their sufferings. But in most cases, silence prevailed, never to be dispelled. The perpetrators, too, were mostly forgotten. Only in the few cases where the genocidal regime was completely defeated were some killers identified, put on trial, convicted, and punished. Most of what is known about mass annihilation comes from these court cases. In front of their judges, the genocidaires negated the charges whenever they could, and when the facts appeared irrefutable, they denied responsibility for their acts and tried to appear as insignificant, blank, and passive as they could.

The sum total of scholarly findings on the perpetrators mirrors this image. The killers appear as ordinary men, exceptional only in their utter banality, their conduct determined entirely by the impact of the genocidal situation that had entrapped them. Recently, some authors have again stressed the impact of collective historical experience and shared culture on the *mentalité* of the population in general, including the perpetrators: for example, in Germany, the defeat in war, the economic crisis, and the relentless eliminationist anti-Semitic propaganda; or, in Rwanda, the heritage of colonialism, authoritarian Catholicism, and the perennial dearth of arable land. Genocidal regimes eagerly exploited the destructive aspects of such a shared mentality.

But the killers did not just share in the collective past of their nation; they had a biography of their own. They had their particular experiences, developed their individual inclinations and opinions—they were, after all, persons in their own right. The critical question is whether the killers differed from others who lived through the same times, in the same society, but who did *not* join the murderers' ranks. The search for such differences has been neglected for over half a century because of this insistence that the genocidaires were all "ordinary men." Rather than look more closely at the perpetrators, people were told to search their own soul, since "you and I or anyone under the same circumstances might have done the same thing."

In fact, no one knows what "anyone" might do under these circumstances. The question is at once haunting, and meaningless. First of all, the fateful phrase, "If you and I had been in the same circumstances," is a counterfactual and cannot be shown to be either true or false, since you and I were not in the same circumstances, which, moreover, are unlikely to recur in our lifetime. The question is also counterintuitive, because people find it very hard to imagine themselves as mass executioners. Yet the idea that in a certain social context, in a given situation, people will commit acts that they would not dream of otherwise is quite plausible. Some people are more likely to do so than others, and some will resist even at considerable personal risk. Others may be willing and even eager to follow orders. That depends not only on the situation of the moment but also on their prior experience and personal history, in a word, a term that with so many words has been declared out of bounds: on their personal disposition. And in other words: on their particular personality.

I very much doubt that I, or most of my readers for that matter, on being brought into the killing site would have started, like automatons, clubbing, knifing, shooting, gassing people to death by the thousands, for weeks and months at a stretch. It would have taken more than that: it would require deadly threats and ineluctable force to turn us into executioners, or a very different past.

To make me or you into mass killers without extreme duress would require more preparation. If, for example, we had been brought up by authoritarian and unfeeling parents, as churchgoing, anti-Semitic German Lutherans or Catholics, had survived the trenches and the mustard gas of World War I, if we had lived through the hyperinflation and the political chaos of the Weimar

Republic, if you and I had lost our jobs or our business as a result of the Great Crisis, had had to adapt to the Nazi tyranny under a constant bombardment of the vilest racist propaganda, if we found ourselves in the utterly destructive battles at the Eastern Front, if this had been the course of our lives, then, yes, maybe then, some of us might have become genocidal killers. But then, you or I, we would have been someone else.

The impact of the genocidal situation on the behavior of the perpetrators has rightly been stressed in the past half-century. There is a renewed interest in the influence of historical-cultural conditions on the formation of a genocidal mentality. What is overdue is an assessment of the importance of personal biography, of the individual dispositions that may lead to genocidal actions.

This is a tall order. Ideally, such research would require the observation of cohorts of subjects, part of whom at some point become genocidal perpetrators, another part of whom never gets involved in mass murder, and maybe even a third part who join the resistance against it.

Such research could have produced data on the personalities of the subjects that should help explain their itineraries in later life. But no one can tell where mass annihilation is likely to occur in the next ten years, so that we can conduct surveys before, during, and after the fact. And yet the few existing retrospective studies do reveal differences between perpetrators and the population at large: the killers more often had an authoritarian background and came more often from the police, the military, or the ranks of violent criminals.

In order to understand how perpetrators cope, once they find themselves in a genocidal environment, requires sustained, close, "thick" observation. Such research is, of course, impossible. Instead, there are the recollections of the victims who survived and of "innocent" bystanders. But these individuals rarely saw the perpetrators "backstage," relaxing among their peers or relatives or being drilled by their commanders.

In the killing compartments there were the reluctant, the indifferent, and the eager perpetrators. But these distinctions are based on rather haphazard reports, since systematic research is not feasible. There is no way to directly relate differences in genocidal conduct with differences in preexisting personality traits.

Last, there is little information about how the perpetrators coped with life *after* their genocidal period. Did they suffer any symptoms reminiscent of post-traumatic stress? Perhaps not, since they had never had to fear for their lives, as combat veterans or survivors had to. Now that their new social environment might condemn the preceding campaigns of mass extermination, were they afraid, ashamed, or remorseful? Maybe not, for they found shelter in the bosom of their denying and forgiving family or among their like-minded former comrades.

A few high-ranking Nazi perpetrators left their memoirs, and some were the subject of detailed biographies. There are studies of rank-and-file genocidaires and increasingly also documentary films about mass killers. There are also the documents from trials, first in Germany and in more recent years from the International Criminal Tribunals and other UN courts.

What if anything can be learned from the existing literature on genocidal perpetrators? Genocidaires, in general, profess high standards of obedience to their superiors and of loyalty to their peers; often they also show commitment to their family. But anyone outside these rather narrow circles of identification is beyond their bounds of moral conscience, and against those people anything is allowed.

Before their judges or their biographers, perpetrators rarely acknowledge that they made any choices at all. "It all just happened to them." They display little sense of agency. Nor do they accept responsibility for their actions. They maintain that they were ordered to do what they did, or were pressured to do so because everyone else did the same. Had they refused, they would have suffered their victims' fate (which is true in quite a few cases but not in the case of the Nazi perpetrators).

Most important, only in exceptional instances do genocidaires show remorse, shame, or compassion. If they do, it is usually because they hope that by openly repenting they will receive a more lenient sentence. Rarely do they show any sign of compassion with their victims. This striking lack of sympathy reveals an inability to identify with their victims: an absence of empathy.

Their restricted moral conscience, low sense of agency, and lack of empathy may yet provide a clue to the differences between most perpetrators and most other people. According to current thinking about early childhood development, infants learn that they have an inner, mental life that is separate from the world around them. Next, they come to understand that other people, too, might have minds of their own. On this basis, the very young child learns to empathize with the feelings of others. This is a necessary condition for the development of sympathy or compassion, when the child vicariously suffers with the perceived suffering of others. Peter Fonagy calls this entire process "mentalization." Wouter Gomperts proposes the term *dysmentalization* for stunted mentalization or regression from an achieved level of mentalization. That might well be the condition of many perpetrators in the genocidal setting.

The perpetrators lacked any feelings of empathy for victims who had been dehumanized by relentless hate propaganda and by the inhuman conditions of the killing compartments. They increasingly indulged in fantasies of omnipotence, although they only did what they were ordered or allowed to do. They could let themselves go, with impunity, without responsibility: a *regression in the service of the regime.* Within the confines of the killing compartments, the regime encouraged and exploited the perpetrators' regression for its own purposes.

In times of upheaval people are more often confronted with a sequence of events that changes the direction of their life course. An almost invisible selection mechanism operates in the manner of a vibrating sieve, gradually sorting out persons who are only slightly more disposed to violent abuse than others, until they end up in a genocidal setting. Once they find themselves in such a situation, the perpetrators may regress much further than they themselves had ever believed possible. They often feel that this killer persona is not really "them." After the genocidal episode is over, if they look back at all, they like to think that they were a different person then, living in a different world.

There is nothing "banal" about such an experience. It is not an ordinary fate, and even if the perpetrators once were ordinary in most respects, they no longer are. They have had to find ways to cope with their killing task, and after it was over, they had to cope with their murderous past. Even mass murderers are persons, in many respects different persons, distinct like everyone else.

Notes

Chapter 1. Introduction

1. See Suedfeld, "Theories of the Holocaust," 51.

2. Thus, the people at the controls, doing the killing at a distance, are not usually called "executioners" or "perpetrators," let alone "genocidaires," but just that: "operators."

3. Davis, *Late Victorian Holocaust*, 7, quotes estimates for the casualties of famine in India between 1876 and 1902 ranging from 12 million to 29 million and mentions similar numbers for China during the same period. As late as 1943, British authorities allowed a famine of comparable scale to happen in Bengal, again without providing aid to peasants who were starving by the millions.

4. "Mass annihilation" is used interchangeably with "mass extermination," "mass destruction," and "mass murder."

5. See a more detailed discussion of these terms in chapter 4. For an early sociological definition of *genocide*, see the pioneering study by Helen Fein, *Genocide*.

6. "In the twentieth century, however, no country has acknowledged that it engaged in genocide" (Smith, "Human Destructiveness and Politics," 28). Yet in countries that were decisively defeated, a radically different successor regime did recognize the crimes committed by its predecessor: for example, (East and West) Germany and Rwanda.

7. See Chirot and McCauley, *Why Not Kill Them All?*, 47: "The identification of state with nation has meant that the modern nation has become the village, the clan, the tribe, or the small city-state with which most people identified in the past."

8. On the contrary, Erich Fromm, writing from a psychoanalytic background, and one of the few students of Nazi personalities presented an elaborate and cautious

portrait of Hitler using evidence available at the time (*Anatomy of Human Destructiveness*, 369–434).

9. Waller, *Becoming Evil*, 18, states: "My central argument is: *it is ordinary individuals, like you and me, who commit extraordinary evil*" (emphasis in original); Mann, *Dark Side of Democracy*, 9, writes: "Placed in comparable situations and similar social constituencies, you or I might also commit murderous ethnic cleansing."

10. Waller, *Becoming Evil*, 133, writes: "We need no longer ask *who* these people are. We know who they are. They are you and I." Or see the very title of Roth: "Hearts of Darkness: 'Perpetrator History' and Why There Is No Why."

11. Much worse, intellectuals have all too often ignored, denied, glossed over, condoned, justified, and even encouraged or glorified mass annihilation: "Put simply, we must recall that scholars and intellectuals have not infrequently found themselves at the forefront of support for mass crimes and inhumanity and have often distinguished themselves by their extraordinary political blindness and moral callousness" (Bartov, "Extreme Violence and the Scholarly Community," 511).

12. See Neitzel and Welzer, *Soldaten*, 89.

13. The notion of completely senseless, "autotelic" violence, violence for its own sake, springs from the imagination of romantic philosophers. Anthropologists and psychologists have found meaning even in apparently meaningless, seemingly unmotivated acts, unless the perpetrators were psychotics. See Blok, "Zinloos en Zinvol Geweld"; and Reemtsma, *Trust and Violence*, 56: "Every action gives us information about the doer—who he is and what he wants to be. Every action, in other words, *possesses a communicative aspect*" (emphasis in original).

14. Zajonc, "Zoomorphism of Human Collective Violence," 238.

15. Baumeister, "Holocaust and the Four Roots of Evil," 243.

16. See Devereux, *From Anxiety to Method in the Behavioral Sciences;* and Heilbron, "Tegenoverdracht en mensenwetenschap."

17. Lifton, *Nazi Doctors*, 502.

Chapter 2. Ordinary Perpetrators and Modernity

1. Baron-Cohen, *Zero Degrees of Empathy*, 67, writes: "3% of US males, 1% of females have antisocial personality disorder," one of the conditions that comes with "zero empathy."

2. Browning, *Ordinary Men;* Welzer, *Täter;* Dutton, *Psychology of Genocide;* Mann, "Perpetrators of Genocide"; Waller, "Perpetrators of the Holocaust"; Goldhagen, *Hitler's Willing Executioners;* Katz, *Ordinary People and Extraordinary Evil;* Conroy, *Unspeakable Acts, Ordinary People;* Askenasy, *Are We All Nazis?;* Jensen and Szejnmann, *Ordinary People as Mass Murderers;* Hughes, "Good People and Dirty Work"; Zimbardo, *Lucifer Effect;* Todorov, *Face à l'extrême*, 131ff.: "Des gens ordinaires." To be continued . . . .

3. Gustave Gilbert, the psychologist who visited the accused in prison, believed most of them to have severe mental pathologies on the basis of extensive conversations

and psychological tests such as the Rorschach. His colleague, Douglas M. Kelley, came to the opposite conclusion. The controversy continued off and on, until Eric A. Zillmer and colleagues concluded in the mid-1980s from a thorough reanalysis of the test data that the defendants had not displayed "diagnosable impairments" (quoted in Waller, *Becoming Evil*, 66).

4. Charny, "Genocide and Mass Destruction," 155, agrees that "the potential for being genociders and accomplices is in all of us," but he argues that we should revise our concept of normalcy and decide that "wanton destruction of life is an act of madness." He proposes to include disorders of pseudocompetence, invulnerability, and doing harm to other people and take into consideration the extent to which people abandon their individual identity and self to any collective process.

5. See Waller, *Becoming Evil*, 74.

6. See De Mildt, *In the Name of the People*, 21. For prosecution by the Allies, see *Encyclopaedia Judaica*, 2nd ed., s.v. "War Crimes Trials," 634–649; for the Federal Republic, see De Mildt, *In the Name of the People*, 21.

7. On Arendt, see Browning, "Revisiting the Holocaust Perpetrators," 12; and Browning, "Introduction," 4: "Most historians would now agree, I think, that Arendt had uncritically accepted Eichmann's misrepresentation of himself, and that he was in fact a Nazi activist, motivated by both his ideological identification with the regime and his unquenchable ambition." But he continues: "Arendt had arrived at a powerful insight that the ability of a state to organize mass murder owes much to the accommodation and compliance of petty and dutiful civil servants, even if she misunderstood her star example."

Mulisch, *Criminal Case 40/61*, 119, concludes at the end of his account of the Eichmann trial: "He is nothing. This extremely useful, absolutely uncorrupted, highly dangerous man is the precise opposite of a 'rebel.' He is precisely the opposite of a man who wants to be bad. He is a machine that is good for anything. He is the right man in the right place. He is the ideal of psycho-technology. Millions like him are roaming the earth." Other writers who attended the trial, with fewer pet theories to launch, avoided these errors. See the always perceptive Herzberg, *Eichmann in Jeruzalem*, who mentions numerous instances of initiatives by Eichmann above and beyond the call of duty.

8. Cesarani, *Eichmann*, 119.

9. Arendt, *Eichmann in Jerusalem*, 46, adds that Eichmann always claimed to have said "Reichsfeinde" (enemies of the Reich), rather than "Jews," but this was most likely untrue.

10. In fact, until late in the 1960s, in order to get the accused convicted in German war crime trials, the prosecutor had to prove that a particular defendant committed criminal acts above and beyond what he was ordered to do. In later jurisprudence, the plea of obedience to superior orders was no longer accepted and the defendants could be sentenced for committing criminal acts even if they had been ordered to do so. Moreover, if the evidence left room for doubt, initially the German courts decided in favor of the defendant (*in dubio pro reo*). See De Mildt, *In the Name of the People*, 302–325.

11. Arendt, *Eichmann in Jerusalem*, 48.

12. See Arendt, *Eichmann in Jerusalem*, 57; and Lipstadt, *Eichmann Trial*, 169: "However, in Eichmann's case her analysis seems strangely out of touch with the reality of his historical record."

13. For an overview of intellectual opinion at the time, see Shapira, "Eichmann Trial." For an early refutation of Arendt's views on Eichmann, exhaustive, painstaking, and at times nitpicking, see Robinson, *Dark Side of Paradise*, 1965.

14. The subtitle of Arendt's book was *A Report on the Banality of Evil*. It is hard to imagine that Arendt thought the murder of some six million people was in any sense "banal," that is, "so lacking in originality as to be obvious and boring" (*OED*). Probably she wanted to convey not so much that "evil" was "banal" but that the "evildoers" were, which would at least be consistent with her book's point of view.

15. In her introduction to Bernd Naumann's book *Auschwitz* on the 1963 Frankfurt trial of twenty-two SS Auschwitz guards, Arendt did not retract her prior opinions on Eichmann, but it seems that she had now finally realized what happended in the annihilation camps, for she stresses the "monstrous deeds," the willful brutality, and the sadistic perversity of the "grotesquely unrepentant" guards (v–xxx).

16. For an extensive and devastating critique of Arendt on Eichmann, founded on much more recent evidence, see Cesarani, *Eichmann*.

17. Hannah Arendt's account of the part played by the "Jewish Councils" is harsh. Waller, *Becoming Evil*, 254, comments: "Hannah Arendt was the first notable scholar to suggest that victims of the Holocaust contributed to their own demise." Arendt thought Jews should have resisted more actively (she was not aware of the actual incidence of Jewish resistance), even though the Nazis punished the slightest opposition with mass killings of inmates, hostages, and random citizens. Also, she argues, the Jews should have fled or gone into hiding. If only such opportunities had been available to the vast majority of prosecuted Jews. . . . Of course, most of them wanted to, many tried, but only a very few found compatriots ready to hide them or a foreign country willing to take them in. Once again, Arendt's opinion echoes a widespread parti pris of the time: the Jews let themselves be led to the gas chambers like sheep to their slaughter.

18. Johan Goudsblom points out that even more obedient than the experiment's subjects were the experimenter and the actor who carried out Milgram's instructions for the full 100 percent, inflicting severe mental shocks on the unsuspecting participants (*Fire and Civilization*, 157).

19. Milgram, *Obedience to Authority*, 85.

20. Milgram himself was not at all a pure situationist: "I am certain that there is a complex personality basis to obedience and disobedience. But I know we have not found it" (*Obedience to Authority*, 205).

21. Milgram, *Obedience to Authority*, 46–47. Even in these few sentences, the subject succeeds in blaming the victim and the experimenter while ignoring his own part in the proceedings.

22. James Waller reduces the position that the subjects' past experience and

psychological makeup might account at least in part for their present behavior to the "fundamental attribution error" of "dispositional thinking" (*Becoming Evil*, 228).

23. One secret experiment that still went on during Milgram's studies and in which poor southern black males were purposely and seriously harmed became a cause célèbre in 1971 and for good reason, yet it did not come anywhere near the willful electrocution of its subjects. The Tuskegee syphilis study was a clinical experiment conducted between 1932 and 1972 in Tuskegee, Alabama, by the US Public Health Service to study the natural progression of untreated syphilis in uninformed patients who thought they were receiving free health care from the federal government. It was precisely this experiment that led to the "complete revamping of HEW [Department of Health, Education, and Welfare] regulations in human experimentation" (see Jones, *Bad Blood*, 214).

24. Milgram asked his subjects after the experiment whether they had believed the shocks were real, and indeed, a majority of the respondents firmly thought so (and among the "defiant" that percentage was higher than among the "obedient") (Milgram, *Obedience to Authority*, 172).

25. The set phrase was: "Although the shocks may be painful, there is no permanent tissue damage. So please go on" (Milgram, *Obedience to Authority*, 21).

26. See Blass, "Psychological Perspectives on the Perpetrators of the Holocaust," 34.

27. Burger, "Replicating Milgram," 10.

28. Most likely the changed setup made little difference in the results, since in the original experiment 80 percent of the subjects who had given a 150V shock continued to the maximum 450V jolt.

29. Blass, "Understanding Behavior in the Milgram Obedience Experiment"; Blass, "Milgram Paradigm After 35 Years"; Blass, "Psychological Perspectives on the Perpetrators of the Holocaust," sketches the application of this "interactionist" approach to the subject of Holocaust perpetrators.

30. Milgram, *Obedience to Authority*, 204, mentions the outcome of test research by his assistant, A. C. Elms, who found "that the subjects who had obeyed showed a greater degree of authoritarianism (a higher F score) than those who refused to obey."

31. Burger, "Replicating Milgram," 2–3.

32. Zimbardo, *Lucifer Effect*, 211. In almost identical terms also in Waller, *Becoming Evil*, 228.

33. For example, Zimbardo, *Lucifer Effect*, 104–110.

34. Their anti-Semitism may have been, in part, a consequence, rather than a cause of their behavior: hatred of Jews could serve as a justification afterward of their deeds in terms that were quite acceptable, even demanded at the time.

35. In an essay on "German-bashing," Randall Collins denies that anti-Semitism was particularly strong or widespread in Germany as compared to its neighbors (*Macrohistory*, 173–175).

36. "Perhaps most important, Goldhagen's work should force scholars to recognize what most survivors have always known, that the killers were primarily motivated by a visceral hatred of the Jews. And this too should lead to a reevaluation of the

force of anti-Semitism in German history" (Weiss, "Review of Goldhagen, *Hitler's Willing Executioners*," 268).

37. This is roughly the argument Norbert Elias advances with much historical detail in *The Germans.*

38. See, however, Desbois, *Holocaust by Bullets.* Desbois and his team interviewed elderly Ukrainians to reconstruct the Nazi extermination of the Jews and located many of the victims' mass graves.

39. Wrong, "Oversocialized Conception of Man."

40. Despite his provocative title, *Ordinary Men,* Christopher Browning, who comes to a situationist conclusion, includes historical and cultural aspects and allows for differences in personal disposition in a very nuanced explanation (159–189). For another situationist but open position, see Frijda, "Emotions and Collective Violence," 30: "One has to agree with Browning's conclusion that many of us, if not most of us, would have acted as the men of Police Battalion 101." And Frijda adds: "For myself, I do not know."

41. "In particular, the banality perspective on evil, which tends to portray evildoers as merely dutiful bureaucrats (e.g. see Milgram, 1974; Zimbardo, 1995), needs dramatic revision because it presently offers an oversimplified situationist account that is especially likely to be misconstrued as exculpatory" (Mandel, "Instigators of Genocide," 279). But compare Browning's reminder that "explaining is not excusing, understanding is not forgiving" (*Ordinary Men,* xviii). See also Miller, "Explaining the Holocaust."

42. Bauman, *Modernity and the Holocaust,* xiii, 28.

43. Bauman, *Modernity and the Holocaust,* 29.

44. Vetlesen, *Evil and Human Agency,* 44: "Bauman commits the error of mistaking the bureaucratic design for the reality." Dan Stone, "Holocaust and Historiography," 371–372, comments: "In other words, in modernity, violence continues to exist in forms which are not *Zweckrational* (purposive-rational), but because of modernization's rhetoric of self-styled civility, it refuses to admit the fact. . . . Ironically, the majority of commentators repeat the same suppression, and accept the murderers' own interpretations too quickly." And he continues: "But far from testifying to 'the murderers' fanatical zeal,' these reports [by the Einsatzgruppen] were designed to conceal any sense of fanaticism. . . . Hiding the fact that the violence of the Holocaust was an outburst of affect, a transgression from norms of society. But the nature of fascism, with its rigidly steeled warrior men, its severe military trammeling of the body and its emotions, had to conceal this fact from itself. It was not the killing of Jews that was problematic for the murderers, it was acknowledging that the killing might be connected to the desire to transgress that had to be suppressed."

45. Vetlesen, *Evil and Human Agency,* 44, writes: "The Nazi regime parasitically and progressively transformed and (even) revolutionized the institutional apparatus it had inherited from the democratic Weimar era. As attested to by the bypassing of established procedural norms and by the blatant disregard for the rule of law, what facilitated and accompanied the extermination policies was a thoroughgoing process of de-bureaucratization."

46. Joas, "Sociology After Auschwitz," 168, writes: "First, one may wonder whether Zygmunt Bauman should not emphasize more than he did in his masterly book on the Holocaust that it took place during the war." Zwaan, "'Modernity' and 'Barbarity' in Genocidal Processes," compares the diametrically opposed views of Zygmunt Bauman and Norbert Elias on the relation between "civilization" and the Holocaust. See also De Swaan, "Dyscivilization, Mass Extermination and the State."

47. Levene, *Meaning of Genocide*, 121, after quoting some examples of wanton, gratuitous cruelty, concludes: "Something other than a straightforward utilitarian approach to mass murder seems to be demanded by way of explanation here."

48. Desbois, *Holocaust by Bullets;* Snyder, *Bloodlands;* Berkhoff, *Harvest of Despair.*

49. See Stone, "Holocaust and Historiography," 375: "One of the good things to emerge out of the Goldhagen debate was proof of a widespread reluctance to admit that the killers could enjoy their violence, or at least to admit that the endless catalogue of atrocities found in survivor testimonies amounts to more than anecdotes of unusual, isolated incidents." See also Weitz, *Century of Genocide*, 135: "The killing of the Jews was never a clean 'sanitized' act, not even in the extermination camps. 'Industrial killing' signifies that Jews were murdered on a massive scale through organized, repetitive procedures, but these actions were not devoid of personalized brutality or of public spectacle." And he adds: "For the men observing the events, the thrill of such power freely dispensed could be intoxicating, as when Mengele and his aides casually inspected five hundred naked women, ordering them to turn around so they could have a total view of the bodies at their disposal . . . prior to gassing their genitals were shaved as well" (137–138).

50. Stone, "Holocaust and Historiography," 375.

51. Indeed, there are precedents, also outside the European sphere of influence. For example, the campaigns of terror and conquest waged by the Zulu leader Shaka in the 1820s in Southern Africa, which in many respects anticipated Nazi practices in their calculated and disciplined destruction of human life en masse; see Walter, "Terror Under Shaka": "Shaka had anticipated the Nazis" (225), and "The violence was wrought by highly disciplined impi, similar to hoplite formations, executing massed attacks in precise evolutions, using the short, stabbing assegai" (227).

52. In fact, Collins, in *Interaction Ritual Chains,* develops a scenario in which economic crisis and defeat in war combine to bring to power an "antimodernist movement" (such as the Nazi Party in Germany).

53. Bauman, *Postmodern Ethics*, 227.

54. See Bernard and Gruzinski on Bartolomé de las Casas and the impact of his and others' writings in both the new colonies and Spain (*Métissages*, 53ff.). See also the comment quoted there (164) from Montaigne ("les Coches"), evoked by his readings on the subject: "Tant de villes rasées, tant de nations exterminées, tant de millions de peuples passés au file de l'épée et la plus riche et plus belle partie du monde bouleversée pour la negociation des perles et du poivre" (So many towns razed, so many nations exterminated, so many millions of people put to the sword and the richest, most beautiful part of the world thrown in disarray by the commerce in pearls and pepper).

55. Rummel, *Death by Government,* 1; a variation of Lord Acton's words.

56. Mann, *Dark Side of Democracy*, 2. Or see his quoting of Andrew Bell-Fialkoff: "The real culprits are the ideals of freedom, self-determination, and representative democracy." And Mann adds: "Democratization has its dark sides" (69).

57. Berenschot, *Riot Politics;* see Wilkinson, "Froids calculs et foules déchaînées."

58. See Arnold Toynbee quoted in Rummel, *Death by Government*, 400.

59. Mann, *Dark Side of Democracy*, does quote some unsettling comments by American presidents, such as Thomas Jefferson (ix), and Theodore Roosevelt, who thought the extermination of the North American Indians had been "as ultimately beneficial as it was inevitable" (94).

60. Mann, *Dark Side of Democracy*, 4.

61. A pertinent counterexample of Mann's thesis, and not the only one of its kind, is the massacre of Highland Indians in Guatemala in the 1980s. After a US-supported coup abolished the democratic government there and brought to power a right-wing military regime, the army much intensified the ongoing raids against Indians and ended up wiping out "almost one third of Guatemala's 85,0000 Ixil Maya Indians" (Totten, *Dictionary of Genocide*, 282). See also Mann, *Dark Side of Democracy*, 512; and chap. 7, below.

62. Mann, *Dark Side of Democracy*, 9.

63. Mann, *Dark Side of Democracy*, 9. He adds: "Our capacity for evil becomes realized only in the circumstances explored in this book" (9). Most of us will agree with Mann that mass annihilation is the worst of evils, but would it really be the *only* setting in which the human capacity for evil manifests itself?

64. Lacoste, *Séductions du bourreau*, 4.

Chapter 3. Widening Circles of Identification and Disidentification

Epigraph: "Die Reichweite der Identifizierung wächst": Elias, "Society of Individuals III," 225.

1. See McCauley, "Psychology of Group Identification," 343ff.

2. Frijda, *Emotions*. Among the "source concerns," Frijda explicitly mentions concern "for the welfare of others, and particularly of close relatives" (344).

3. Freud, *Group Psychology*, 60.

4. Stein, "Indispensable Enemy," 71. On projective group identification, see also Bion, *Experiences in Groups*, 149.

5. Horowitz, *Deadly Ethnic Riot*, 75.

6. Anton Blok, "Narcissism of Minor Differences," referring, among others, to Freud, *Civilization and Its Discontents*. See also Jacoby, *Bloodlust*, 153–154, for a similar point of view, with references to Freud and René Girard's notion of "mimetic desire" (*La violence et le Sacré*). These authors all define "small differences" from the viewpoint of the outsider looking at another society. They also conveniently ignore the massive violence of conquerors against people in remote and alien societies whom they consider as very different.

7. Lasswell, *Psychopathology and Politics*, esp. 256–259; Lasswell, *World Politics and Personal Insecurity*. See also Parsons, *Social Structure and Personality*, 106–107.

8. Lasswell, *World Politics and Personal Insecurity*, 37.

9. Lasswell, *Psychopathology and Politics*, 257.

10. Lasswell, *World Politics and Personal Insecurity*, 245.

11. Volkan, "Overview of Psychological Concepts," 33.

12. Huizinga, *Geschonden wereld*.

13. Elias, *Germans*.

14. See Vansina, *Antecedents to Modern Rwanda*, 39, about tensions between kin-based cult associations and territorially organized cult congregations in seventeenth-century Rwanda.

15. See Black-Michaud, *Cohesive Forces;* and Black-Michaud, *Sheep and Land*.

16. See Goudsblom, *Fire and Civilization*, 55–71.

17. See Scott, *Weapons of the Weak*.

18. See Simmel, *Sociology*.

19. See De Swaan, *In Care of the State*.

20. See Nirenberg, *Communities of Violence*.

21. See Elias, "Society of Individuals III."

22. Anderson, *Imagined Communities*.

23. See Elias, *Collected Works*, "Introduction" (to volume 1) on the German concept of "Kultur" as marking (and producing) the distinction from the French idea of "civilisation."

24. De Swaan, *In Care of the State*, 26–28.

25. Jobson, *Golden Trade*, 112.

26. Haskell, "Capitalism and the Origins of the Humanitarian Sensibility," 342, 550–551.

27. Elias, "Society of Individuals III," 270.

Chapter 4. The Transformations of Violence in Human History

1. See Staub, "Roots of Evil," 179: "How would the meaning of evil be differentiated from the meaning of 'violence'? Is evil the end point in the evolution of violence?" See also McCauley, "Psychology of Group Identification," 343ff. For a fundamental discussion of the terms *identity* versus *identification*, see Brubaker and Cooper, "Beyond 'Identity,'" 14: "As a processual, active term, derived from a verb, 'identification' lacks the reifying connotations of 'identity.' It invites us to specify the agents that do the identifying. . . . Identification—of oneself and of others—is intrinsic to social life; 'identity' in the strong sense is not."

2. Ardrey, *African Genesis*, is another example.

3. See Gat, *War in Human Civilization*, 6ff., for an overview of recent literature on the subject.

4. On competing males, see Wrangham and Peterson, *Demonic Males*, 5–6: "The attack on Godi was a first—the first time that any human observer had watched them do it." That is an implausible claim, as local human observers must have watched their chimpanzee neighbors for tens of thousands of years.

5. See De Waal, *Chimpanzee Politics*.

6. Collins, *Violence,* 27.

7. Collins, *Violence,* 43ff. According to most of the relevant literature, human beings, males especially, do bluster and threaten, but most of the time refrain from actual physical attack; soldiers, even under enemy fire, find it hard to actually shoot at their opponents. See also Grossman, *On Killing.* And see van Doorn and Hendrix, *Het Nederlands/ Indonesisch conflict,* 176: "This ignores what a man experiences when he is ordered to kill people. The average soldier brings himself to do so only with effort. If such an order is executed without hesitation, it usually involves 'volunteers' and specialists who are selected for their extraordinary harshness." A study of trained killing professionals shows that these shooters do not hesitate to fire at a distance yet are often quite disturbed by the death of the target, despite experiencing a certain elation at their power to kill the opponent (Bar and Ben-Ari, "Israeli Snipers in the Al-Aqsa Intifada"). The strong reluctance of "ordinary" (that is, "unprepared") men to kill, even in situations that seem to provoke it, goes squarely against the "situationist" view.

8. In Marx's famous phrase: "In actual history it is notorious that conquest, enslavement, robbery, murder, briefly force, play the great part. In the tender annals of Political Economy, the idyllic reigns from time immemorial." Marx and Engels, *Capital,* 8.26.1.

9. Marx and Engels, *Capital.*

10. Keeley, *War Before Civilization,* 33.

11. Keeley, *War Before Civilization,* 174–175 (the paramount limiting factor in primitive warfare was logistics, 175). Since then, Keeley's conclusions have been confirmed by several paleoanthropological studies; see, among others, Walker and Bailey, "Body Counts in Lowland South American Violence," 29–34.

12. Gat, *War in Human Civilization,* 406, 408 (emphasis in original). Gat refers here to Thomas Hobbes's concept of "warre of everyone against everyone." Hobbes argued that this was the natural condition for human beings before they decided to submit to a single authority, the "Leviathan," which henceforward would monopolize the exercise of violence in their society.

13. Leadbetter, "Genocide in Antiquity," 275 (emphasis in original).

14. Probably the most extensive survey of premodern episodes of mass annihilation is Steven T. Katz, *Holocaust in Historical Context.*

15. Quoted in Chalk and Jonassohn, *History and Sociology of Genocide,* 58.

16. See Chirot and McCauley, *Why Not Kill Them All?* for Old Testament examples: in Number 31, Moses' warriors' exterminate the defeated Midianites (29); in 1 Samuel 15, the Lord is furious at Saul for not having exterminated the Amalekites to the last man (39); and in Genesis 34:25, Jacob's sons exterminate the Hivite men (63). Other writers, such as Kiernan, *Blood and Soil,* include less familiar material from South and Southeast Asian history.

17. Smith, "Human Destructiveness and Politics," 28. Even as late as 1864, Colonel John Milton Chivington boasted that he had killed "400 to 500, or 600" Cheyennes during the Sand Creek Massacre, whereas most likely he made some 150 casualties. Quoted in Waller, *Becoming Evil,* 26.

18. Quoted in Riley-Smith, *Oxford Illustrated History of the Crusades,* 47.

19. Strayer, "Albigensian Crusades"; Ruthven, "Albigensian Crusades."

20. See Saunders on Genghis Khan's conquest of Iran in *History of the Mongol Conquests*, 56: "The cold and deliberate genocide practised by the Mongols, which has no parallel save that of the ancient Assyrians and the modern Nazis."

21. See the accounts by Kiernan, *Blood and Soil*, 129–133, of Vietnamese massacres of the Cham in 1470 (109), and of Japanese massacres in Korea in 1592: "Kill Koreans one by one and empty the country."

22. Stannard, *American Holocaust*. In "Uniqueness as Denial," Stannard violently attacks the claim that the Nazi genocide of the Jews was "unique," calling such claims "intellectual thuggery" (300) because they do injustice to so many other instances of genocide, such as the extermination of Indians in the Americas.

23. See Barkan, "Genocides of Indigenous Peoples." Lewy, *Nazi Persecution of the Gypsies*, maintains that, some deliberate massacres aside, most casualties among the North American Indians were not intended by the federal and local governments but rather resulted from ignorance and negligence in the face of rampant contagious disease.

24. Chalk and Jonassohn, *History and Sociology of Genocide*, 199; see also the authors' conclusion in the case of the Yuki people: "The governor of California sanctioned a Yuki genocide" (199). On the wars with the Apaches, see Cocker, *Rivers of Blood, Rivers of Gold*, 185–268.

25. See Kiernan, *Blood and Soil*, 249–309.

26. For Namibia and Kenya, see Hull, "Military Culture and the Production of 'Final Solutions'"; Olusoga and Erichsen, *Kaiser's Holocaust;* and Silvester and Gewalt, *Words Cannot Be Found*. For Aceh, see Van 't Veer, *Atjeh-oorlog*. Rummel, *Death by Government*, 403, counts imperial Russia among the "megamurderers," with more than a million victims between 1900 and 1917. And for King Leopold's conquests, see Ascherson, *King Incorporated;* Hochschild, *King Leopold's Ghost;* and Van Reybrouck, *Congo*.

27. See Knight, "Shaka Zulu," 226.

28. Much higher numbers have been mentioned: Jen, *Taiping Revolutionary Movement*, 8: "A total of twenty million died during this period. . . . [Some] accounts give estimates as high as fifty million. . . . The highest figure, is one hundred million, or about a third of China's population at the time"; and Spence, *God's Chinese Son*, xix: From 1853 on, Nanjing remained the base of the Taiping movement "until in 1864—after twenty million people or more in the regions under their sway had lost their lives in battle or from starvation—Hong and the remnants of his army perished in their turn from famine, fire, and sword."

29. For example, Jen, *Taiping Revolutionary Movement*, 425–427: immediately after a massacre of ten thousand rebels who had already surrendered, Nanjing fell and the imperial army slaughtered another sixteen thousand fighters and ten thousand civilians.

30. Whitaker, "Tonghak Rebellion (Korea)."

31. Kiernan, *Blood and Soil*, 2.

32. Collins, *Interaction Ritual Chains*, 29, writes: "If there is a historical pattern, it is that the capacity for violence has increased with the level of social organization. Violence is not primordial, and civilization does not tame it; the opposite is much nearer the truth." The first sentence fits the known facts. The second seems to confuse the individual and the societal level.

33. This is why the more general term for the victims, "unorganized and unarmed people," is preferred to the oft-used expression "noncombatants," a much-contested juridical concept that excludes the mass killing of military men (and women) rendered defenseless. See, however, Sémelin, *Purify and Destroy*, 4, who chooses as his key term *massacre*, "a form of action that is most often collective and aimed at destroying non-combatants."

34. Rummel, *Death by Government*, 31ff.

35. Article II of the United Nations Convention on Genocide defines the term: "acts committed with intent to destroy, in whole or in part, a national, ethnical, racial or religious group" by killing or seriously harming its members, imposing conditions that might result in its physical destruction, preventing births or taking away the children (Charny, *Encyclopedia of Genocide*, 578). The one term missing in the UN definition is precisely *state*, as Kuper, *Genocide*, 161, among others, has pointed out. See also Levene, *Meaning of Genocide*, 42.

36. The Nazi regime was a good case in point. Hitler avoided committing any orders for the deportation and extermination of the Jews to paper. His role as initiating and driving force behind the Holocaust has nevertheless been firmly established. See, e.g., Browning, *Origins of the Final Solution*, esp. 370, 425–427.

37. See chaps. 6 and 7, below.

38. Thus, I do not consider *ethnocide* or *linguicide* or *linguistic genocide* (attempts to destroy the cultural heritage or the language of a group) as instances of mass annihilation.

39. See Chalk and Jonassohn, *History and Sociology of Genocide*, 23: "one-sided mass killing"; and Chirot and McCauley, *Why Not Kill Them All?*, 19: "one group has an overwhelming superiority in power."

Chapter 5. Rwanda

1. Power, *"Problem from Hell"*; Cohen, *States of Denial*; Dallaire, *Shake Hands with the Devil*.

2. See Mamdani, *When Victims Become Killers*.

3. Berkeley, *Graves Are Not Yet Full*, 10.

4. Sagan, *Dawn of Tyranny*, 3–58; Reid, *History of Modern Africa*, esp. 52–60; Lemarchand, *Burundi*; Newbury, *Cohesion of Oppression*; Prunier, *Rwanda Crisis*. For a political history of colonial conquest on the African continent, see Wesseling, *European Colonial Empires*, esp. 147–190.

5. Bäck, "Traditional Rwanda," 30; Trouwborst, "Political Economy of the Interlacustrine States," 99, 105.

6. Vansina, *Antecedents to Modern Rwanda*, 134–135.

7. Vansina, *Antecedents to Modern Rwanda*, 195.

8. See Bayart, *State in Africa*.

9. Straus, *Order of Genocide*, 68.

10. Hoetink, *Two Variants in Caribbean Race Relations*.

11. See Prunier, *Rwanda Crisis*, 5–13, for a review of the early accounts of Tutsi origins.

12. Mamdani, *When Victims Become Killers*, 80.

13. Gourevitch, *We Wish to Inform You*, 56.

14. Mamdani, *When Victims Become Killers*, 41, mentions that certain genetic features differ. Tutsis more often produce the enzyme lactase necessary to break down lactose (milk sugar) and less often carry the gene for sickle cell anemia. Both traits point to a relatively more pastoral and less agricultural heritage among Tutsis than among Hutus, although the two groups practiced agriculture and pastoralism, be it in different proportions. Both genetic traits have been selected for as a result of long-standing *cultural* practices.

15. Bäck, "Traditional Rwanda," 15–33, 18; Lemarchand, *Burundi*, 1–16.

16. De Lame, "Une colline entre mille," 73, on the village of Murundi.

17. Lemarchand, *Burundi*, 30–33.

18. See Dawkins, *Blind Watchmaker*, 199–216.

19. See Blok, *Wittgenstein en Elias*.

20. Malkki, *Purity and Exile*, 71.

21. Newbury, *Cohesion of Oppression*, 115–140.

22. Lemarchand, *Burundi*, 10; see Mamdani, *When Victims Become Killers*, 62–76.

23. Malkki, *Purity and Exile*, 82–88.

24. These phrases were written in Kinyarwanda and French in the Hutu Power review *Kangura*, 6, and are quoted from Chrétien, *Rwanda*, 39–40, translated into English by the author.

25. Chrétien, *Rwanda*, 40.

26. Van Bruggen, *Hedendaagsch fetischisme*, 64–76.

27. Chrétien, *Rwanda*, 98. Translation by the author. Note the use of place-names—i.e., the references to the national map—in constructing a nationwide brotherhood of Hutus.

28. Chrétien, *Rwanda*, 57. For an extensive political history of the genocide, see Des Forges.

29. See Fujii, *Killing Neighbors*, 2–3; Straus, *Order of Genocide*, 7–9; and Mironko, "Social and Political Mechanisms of Mass Murder," 2–3.

30. This is the psychological mechanism Fujii, *Killing Neighbors*, 188, found among the Hutu "Joiners" (participants in the killings).

31. See Kroslak, *Role of France in the Rwandan Genocide*.

32. See Kroslak, *Role of France in the Rwandan Genocide;* Prunier, *Rwanda Crisis*, 281–311; and Ba, *Rwanda*.

33. For eyewitness accounts, see Braeckman, *Rwanda;* Keane, *Season of Blood;* and de Temmerman, *Doden zijn niet dood*.

34. Lemarchand, *Burundi*, 76ff.

35. Sémelin, *Purify and Destroy*, 251–252.

36. Prunier, *Rwanda Crisis*.

37. See Powell, *Barbaric Civilization*.

38. Mironko, "Social and Political Mechanisms of Mass Murder"; Straus, *Order of Genocide*.

39. Straus, *Order of Genocide*, 142.

40. Straus, *Order of Genocide,* 145, cites a Hutu businessman: "They found me there. They began to call me an accomplice. They said they even would eat my cows. . . . *Did they try to forcibly take you?* They tried and I refused. They said that if I didn't go with them, they would cut me, but I refused. *It was possible to refuse?* Yes, if you were not afraid. They threatened me with their machetes." This man finally got away by paying them off.

41. See Straus, *Order of Genocide,* 10: "My findings support 'ordinary men' theories of genocide perpetrators."

42. See Straus, "How Many Perpetrators Were There?"

43. Kimonyo's title, *Rwanda: Un génocide populaire.* All in all, out of 3.4 million inhabitants between fifteen and fifty-four years of age, almost half a million Rwandans were indicted for violent crimes by judicial courts or village tribunals ("Gacaca," 8).

44. See African Rights, *Not So Innocent.*

45. Many of these testimonies were recorded immediately after the events in African Rights, *Not So Innocent.*

46. Fujii, *Killing Neighbors,* 185.

47. Mironko, "Social and Political Mechanisms of Mass Murder," 197.

48. Fujii, *Killing Neighbors,* 172.

49. For detailed descriptions, see the anthropological account by Fujii, *Killing Neighbors,* 171ff.

50. Mironko, "Social and Political Mechanisms of Mass Murder," 200.

51. This notion is discussed at length in chap. 6.

52. Fujii, *Killing Neighbors,* 55.

53. Straus, *Order of Genocide,* 161. Kimonyo, *Rwanda,* 8, mentions that while hundreds of thousands of Hutus were busy chasing and killing Tutsis, only fifty thousand were part of the Rwandese army that confronted the RPF marching toward Kigali.

54. Straus, *Order of Genocide,* 11: "They chose genocide as an extreme, vengeful, and desperate strategy to win a war that they were losing." Even this interpretation attributes too much to the Hutu Power cabal in government, since there was no way the "strategy" could ever improve the odds of winning the war. Rather, as Kimonyo, *Rwanda,* 504, writes: "For the architects of the genocide, the continuation of the massacres was more important than putting a halt to a war they were losing." See also Des Forges, *Leave None to Tell the Story,* 344ff.

55. This is discussed in detail in chaps. 6 and 7.

56. Fujii, *Killing Neighbors,* 55.

57. For a full discussion of the compartmentalizing process and mass annihilation, see chaps. 6 and 7, below.

58. Hatzfeld, *Machete Season.*

59. Fujii, *Killing Neighbors,* 175–177.

Chapter 6. Genocidal Regimes and the Compartmentalization of Society

1. Tilly, *Coercion, Capital, and European States,* 20–28.

2. Elias, "On the Process of Civilisation," 403–417, called this "the social con-

straint to self-constraint." The use of the term *regulation* in place of *constraint* is meant to convey that what is at stake is not only reining in impulsive behavior, e.g., aggression, but also *overcoming* inclinations, often equally impulsive, that inhibit certain actions, such as fear, shame, and pity.

3. See Muchembled, *Histoire de la violence;* Pinker, *Better Angels of Our Nature;* and Body-Gendrot and Spierenburg, *Violence in Europe.*

4. See Bourdieu, *Raisons pratiques,* 107–120, 186–200; and Bourdieu, *Sur l'état.*

5. Shaw, "General Hybridity of War and Genocide," has argued that the dividing line between "war" and "genocide" is rather arbitrary. The distinction between "war" and "mass annihilation" as defined here is not. It is gradual, depending by the degree of asymmetry between the two sides.

6. Conversely, the attempt to prevent or cure disease is perceived as a battle, a fight against nonhuman pathogens; see Sontag, *Illness as Metaphor.*

7. Staub, "Psychology of Bystanders, Perpetrators and Heroic Helpers," 24. And he adds: passive bystanders "encourage perpetrators, who often interpret silence as support for their policies" (27).

8. Cohen, *States of Denial,* 153, qualifies this as "double discourse": "the balance between making state terror known, yet hiding or denying its details."

9. De Swaan, "Terror as a Governmental Service," 44.

10. See also Kürsat-Ahlers, "Über das Toten in Genoziden," 184.

11. Klee, Dressen, and Riess, *"The Good Old Days,"* 107–137.

12. Browning, *Ordinary Men;* Desbois, *Holocaust by Bullets;* Snyder, *Bloodlands.*

13. Sereny, *Into That Darkness,* 193.

14. Sereny, *Into That Darkness,* 238.

15. See Desbois, *Holocaust by Bullets,* 183, on the German extermination of the Jews in the Ukraine. See also chap. 5, above, on Rwanda.

16. Sofsky, *Traktat über die Gewalt,* 104: "Der Unbeteiligte ist keineswegs ahnungslos. Er weiss so viel, wie er wissen will. Wass er nicht weiss, das will er nicht wissen. Das aber heisst, dass er sehr wohl genug weiss, um zu wissen dass er nicht mehr wissen will."

17. "Er macht sich nicht wissen," a survivor's son told me, quoting his father.

18. Danner, "America and the Bosnia Genocide," 59.

19. Levene, *Meaning of Genocide,* 121, 124–125. Levene, "Changing Face of Mass Murder," 446, on the killings of Armenians: "While participants may be allowed or enabled to inflict whatever disorganised tortures they can dream up, the context in which they do so is an organised one." See also Dadrian, *History of the Armenian Genocide;* and Sorabji, "Very Modern War."

20. Elias, *Germans,* 403–433.

21. This is a variation on the psychoanalytic expression "regression in service of the ego"; see Ernst Kris, *Psychoanalytic Explorations in Art,* 312: "Under certain conditions the ego regulates regression."

22. Sofsky, *Traktat über die Gewalt,* 226, radically rejects the notion of regression in this context: "that the unleashing of absolute violence is not a regression to the primitive, primal condition of the psyche [*Seele*]. Violence itself is a product of human culture, a result of the culture experiment."

23. Sémelin, "Rationalités de la violence extrême," speaks of the "'instrumentalisation de l'irrationnel." Or see Friedländer, *Years of Extermination*, 472, on Nazi Germany: "the epitome of the regime's propaganda style: the unleashing of demented passion controlled by the most careful staging and orchestration."

24. See De Swaan, "Dyscivilization, Mass Extermination and the State," some parts of which are reproduced here.

25. Elias, *Germans*, 41.

26. Elias, *Germans*, ch. 4.

27. Sofsky, *Ordnung des Terrors*, 262: the more secluded the perpetrators are, the more their norms will prevail without question. Sémelin, "Rationalités de la violence extrême," 123, speaks of a "situation de huis clos," where violence can exceed any limit. But, as has been noted before: seclusion is not a *necessary* condition for extreme collective violence.

28. See Goffman, *Presentation of Self*, on "front stage" and "backstage."

29. See an unpublished report by Bas Heerma van Voss on testimony in the trial of Žigić about the conditions under which he could enter the camp and volunteer to kill and torture at his own whim.

30. These spatial aspects are sometimes mentioned in accounts, but almost always in passing and without comment.

31. Sanders, "Evil Within," 35, quoting from an eyewitness interview.

32. Hinton, *Why Did They Kill?*, 155–156.

33. Sanders, "Evil Within," 36–37.

34. Wacquant, "Elias in the Dark Ghetto."

35. It takes "only one wrong turn" for people to become enmeshed in the decivilizing compartment of the ghetto, as Tom Wolfe shows in *Bonfire of the Vanities*.

36. Fletcher, *Violence and Civilization*, 286, defines civilization as "an expansion in the scope of mutual identification within and between groups."

37. Mann, *Dark Side of Democracy*, 5.

38. Levene, "Changing Face of Mass Murder," 450.

39. The sarcastic title of a collection of letters, diaries, and photos by Holocaust perpetrators: Klee, Dressen, and Riess, *"The Good Old Days."*

40. Sémelin, *Purify and Destroy*, 45–48.

41. Collins, *Violence*, 88.

42. Collins, *Violence*, 127–132, 97. Collins excludes massacres perpetrated on the express orders of superior commanders (e.g., the German mass execution of Jews behind the Eastern Front). Since such orders are usually tenaciously denied, in practice this criterion is unsuitable to distinguish one case from another (99–100).

43. Van Doorn and Hendrix, *Nederlands/ Indonesisch conflict*, 221ff.

44. Recent facts may be found in the (interim) reports by the UN Commission of Inquiry on Human Rights in the Democratic People's Republic of Korea: http://www.ohchr.org/Documents/HRBodies/HRCouncil/CoIDPRK/Report/coi-dprk-q-and-a.pdf.

45. Horowitz, *Deadly Ethnic Riot*, 1: "A deadly ethnic riot is an intense, sudden, though not necessarily wholly unplanned, lethal attack by civilian members of one

ethnic group on civilian members of another ethnic group, the victims chosen because of their group membership." See also p. 20.

Chapter 7. The Four Modes of Mass Annihilation

1. Van 't Veer, *Atjeh-oorlog;* see Reid, *Contest for North Sumatra,* x; see also Schulte Nordholt, "Genealogy of Violence," on the "imperialist expansion of colonial rule" throughout the archipelago during the same period.

2. Schulte Nordholt, "Genealogy of Violence," 36.

3. Wesseling, *European Colonial Empires,* 168.

4. Ascherson, *King Incorporated,* 250ff; Berkeley, *Graves Are Not Yet Full,* 9; Hochschild, *King Leopold's Ghost,* 232ff.; Vangroenweghe, *Rood Rubber,* 64ff.

Reybrouck, *Congo,* 109–110, speaks of "a hecatomb, a carnage on an unbelievable scale, not intended as such, although it could have been understood much more quickly as *collateral damage* of a perfidious, rapacious policy of exploitation, a sacrifice on the altar of a pathological lust for profit" (emphasis in original). Even this assessment is apologetic: the authorities, the king foremost, knew very well what went on and deliberately allowed villagers who did not collect enough rubber to be executed in order to terrorize the survivors into exerting themselves to death in meeting the ever-rising quotas.

5. Wesseling, *European Colonial Empires,* 169.

6. Van den Braembussche, "Silence of Belgium," discusses the blanket denial of the "Holocaust" in Congo in Belgian collective memory.

7. Kiernan, *Blood and Soil,* 35–37; Silvester and Gewald, *Words Cannot Be Found;* Olusoga and Erichsen, *Kaiser's Holocaust,* 282–292; Lindquist, *Exterminate All the Brutes.*

8. Rummel, *Death by Government,* 403.

9. See Katsuichi, *Nanking Massacre,* 285; and Chang, *Rape of Nanking.* For once, Rummel, *China's Bloody Century,* 145, comes up with a lower estimate: two hundred thousand casualties. He emphasizes, however, that such massacres happened each time the Japanese army conquered new territory.

10. Katsuichi, *Nanking Massacre,* 243–244.

11. Rummel, *China's Bloody Century,* 137–168. See Fogel, *Nanjing Massacre;* and Chang, *Rape of Nanking,* on silence and denial in Japan.

12. See Mann's chapter "Genocidal Democracies of the New World" in *Dark Side of Democracy,* 70–110. French North Africa and South Africa might also be relevant cases.

13. Mann, *Dark Side of Democracy,* 109.

14. These settler democracies ("ethnocracies") are the crowning evidence for Mann's thesis on the "dark side of democracy."

15. Gilly, *Mexican Revolution,* 83. For a discussion of the social and political implications of the revolution, see Wolf, "Mexico," *Peasant Wars of the Twentieth Century,* 3–50.

16. McCaa, "Missing Millions."

17. Browning, *Origins of the Final Solution*, 314.

18. Desbois, *Holocaust by Bullets*, vii.

19. Browning, *Origins of the Final Solution*, 299.

20. This later phase of the Nazi extermination is discussed in chap. 5, above.

21. Snyder, *Bloodlands*, 185.

22. See Wielek, *Oorlog die Hitler won*.

23. Campbell and Brenner, *Death Squads in Global Perspective*, 153.

24. Weitz, *Century of Genocide*, 69.

25. Naimark, *Fires of Hatred*, 55-107.

26. See Wheatcroft, "Scale and Nature of German and Soviet Repression." Snyder, *Bloodlands*, discusses the period 1933-1945, when both Hitler and Stalin were in power, and concludes on the basis of recent evidence that about one million people died in the Gulag in those twelve years (and between two and three million during the entire Stalinist period of 1928-1953). The Great Terror (of 1937) and other shooting actions killed another million people. The largest catastrophe was the famine of 1930-1933, which all in all took five million lives. There is little doubt that the large majority died because of deliberately imposed starvation. Compare Werth, "Stalinist State Violence," whose estimates are not much different.

27. Weitz, *Century of Genocide*, 64.

28. Marples, "Ethnic Issues in the Famine of 1932-33," 515. See also the most careful discussion of these issues in Ellman, "Soviet Repression Statistics," 411, who mentions "3.3 million Soviet citizens (mostly Ukrainians) deliberately starved by their own government in Soviet Ukraine in 1932-1933." On the legal attribution of (criminal) responsibility for famines to governments, see Marcus, "Famine Crimes in International Law."

29. See also Snyder, *Bloodlands*, 21-58. Werth, "Stalinist State Violence," mentions a total estimate of "circa 6 million deaths" in the years 1931-1933 from famine in Kazakhstan, western Siberia, the north Caucasus, and the Ukraine.

30. See Rummel, *China's Bloody Century*.

31. Dikötter, *Mao's Great Famine*, 179n.

32. Becker, *Hungry Ghosts*, xi, mentions an estimate, based on the analysis of Chinese mortality statistics published in the mid-1980s, of thirty million people who starved to death, "far more than anyone, including the most militant critics of the Chinese Communist Party had ever imagined." He concludes that this famine "was entirely man-made" (273). Dikötter, *Mao's Great Famine*, 325ff., puts the "final tally" at forty-five million on the basis of internal Communist Party reports that have since become available. And this number may still be on the conservative side: one independent Chinese expert puts the figure at fifty-five million (334).

33. A procession of Western luminaries and China experts allowed themselves to be fooled by the Great Leap Forward or lustily lied along with their Chinese hosts: Felix Greene, Edgar Snow, Gunnar Myrdal, Han Suyin, François Mitterrand, and Anna Louise Strong (and, for that matter, Joris Ivens and W. F. Wertheim). See Becker, *Hungry Ghosts*, 287-306.

34. White, *Politics of Chaos*, 40. See Gong, "Logic of Repressive Action."

35. Thurston, "Urban Violence During the Cultural Revolution," 140. Su, *Collective Killings in Rural China*, 2, mentions that in the countryside villages alone "at least four hundred thousand and possibly as many as three million" people were killed.

36. Su, *Collective Killings in Rural China*, 154.

37. Wachsmann, "Dynamics of Destruction," 19.

38. Howard-Hassman, "State-Induced Famine and Penal Starvation," 153.

39. Howard-Hassman, "State-Induced Famine and Penal Starvation," 151.

40. Haggard and Noland, *Famine in North Korea*, 50, 169ff.

41. Haggard and Noland, *Famine in North Korea*, 153–154.

42. See Amartya Sen, "Preface," in Haggard and Noland, *Famine in North Korea*.

43. Fings, "Public Face of the Camps," 110.

44. Elisabeth Noelle-Neuman quoted in Sémelin, *Purify and Destroy*, 95.

45. De Swaan, "Terror as a Governmental Service."

46. Suharto alleged that President Sukarno's men had brutally murdered and mutilated General Yani and five other senior army generals in order to forestall a coup attempt on their part. However, Yani and his "co-conspirators" were unlikely putschists as they were not squarely opposed to Sukarno or the PKI (Communist Party of Indonesia). A plausible scenario is that they were killed by Suharto's men. Suharto then blamed the Sukarno regime and the PKI for the murders as a pretext to take power and create an atmosphere of "killed or be killed" that set the tone for the subsequent mass extermination. See Cribb, "Unresolved Problems in the Indonesian Killings of 1965–1966"; Scott, "United States and the Overthrow of Sukarno."

47. Cribb, "Problems in the Historiography of the Killings in Indonesia," 22–23.

48. Cribb, "Genocide in Indonesia"; Colombijn and Lindblad, *Roots of Violence in Indonesia;* Robinson, *Dark Side of Paradise;* Anderson, *Violence and the State in Indonesia.*

49. Van Langenberg, "Gestapu and State Power in Indonesia," 58.

50. Hughes, *End of Sukarno*, 180.

51. Hughes, *End of Sukarno*, 180.

52. Young, "Local and National Influences in the Violence of 1965," 80.

53. Cribb et al., "Mass Killings in Bali," 241.

54. Robinson, *Dark Side of Paradise*, 298.

55. Dwyer and Santikarma, "'When the World Turned to Chaos.'"

56. For the period from 1960 until the peace agreement of 1996, the total number of executions and "disappearances" has been estimated at 200,000, and in the final years from 1978 alone at 132,000. See also Grandin, "Politics by Other Means," 198.

57. From testimonies quoted in Grandin, "Politics by Other Means," 121.

58. Grandin, "Politics by Other Means," 13.

59. See Jonas, "Guatemala"; Totten, "Genocide in Guatemala"; Valentino, Huth, and Balch-Lindsay, "'Draining the Sea.'"

60. *New York Times*, February 3, 2013. In 2011 four "Ksibiles," counterguerrilla soldiers, were sentenced to six thousand years of prison.

61. Gourevitch, *We Wish to Inform You*, 156.

62. Fenichel, *Psychoanalytic Theory of Neurosis,* 542–543; Corradi, "Turning Passive into Active." In children's play, as in adult dreams and fantasies, and not so seldom in real life, painful or frightful events, remembered or anticipated, are transformed into scenes in which the person actively commits or inflicts something similar on others (or sometimes even on him- or herself), in order to avoid the anxiety that comes with helplessness.

63. Levene, *Meaning of Genocide,* 35: "Genocide occurs when a state, perceiving the integrity of its agenda to be threatened by an aggregate population—defined by the state as an organic collectivity, or series of collectivities—seeks to remedy the situation by the systematic, *en masse,* physical elimination of that aggregate, *in toto,* or until it is no longer perceived to represent a threat." On the face of it, this is a more rational perspective, but the state's perception of the threat may have little or no foundation in the facts.

64. Dadrian, *History of the Armenian Genocide,* 155, basing himself on an analysis of French diplomatic documents of the time.

65. Akçam, *Shameful Act,* 102–108.

66. Üngör, *Making of Modern Turkey,* 55–106; see also Mann, *Dark Side of Democracy,* 168–173.

67. Üngör, *Making of Modern Turkey,* 108–122.

68. Dadrian, "Armenians in Ottoman Turkey and the Armenian Genocide," 74–75.

69. Üngör, *Making of Modern Turkey,* 71–100.

70. Dadrian, "Armenians in Ottoman Turkey and the Armenian Genocide," 74–75.

71. Enver Pasha, the leader of the ruling party, confirmed the government's responsibility for the killings (Melson, "Provocation or Nationalism," 66). In 1919, during the short-lived postwar rule of Sultan Mehmet V (and under pressure of the victorious British), a tribunal convicted the entire leadership of the wartime cabinet of a systematic attempt to destroy the Turkish Armenian population in its entirety and sentenced them to death. Three officials were indeed executed, but in the subsequent period of political and military confusion, the main culprits escaped punishment, and most assumed positions of power and responsibility in the successor regime. See Üngör and Polatel, *Confiscation and Destruction,* 96.

72. See Hovannisian, *Armenian Genocide,* 28.

73. Üngör, *Making of Modern Turkey,* 51ff.

74. Mann, *Dark Side of Democracy,* 8: "For the Young Turks, however, the final solution to the Armenian problem seems much more contingent, flowing out of what they saw as their suddenly desperate situation in 1915." See also 145–153.

75. Lewy, *Nazi Persecution of the Gypsies,* 222, quotes estimates of the number of victims: some two hundred thousand out of a Gypsy population of eight hundred thousand to one million in territories under Nazi rule. He also mentions higher estimates, such as half a million casualties by an official spokesman for the federal German government. Lewy, however, does not consider the extermination of the Gypsies

a "genocide" or even part of the "Holocaust," a term he reserves for the extermination of the Jews. For an opposing view, see among others Hancock, "Responses to the Porrajmos," 81.

76. Burrin, *Hitler and the Jews*, 97, writes: "There is a world of difference in the thinking behind the covert and rational organization of the genocide and the open use of the most savage violence [behind the Eastern Front]."

77. Snyder, *Bloodlands*, 427.

78. Gerlach, "Wannsee Conference," esp. 760.

79. Burrin, *Hitler and the Jews*, 79, writes: "The years of success, at any rate, did not bring Hitler to decide on extermination. The departure of the European Jews, and their confinement in a distant territory, would suffice to solve the problem." But then the odds of war turned against him: "[Hitler] would conduct this exercise of vengeance, as it turned out, with mounting determination as the situation worsened, and he advanced toward an apocalyptic end" (147). See also p. 151: "Confronted by the probable failure of his plan for world domination, he burned his bridges by deciding to destroy those responsible for his downfall; he would persevere in the military conflict and in the massacre of the innocents until he had reduced Germany to ruins." And p. 152: "Here once again, Hitler was master of the situation." The Nazi regime had turned passive into active in a huge campaign of autodestructive destruction. For an extensive presentation of the documentary evidence of the Nazi decision-making process on the extermination of the Jews of Europe, see Brayard, *"Solution finale de la question juive."*

80. Wachsmann, "Dynamics of Destruction," 32.

81. Goldhagen, *Hitler's Willing Executioners*, 371.

82. According to Fromm, *Anatomy of Human Destructiveness*, 384, possibly Hitler never thought Germany would win the war and did not even really want victory. See also Haffner, *Meaning of Hitler;* and Von der Dunk, *Voorbij de verboden drempel*, 172–176.

83. Jaffrelot, *Syndrome pakistanais*, 138, 240.

84. Horowitz, *Deadly Ethnic Riot*, 164; Rummel, *Death by Government*, 334, puts their number at 150,000.

85. Chalk and Jonassohn, *History and Sociology of Genocide*, 396, mention "between one million and three million" casualties. Baxter, "Bangladesh/East Pakistan," 118, states: "Estimates by Bangla Deshi sources" amount to "up to three million." Similar estimates are in Totten and Bartrop, *Dictionary of Genocide*, 1:34–35; and in Charny, *Encyclopedia of Genocide*, 1:115–116. The (West) Pakistani campaign is qualified as "genocide" in both. See also Mascarenhas, *Rape of Bangla Desh*.

86. Since 2010, there have been contested attempts to bring some of the major perpetrators to trial before a court, so far resulting in a few major convictions, some of which are being appealed before the supreme court.

87. In December 2013, after a controversial trial, Abdul Quader Molla, one of the leaders of the pro-Pakistani Jamaat-e-Islami Party in Bangladesh, was hanged for his part in the massacres of 1973. Four other leaders were also condemned to death.

88. See Hinton, *Why Did They Kill?;* Heder, "Cambodia."

89. Kiernan, *Pol Pot Regime*, 24.

90. Kiernan, *Blood and Soil*, 547.

91. Heder, "Cambodia," 142.

92. Hinton, "Why Did You Kill?" 114.

93. By February 2014, only Comrade Deuch (Kaing Guek Eav), the director of the S21 Tol Sleng interrogation center, where almost no detainee survived, had received a definitive prison sentence, for life. Trials against some major instigators of the mass killings have started but have been hampered by interference from the present regime.

94. Chirot, "Introduction," 4, speaks of an "auto-genocide": "The Vietnamese were identified as the main enemy, and the fiercely barricaded Khmer Rouge leadership lived in deadly fear of being exterminated by the Vietnamese."

95. See also Kleinen, "Cambodia."

96. Sémelin, *Purify and Destroy*.

97. Zwaan, "Crisis and Genocide in Yugoslavia," 123.

98. There is another area of Europe, equally torn asunder by the border between the two most numerous religious groupings of the subcontinent, carved up, moreover, by the divide between the largest language families of Europe, and, to boot, parceled up in several state territories. And yet this region—the Low Countries—may well be the most peaceful in Europe. Apparently, such historical chasms are not sufficient cause for recurrent and bloody conflagrations. On the contrary, the fact that in the Low Countries these "cleavages" do not coincide but cross-cut may help to prevent a mobilization across a single front, whereas in the former Yugoslavia state territories, "nationalities," and "religious affiliations" mostly did coincide and prompted partisan division on all three dimensions at once. See Lipset and Rokkan, "Cleavage Structures, Party Systems, and Voter Alignments."

99. Rummel, *Death by Government*, 344. See Tomasevitch, *War and Revolution in Yugoslavia*, 259ff.; and Mann, *Dark Side of Democracy*, 274–276.

100. Rummel, *Death by Government*, 354–357; these are very rough estimates.

101. Saideman, *Ties That Divide*, 122–131, 141.

102. See among others Mann, *Dark Side of Democracy*, 356–358.

103. Tomasevitch, *War and Revolution in Yugoslavia*, 256: "The peoples of the South Slav nations grew accustomed to the use of terror as a means of dealing with an enemy."

104. The Dutch government commissioned an extensive report on the events in and around Srebrenica (where the United Nations had stationed Dutch units at the time, NIOD, 2002; English version at www.srebrenica.nl).

105. Mann, *Dark Side of Democracy*, 353, 356.

106. Kaldor, *New and Old Wars*, 53.

107. Kaldor, *New and Old Wars*, 46–59.

108. See De Swaan, "State of Outrage."

109. Schelling, *Strategy of Conflict*, 90, speaks of a "focal point" in which the expectations of all participants converge. See also Horowitz, *Deadly Ethnic Riot*, 268.

110. MacDonogh, *After the Reich;* Naimark, *Fires of Hatred;* Snyder, *Bloodlands*.

111. Respectively, Snyder, *Bloodlands;* and Mann, *Dark Side of Democracy,* 353.

112. Lowe, *Savage Continent,* 243; Snyder, *Bloodlands,* 331.

113. The fatality rate of German POWs in Soviet camps was 11.8% as compared to 57.5% for Soviet soldiers in German captivity; see Snyder, *Bloodlands,* 318, 181. See also Bartov, *Hitler's Army,* 78ff.: 3.3 million out of 5.7 million Soviet POWs died in German captivity. And see Snyder, *Bloodlands,* 323–324. Snyder mentions 3.1 million Soviet prisoners of war killed in German captivity and comments that this in no way served the German war effort; on the contrary, it strengthened the fighting spirit of Soviet troops, who would fight to death rather than be taken prisoner (184).

114. Snyder, *Bloodlands,* estimates that almost a million German civilians died at the end of the war, some 700,000 as a result of mob violence and expulsion (332), another 200,000 in Soviet and Polish camps (318). According to Mann, *Dark Side of Democracy,* 353, "Over 2 million died en route, the targets of murderous vengeance by the locals."

115. For the "vengeance" perpetrated on Germans by Poles and Czechs, see Lowe, *Savage Continent,* 125–144.

116. Schlögel, "Nach der Rechthaberei," 12: "Wie spricht man über Verbrechen im Schatten eines anderen Verbrechens?"

117. Khan, *Great Partition,* 206ff.

118. It became the Islamic Republic of Pakistan in 1956.

119. And most rioters implicitly trusted that local authorities would let them get away with murder. Horowitz, *Deadly Ethnic Riot,* 350, quoting Richard Lambert, "Hindu Muslim Riots" (PhD diss., University of Pennsylvania, 1951), 219–20.

120. Talbot and Singh, *Partition of India,* 89; see also 84ff.

121. Kumar, "Settling Partition Hostilities."

122. Horowitz, *Deadly Ethnic Riot,* 537, quoting Jack Katz, *Ordinary People and Extraordinary Evil,* 180, who in turn quotes Franklin Zimring and James Zuehl, "Victim Injury and Death," *Journal of Legal Studies* 15 (1986): 30.

123. Horowitz, *Deadly Ethnic Riot,* 537.

124. Talbot and Singh, *Partition of India,* 21, and see 66–67. See Khan, *Great Partition,* 207: "It is beyond doubt that nationalist politicians and enthusiasts from leading political parties colluded with, and became tangled up in, the massacres."

125. A similar pattern of complicity, in this case on the part of the Gujarati state government in the "communal riots" of 2002, is revealed by, among others, Berenschot, *Riot Politics.* It became known because the all-Indian government did not condone the bloodshed, while Indian media and the federal police reported on it.

Chapter 8. Genocidal Perpetrators and the Compartmentalization of Personality

Epigraph: Frijda, "Emotions and Collective Violence," 14; see also Hoffman, *Empathy and Moral Development,* 282.

1. Hinton, *Why Did They Kill?,* 279.

2. Waller, *Becoming Evil*, 228.

3. Steiner, "SS Yesterday and Today," 431n.

4. Elias, *Germans*.

5. Goldhagen, *Hitler's Willing Executioners*, 32, emphasis in original.

6. See the polemic in Browning, *Ordinary Men*, "Afterword," 191–223; and in Waller, *Becoming Evil*, 37–41.

7. Welzer, "Mass Murder and Moral Code," 17.

8. Roth, "Hearts of Darkness," 225.

9. The expression is used in a somewhat different sense as in McAdam, Tarrow, and Tilly, *Dynamics of Contention*, 81–99, esp. 84, where it refers to "incentives for people to undertake collective action."

10. Erber, "Perpetrators with a Clear Conscience," 290ff.

11. Walter, "Politics of Decivilization," 304.

12. For similar reasons, many Germans continued to support Hitler against all misgivings, because turning away from him would be tantamount to recognizing their mistake. Neitzel and Welzer, *Soldaten*, 270.

13. Hatzfeld, *Machete Season*, 50; Snyder, *Bloodlands*, 205: "During the first try, my hand trembled a bit as I shot, but one gets used to it. By the tenth try, I aimed calmly and shot surely at the many women, children and infants."

14. Sémelin, *Purify and Destroy*, 226ff.

15. Frijda, "Emotions and Collective Violence," 16.

16. McNeill, *Keeping Together in Time*, 147–149. Collins, *Interaction Ritual Chains*, discusses the emotional energy and collective bonding that comes from acting together in "interaction ritual chains."

17. Milgram, *Obedience to Authority*, 132–134.

18. This notion is very close to the psychoanalytic idea of surrender of the superego to an external authority, coupled to the unleashing of the inward superego aggression on outward targets indicated by the authority. See Pohl, "Normalität und Pathologie," 175.

19. Steiner, "SS Yesterday and Today," 432.

20. Staub, "Psychology of Bystanders, Perpetrators and Heroic Helpers," 21 (emphasis in original).

21. Lifton, *Nazi Doctors*, 492–493.

22. For example, Kimonyo, *Rwanda;* and Hatzfeld, *Machete Season*.

23. Horowitz, *Deadly Ethnic Riot*, 265–266. He adds: "That ordinary people rather than deviants engage in deadly riots is probably related to the deindividuation that occurs in crowds, but it also suggests that the violence has social support, otherwise respectable people would not participate, and perhaps more important, could not resume ordinary life, free of social sanction, after the facts." See also Staub, "Psychology of Bystanders, Perpetrators and Heroic Helpers," on self-selection.

24. Hilberg, *Perpetrators, Victims, Bystanders*, 51. In part 1, Hilberg presents a stunning array of vignettes of the perpetrators (3–102).

25. See Dicks, *Licensed Mass Murder;* Mann, *Dark Side of Democracy;* De Mildt, *In the Name of the People;* Orth, *Konzentrationslager-SS;* Steiner, "SS Yesterday and

Today"; Van Roekel, *Nederlandse Vrijwilligers in de Waffen SS;* and Welzer, *Täter.* Dicks discusses a rare collection of "autobiographies" written in 1936 by militants who wanted to join the Nazi Party: they strikingly differ in tone from the trial documents that are the source of almost all historical research, since the applicants present themselves as ideological enthusiasts and militants eager to join the movement. By 1936, the Nazi regime was engaged in terror, not yet in mass annihilation. See also Mann, *Dark Side of Democracy,* 168–173, on Turkish perpetrators.

26. Mann, *Dark Side of Democracy,* 359ff.

27. Steiner, "SS Yesterday and Today," 433: In 1938, only 1 percent of SS men had more than a high school diploma.

28. See also Hilberg, *Perpetrators, Victims, Bystanders,* 65–74, for an enumeration of instances of complicity and corruption of professional standards by lawyers and physicians involved in the annihilation of Jews.

29. See Sémelin, *Purify and Destroy,* 81–89, and Mamdani, *When Victims Become Killers,* 226–227, on Rwanda; Cribb, "Genocide in Indonesia," and Crouch, *Army and Politics in Indonesia,* 156, on Indonesia; and De Mildt, *In the Name of the People,* 308–310.

30. Steiner, "SS Yesterday and Today," 431–434.

31. Mann, *Dark Side of Democracy,* 278.

32. For example, Neitzel and Welzer, *Soldaten,* 45: "It makes a difference who and with which personal make up is confronted with what sort of situation. But the weight of these variations must not be overestimated."

33. Browning, *Ordinary Men,* 41–42; Goldhagen, *Hitler's Willing Executioners,* 203.

34. For example, Goldhagen, *Hitler's Willing Executioners,* 222.

35. For example, Klee, Dressen, and Riess, *"The Good Old Days,"* 126ff.

36. See chap. 2, above.

37. Orth, *Konzentrationslager-SS,* 251–252, remarks that survivors who had experienced such favors often were not aware how the same guard mistreated other inmates elsewhere.

38. See chap. 3, above.

39. For a helpful overview of the bias in judicial documents, see De Mildt, *In the Name of the People,* 40–48.

40. Christopher Browning, conversation with author, January 28, 2012.

41. Dresden, *Vervolging, vernietiging, literatuur,* 185: 'Zij hadden eens en voor altijd gekozen voor het niet kiezen."

42. Dicks, *Licensed Mass Murder,* 112: Höss called himself "an unknowing cog in the great extermination machine created by the Third Reich." Dicks quotes an especially perverse killer as saying: "I came into the general SS," and comments: "The wording conveys a sense of passivity, rather than of his own choosing" (160).

43. Neitzel and Welzer, *Soldaten,* 177, 183: German military in British captivity were secretly recorded while talking among themselves. Speaking about the horrors of the extermination of the Jews, they worried what would happen to themselves when "the world will take revenge." They never expressed feelings of contrition or guilt. But then, they hardly voiced any feelings at all (209ff.).

44. Cesarani, *Eichmann,* 367, on Eichmann: "But he never fully repented." There are, however, exceptions: see Naumann, *Auschwitz,* 262, on Hans Stark's repentance in the Frankfurt Auschwitz trial. Before the International Criminal Tribunal for the former Yugoslavia, defendants Dragan Nikolić, Dragan Obrenović, and Milan Babić apologized and repented. Their sincerity is hard to judge since the accused may have hoped that their statements would gain them a shorter sentence. Here, e.g., is Obrenović: "I am to blame for everything I did at that time and for what I did not, protecting the prisoners. . . . Thousands of innocent victims perished. . . . I bear part of the responsibility for this. Our guilt is individual, not of a nation" (see "Statements of Guilt: Dragan Obrenović," at http://www.youtube.com/watch?v=gjWmkkp9g5I, and several related sites under "ICTY statements of guilt").

45. Lifton, *Nazi Doctors,* 502. See also Cribb, "Genocide in Indonesia," 16, on the Indonesian mass killers of 1965: "There is evidence enough that plenty of mass murderers remain unaffected by what they do." And see the documentary film directed by Joshua Oppenheimer, *The Act of Killing (Jagal),* 2012.

46. Klee, Dressen, and Riess, *"The Good Old Days,"* 154; see also the statement by a member of an extermination squad: "I still recall today the complete terror of the Jews when they first caught sight of the bodies as they reached the top edge of the ravine. Many Jews cried out in terror. It's almost impossible to imagine what nerves of steel it took to carry out that dirty work down there. It was horrible" (67).

47. Frijda, "Emotions and Collective Violence," 21–24.

48. Frijda, "Emotions and Collective Violence," 21. See also Baumeister, *Evil,* 245: "Maximum cruelty makes use of empathy without sympathy. To hurt someone you must know what that person's sensitivities and vulnerabilities are, without having compassion or pity for that person's suffering."

49. Fonagy et al., *Affect Regulation, Mentalization, and the Development of the Self;* Allen and Fonagy, *Handbook of Mentalization-Based Treatment.*

50. Jeremy Holmes quoted in Allen and Fonagy, *Handbook of Mentalization-Based Treatment,* 31–32.

51. Allen and Fonagy, *Handbook of Mentalization-Based Treatment,* 12; Frijda, *Emotions,* 2008, 55n67.

52. Fonagy et al., *Affect Regulation, Mentalization, and the Development of the Self,* 171. The "mother" denotes whoever is the primary caretaker of the infant.

53. Allen and Fonagy, *Handbook of Mentalization-Based Treatment,* 13. Allen continues: "Sometimes when attempting quickly to convey the gist of mentalizing, I point out that if we extended the concept of empathy to include empathy for oneself, the terms would be nearly synonymous" (13).

54. Hoffman, *Empathy and Moral Development,* 29. Hoffman explains altruism on the basis of empathy.

55. Allen and Fonagy, *Handbook of Mentalization-Based Treatment,* 12, distinguish empathy from *emotional contagion,* in which there is no "self-other differentiation."

56. Frijda, *Laws of Emotion,* 53.

57. Baron-Cohen, *Zero Degrees of Empathy,* 64 (emphasis in original).

58. Gomperts, "Dysmentalization and Mentalization," 2002.

59. Tomasello, *Why We Cooperate*, discussing the evolutionary and neurological roots of helping behavior, stresses that children have a genetic predisposition to help others, shaped by socialization: "But then they learn to be selective about whom to help, inform, and share with" (43). Hoffman, *Empathy and Moral Development*, 206ff., speaks of "familiarity bias" in restricting empathy to the members of "in-groups."

60. The "fragility of compassion": Frijda, "Emotions and Collective Violence," 14; the "erosion of empathy": Baron-Cohen, *Zero Degrees of Empathy*, 6.

61. Grossman, *On Killing;* Bar and Ben-Ari, "Israeli Snipers in the Al-Aqsa Intifada."

62. See, however, the documentary films on Cambodian perpetrators by Rithy Panh, *Duch, Master of the Forges of Hell*, 2012, and Rob Lemkin and Thet Sambath, *Enemies of the People*, 2009.

63. In Joshua Oppenheimer's documentary *The Act of Killing* (2012) on gangster perpetrators of the massacres in Sumatra in 1965, one murderer reminisces about the rape of a young girl: "It was hell for her, but it was heaven for me."

64. Schorsch, "Perversion, Liebe, Gewalt," 53, defines sadism as "sexualized destructivity"—that is, a "perverse defense structure that consists in shielding by a sort of dam the magic imaginary world of perversion from social reality." This amounts to a mental compartmentalization. He next points out that in a setting where human beings are dehumanized, made unconditionally dependent and completely defenseless, and where they are declared to be unworthy and dangerous, sadism becomes the normal behavior (56). In other words, social compartmentalization undoes mental compartmentalization once the imaginary world of cruelty has become social reality.

65. Heerma van Voss, "Report on the Case Against Zoran Žigić."

66. Heuer, *Geheime Staatspolizei*, 162–169.

67. Pohl, "Normalität und Pathologie," 175.

68. See Waller, *Becoming Evil*, 119, also quoting De Mildt, *In the Name of the People*, and Steiner, "SS Yesterday and Today," on the perpetrators' relatively easy readaptation after the war.

69. Todorov, *Face à l'extrême*, 145–149.

70. See Levene, *Meaning of Genocide*, 135, on the "superhuman" powers ascribed to Jews and Gypsies as "all-powerful victims."

71. For example, Goldhagen, *Hitler's Willing Executioners*, 338: "In their postwar testimony they are practically devoid of sympathy of the plight of the victims." See also, among others, Overy, *Interrogations*, 188; and Bar-On, *Did Holocaust Perpetrators Feel Guilty in Retrospect?*, 29.

72. Klee, Dressen, and Riess, *"The Good Old Days";* cf. Steiner, "SS Yesterday and Today."

73. Steiner, "SS Yesterday and Today," 416–417.

74. Bar-On, *Did Holocaust Perpetrators Feel Guilty in Retrospect?*, 8–11, 13.

75. Bar-On, *Did Holocaust Perpetrators Feel Guilty in Retrospect?*, 14.

76. Holocaust survivors, on the contrary, did confide their tales of suffering in

the privacy of the psychotherapeutic compartment during the 1950s and 1960s when their stories were rarely expressed in public. See De Swaan, "Survivors' Syndrome," 1990.

77. Gottschalk, "Rise and Fall of Apartheid's Death Squads," 251. Clearly, these were the killers of the Apartheid regime, the losing side: "All the death, the suffering, and the oppression, which were used to combat the regime's real and imagined enemies, were useless" (252).

78. Hatzfeld, *Strategy of Antelopes.*

79. Waller, "Perpetrators of the Holocaust," 11, 28. Waller, *Becoming Evil,* 118, claims: "People tend towards integration, not compartmentalization." But there is no evidence for this general tendency.

80. Klee, Dressen, and Riess, *"Good Old Days,"* 105 (emphasis in original).

81. In one instance, the highly educated and very successful daughter of an SS man, who seemed to have completely distanced herself from her father, seriously contended that "the inner life does not exist." That was, apparently, the price she paid.

82. Bergmann and Jucovy, *Generations of the Holocaust,* 162, 175; Volkan, Ast, and Greer, *Third Reich in the Unconscious,* 145–160.

83. Lifton, *Nazi Doctors,* 419–428.

84. Lifton, *Nazi Doctors,* 427, suspects "a certain degree of self-selection. . . . Previous psychological characteristics of a doctor's self had considerable significance." But he continues: "Considerable doubling occurred in people with the most varied psychological characteristics." He concludes that "most of what Nazi doctors did would be within the potential capability—at least under certain conditions—of most doctors and most people."

85. Sereny, *Into That Darkness,* 164. He continues, "[Stangl] revealed the *two* men he had become in order to survive" (176, emphasis in original).

86. See the indictment by the ICTY (International Criminal Tribunal for the Former Yugoslavia) in the case of Ratko Mladić, at www.ictfy.org; and see the indictment, judgment, and sentence by the ICTR (International Criminal Tribunal for Rwanda) in the case of Idelphonse Hategekimana, at www.ictr.org.

87. Sereny, *Into That Darkness,* 349. In Stangl's case, as in those of other perpetrators, the family pretended to know only as much as he had told them, a small part of the record, and refused to believe third-party accusations. As Stangl's daughter said: "Nothing—nothing on earth—will make me believe he has done anything wrong" (350). The dogged denials of many defendants may have been motivated more by the fear of losing the love and respect of their family than by juridical considerations.

Conclusion

1. This is what Christopher Powell's title *Barbaric Civilization* refers to.

Bibliography

African Rights. *Not So Innocent: When Women Become Killers*. London: African Rights, 1995.

Akçam, Taner. *A Shameful Act: The Armenian Genocide and the Question of Turkish Responsibility*. New York: Picador, 2007.

Allen, John G., and Peter Fonagy, eds. *Handbook of Mentalization-Based Treatment*. Chichester, UK: Wiley and Sons, 2006.

Anderson, Benedict. *Imagined Communities: Reflections on the Origin and Spread of Nationalism* [1983]. Rev. ed. London: Verso, 1991.

———. *Violence and the State in Indonesia*. Ithaca, NY: Cornell University, 2001.

Ardrey, R. *African Genesis: A Personal Investigation into the Animal Origins and Nature of Man*. London: Fontana, 1961.

Arendt, Hannah. *Eichmann in Jerusalem: A Report on the Banality of Evil* [1963]. New York: Penguin, 1979.

Ascherson, Neal. *The King Incorporated: Leopold the Second and the Congo*. London: Granta, 1999.

Askenasy, Hans. *Are We All Nazis?* Secaucus, NJ: L. Stuart, 1978.

Ba, Mehdi. *Rwanda: Un génocide français*. Paris: L'Esprit Frappeur, 1997.

Bäck, Lucien R. "Traditional Rwanda: Deconsecrating a Sacred Kingdom." In Henri J. M. Claesen and Peter Skalník, eds., *The Study of the State*, 15–33. The Hague: Mouton, 1981.

Bar, Neta, and Eyal Ben-Ari. "Israeli Snipers in the Al-Aqsa Intifada: Killing, Humanity and Lived Experience." *Third World Quarterly* 26 (2005): 133–152.

Barkan, Elazar. "Genocides of Indigenous Peoples." In Robert Gellately and Ben Kiernan, eds., *The Specter of Genocide: Mass Murder in Historical Perspective*, 117–139. Cambridge: Cambridge University Press, 2003.

Bar-On, Dan. *Did Holocaust Perpetrators Feel Guilty in Retrospect?* Beer-Sheva: Bar-On, 1988.

Baron-Cohen, Simon. *Zero Degrees of Empathy: A New Theory of Human Cruelty.* London: Allen Lane, 2011.

Bartov, Omer. "Extreme Violence and the Scholarly Community." *International Social Science Journal* 54 (2002): 509–518.

———. *Hitler's Army: Soldiers, Nazis, and War in the Third Reich.* New York: Oxford University Press, 1991.

Bauman, Zygmunt. *Modernity and the Holocaust.* Cambridge: Polity, 1989.

———. *Postmodern Ethics.* Malden, MA: Blackwell, 1993.

Baumeister, Roy. *Evil: Inside Human Cruelty and Violence.* New York: Freeman/Holt, 2001.

———. "The Holocaust and the Four Roots of Evil." In Leonard S. Newman and Ralph Erber, eds., *Understanding Genocide: The Social Psychology of the Holocaust,* 241–258. Oxford: Oxford University Press, 2002.

Baxter, Craig. "Bangladesh/East Pakistan." In Dinah L. Shelton, ed., *The Encyclopedia of Genocide and Crimes Against Humanity,* 3 vols., 1:115–119. Farmington Hills, MI: Thomson Gale, 2005.

Bayart, Jean-François. *The State in Africa: The Politics of the Belly.* London: Longman, 1993.

Becker, Jasper. *Hungry Ghosts: Mao's Secret Famine.* New York: Henry Holt, 1996.

Berenschot, Ward. *Riot Politics: Hindu-Muslim Violence and the Indian State.* London: Hurst, 2011.

Bergen, Doris L. "Religion and Genocide: A Historiographical Survey." In Dan Stone, ed., *The Historiography of Genocide,* 194–227. New York: Palgrave Macmillan, 2010.

Bergmann, Martin S., and Milton E. Jucovy. *Generations of the Holocaust.* New York: Columbia University Press, 1982.

Berkeley, Bill. *The Graves Are Not Yet Full: Race, Tribe, and Power in the Heart of Africa.* New York: Basic Books, 2001.

Berkhoff, Karel. *Harvest of Despair: Life and Death in Ukraine Under Nazi Rule.* Cambridge, MA: Harvard University Press, 2004.

Bernard, Carmen, and Serge Gruzinski. *Histoire du nouveau monde,* Vol. 2: *Les métissages, 1550–1640.* Paris: Fayard, 1993.

Bion, Wilfred. *Experiences in Groups.* London: Routledge, 1989.

Black-Michaud, Jacob. *Cohesive Forces: Feud in the Mediterranean and in the Middle East.* Oxford: Blackwell, 1975.

———. *Sheep and Land: The Economics of Power in a Tribal Society.* Cambridge: Cambridge University Press, 1986.

Blass, Thomas. "The Milgram Paradigm After 35 Years: Some Things We Now Know About Obedience to Authority." In Thomas Blass, ed., *Obedience to Authority: Current Perspectives on the Milgram Paradigm,* 35–59. Mahwah, NJ: Lawrence Erlbaum, 2000.

———. "Psychological Perspectives on the Perpetrators of the Holocaust: The Role of Situational Pressures, Personal Dispositions, and Their Interactions." *Holocaust and Genocide Studies* 30 (1993): 30–50.

———. "Understanding Behavior in the Milgram Obedience Experiment: The Role of Personality, Situations, and Their Interactions." *Journal of Personality and Social Psychology* 60 (1991): 398–413.

Blok, Anton. "The Narcissism of Minor Differences." In *Honour and Violence*, 115–135. Cambridge: Polity, 2001.

———. *Wittgenstein en Elias: Een methodische richtlijn voor de antropologie.* Amsterdam: Atheneum, 1975.

———. "Zinloos en zinvol geweld." In Herman Franke, Nico Wilterdink, and Christien Brinkgreve, eds., *Alledaags en ongewoon geweld,* 187–207. Amsterdams Sociologisch Tijdschrift, 18, no. 3. Groningen: Wolters Noordhoff, 1991.

Body-Gendrot, Sophie, and Pieter Spierenburg, eds. *Violence in Europe: Historical and Contemporary Perspectives.* New York: Springer, 2009.

Bourdieu, Pierre. *Raisons pratiques: Sur la théorie de l'action.* Paris: Éditions du Seuil, 1994.

———. *Sur l'état: Cours au Collège de France, 1989–1992.* Paris: Éditions du Seuil, 2012.

Braeckman, Colette. *Rwanda: Histoire d'un génocide.* Paris: Fayard, 1994.

Braembussche, Antoon van den. "The Silence of Belgium: Taboo and Trauma in Belgian Memory." *Yale French Studies* 102 (2002): 34–52.

Brass, Paul R. "The Partition of India and Retributive Genocide in the Punjab, 1946–47: Means, Methods, and Purposes." *Journal of Genocide Research* 5 (2003): 71–101.

Brayard, Florent. *La "solution finale de la question juive": La technique, le temps, et les catégories de la décision.* Paris: Fayard, 2006.

Browning, Christopher R. "Introduction." In Leonard S. Newman and Ralph Erber, eds., *Understanding Genocide: The Social Psychology of the Holocaust,* 3–10. Oxford: Oxford University Press, 2002.

———. *Ordinary Men: Reserve Police Battalion 101 and the Final Solution in Poland* [1992]. Reprint, London: Penguin, 2001.

———. "Revisiting the Holocaust Perpetrators: Why Did They Kill?" Nooit meer Auschwitz Lezing, Amsterdam, January 11, 2011.

Browning, Christopher R., with Jürgen Matthäus. *The Origins of the Final Solution: The Evolution of Nazi Jewish Policy, September 1939–March 1942.* Lincoln: University of Nebraska Press, and Jerusalem: Yad Vashem, 2004.

Brubaker, Rogers, and Frederick Cooper. "Beyond 'Identity.'" *Theory and Society* 29 (2000): 1–47.

Bruggen, Carry van. *Hedendaagsch fetischisme.* Amsterdam: Em. Querido, 1925.

Burger, Jerry M. "Replicating Milgram: Would People Still Obey Today?" *American Psychologist* 64 (January 2009): 1–11.

Burrin, Philippe. *Hitler and the Jews: The Genesis of the Holocaust.* London: E. Arnold, 1994.

Campbell, Bruce C., and Arthur D. Brenner, eds. *Death Squads in Global Perspective: Murder with Deniability.* London: Palgrave Macmillan, 2000.

Cesarani, David. *Eichmann: His Life and Crimes.* London: Heinemann, 2004.

Chalk, Frank, and Kurt Jonassohn, eds. *The History and Sociology of Genocide: Analyses and Case Studies.* New Haven: Yale University Press, 1990.

Chang, Iris. *The Rape of Nanking: The Forgotten Holocaust of World War II.* London: Penguin, 1998.

Charny, Israel W. "Genocide and Mass Destruction: A Missing Dimension in Psychopathology." In Israel W. Charny, ed., *Toward the Understanding and Prevention of Genocide: Proceedings of the International Conference on the Holocaust and Genocide,* 154–174. Boulder, CO: Westview, 1984.

Charny, Israel W., ed. *Encyclopedia of Genocide.* 2 vols. Santa Barbara, CA: ABC-CLIO, 1999.

Chirot, Daniel. "Introduction." In Daniel Chirot and Martin E. P. Seligman, eds., *Ethnopolitical Warfare: Causes, Consequences, and Possible Solutions,* 3–26. Washington, DC: American Psychological Association, 2001.

Chirot, Daniel, and Clark McCauley. *Why Not Kill Them All? The Logic and Prevention of Mass Political Murder.* Princeton, NJ: Princeton University Press, 2006.

Chrétien, Jean-Pierre, ed. *Rwanda: Les médias du génocide.* Paris: Karthala, 1995.

Cocker, Mark. *Rivers of Blood, Rivers of Gold: Europe's Conflict with the Tribal Peoples.* London: Pimlico, 1999.

Cohen, Stanley. *States of Denial: Knowing About Atrocities and Suffering.* Cambridge: Polity, 2001.

Collins, Randall. *Interaction Ritual Chains.* Princeton, NJ: Princeton University Press, 2004.

———. *Macrohistory: Essays in the Sociology of the Long Run.* Stanford, CA: Stanford University Press, 1999.

———. *Violence: A Micro-Sociological Theory.* Princeton, NJ: Princeton University Press, 2008.

Colombijn, Freek, and J. Thomas Lindblad, eds. *Roots of Violence in Indonesia: Contemporary Violence in Historical Perspective.* Leiden: KITLV, and Singapore: ISEAS, 2002.

Conroy, John. *Unspeakable Acts, Ordinary People: The Dynamics of Torture.* New York: Knopf, 2000.

Corradi, Richard B. "Turning Passive into Active: A Building Block of Ego and Fundamental Mechanism of Defense." *Journal of the American Academy of Psychoanalysis and Psychodynamic Psychology* 35 (2007): 393–416.

Creveld, Martin van. *The Culture of War.* New York: Ballantine, 2008.

Cribb, Robert. "Genocide in Indonesia, 1965–1966." *Journal of Genocide Research* 3 (2001): 219–239.

———. "Problems in the Historiography of the Killings in Indonesia." In Robert Cribb, ed., *The Indonesian Killings, 1965–1966: Studies from Java and Bali,* 1–44. Monash Paper on Southeast Asia, no. 21. Clayton, Victoria: Monash University, 1990.

————. "Unresolved Problems in the Indonesian Killings of 1965–1966." *Asian Survey* 42 (2002): 550–563.

Cribb, Robert, et al. "The Mass Killings in Bali." In Robert Cribb, ed., *The Indonesian Killings 1965–1966: Studies from Java and Bali*, 241–260. Monash Paper on Southeast Asia, no. 21. Clayton, Victoria: Monash University, 1990.

Crouch, Harold. *The Army and Politics in Indonesia*. Rev. ed. Ithaca, NY: Cornell University Press, 1998.

Cumberland, Charles C. *Mexico: The Struggle for Modernity*. New York: Oxford University Press, 1968.

Dadrian, Vahakn N. "Armenians in Ottoman Turkey and the Armenian Genocide." In Dinah L. Shelton, ed., *Encyclopedia of Genocide and Crimes Against Humanity*, 3 vols., 1:67–76. Farmington Hills, MI: Thomson Gale, 2005.

————. *The History of the Armenian Genocide: Ethnic Conflict from the Balkans to Anatolia to the Caucasus*. Providence, RI: Berghahn Books, 1995.

Dallaire, Romeo A. *Shake Hands with the Devil: The Failure of Humanity in Rwanda*. Toronto: Random House, 2003.

Danner, Mark. "America and the Bosnia Genocide." *New York Review of Books*, December 4, 1997.

Davis, Mike. *Late Victorian Holocaust: El Niño Famines and the Making of the Third World*. London: Verso, 2001.

Dawkins, Richard. *The Blind Watchmaker*. New York: W. W. Norton, 1986.

Desbois, Father Patrick. *The Holocaust by Bullets*. New York: Palgrave Macmillan, 2008.

Des Forges, Allison. *Leave None to Tell the Story*. New York: Human Rights Watch, 1999.

Devereux, George. *From Anxiety to Method in the Behavioral Sciences*. New York: Humanities Press, 1967.

Dicks, Henry V. *Licensed Mass Murder: A Sociopsychological Study of Some SS Killers*. New York: Basic Books, 1972.

Dikötter, Frank. *Mao's Great Famine: The History of China's Most Devastating Catastrophe, 1958–1962*. London: Bloomsbury, 2010.

Doorn, J. A. A. van, and W. J. Hendrix. *Het Nederlands/Indonesisch conflict: Ontsporing van geweld*. Dieren: De Bataafsche Leeuw, 1985.

Dresden, Sem. *Vervolging, vernietiging, literatuur*. Amsterdam: Meulenhoff, 1991.

Dunk, H. W. von der. *Voorbij de verboden drempel: De Shoah in ons geschiedbeeld*. Amsterdam: Prometheus, 1990.

Dutton, Donald G. *The Psychology of Genocide, Massacres and Extreme Violence: Why "Normal" People Come to Commit Atrocities*. Westport, CT: Praeger Security International, 2007.

Dwyer, Leslie, and Degung Santikarma. "'When the World Turned to Chaos': 1965 and Its Aftermath in Bali, Indonesia." In Robert Gellately and Ben Kiernan, eds., *The Specter of Genocide: Mass Murder in Historical Perspective*, 289–305. Cambridge: Cambridge University Press, 2003.

Elias, Norbert. *The Germans: Power Struggles and the Development of Habitus in the*

Nineteenth and Twentieth Centuries. Edited by Michael Schröter and translated by Eric Dunning and Stephen Mennell. New York: Columbia University Press, 1996. First published in German as *Studien über die Deutschen*, 1989.

———. "On the Process of Civilisation" [1939]. In Norbert Elias, *Collected Works*, vol. 6. Dublin: University College Dublin Press, 2012.

———. "The Society of Individuals III: Changes in the We-I-Balance." In Norbert Elias, *The Society of Individuals*. Dublin: University College Dublin Press, 2010.

Ellman, Michael. "Soviet Repression Statistics: Some Comments." *Europe-Asia Studies* 54 (2002): 1151–1172.

Erber, Ralph. "Perpetrators with a Clear Conscience: Lying, Self-Deception and Belief Change." In Leonard S. Newman and Ralph Erber, eds., *Understanding Genocide: The Social Psychology of the Holocaust*, 285–300. Oxford: Oxford University Press, 2002.

Fein, Helen. *Genocide: A Sociological Perspective. Current Sociology*, special issue, 38 (1990).

———. "Revolutionary and Antirevolutionary Genocides: A Comparison of State Murders in Democratic Kampuchea, 1975–1979, and in Indonesia, 1965–1966." *Studies in Society and History* 35 (1993): 796–823.

Fenichel, Otto. *The Psychoanalytic Theory of Neurosis*. New York: W. W. Norton, 1945.

Fings, Karola. "The Public Face of the Camps." In Jane Caplan and Nikolaus Wachsmann, eds., *Concentration Camps in Nazi Germany: The New Histories*, 108–126. London: Routledge, 2010.

Fletcher, Jonathan. *Violence and Civilization: An Introduction to the Work of Norbert Elias*. Cambridge: Polity, 1997.

Fogel, Joshua, ed. *The Nanjing Massacre in History and Historiography*. Berkeley: University of California Press, 2000.

Fonagy, Peter, et al. *Affect Regulation, Mentalization, and the Development of the Self*. New York: Other Press, 2002.

Freud, Sigmund. *Civilization and Its Discontents* [1930]. Reprinted in Albert Dickson, ed., *The Penguin Freud Library*, vol. 12, 243–340. Harmondsworth, UK: Penguin, 1991.

———. *Group Psychology and the Analysis of the Ego* [1921]. Reprint, New York: Liveright, 1951.

Friedländer, Saul. *The Years of Extermination: Nazi Germany and the Jews*, Vol. 2: *1939–1945*. New York: HarperCollins, 2007.

Frijda, Nico H. *The Emotions*. Cambridge: Cambridge University Press, and Paris: Maison des sciences de l'homme, 1986.

———. "Emotions and Collective Violence." Paper presented at the International Conference on Women and Moral Emotions in Times of War and Peace, University of Haifa, June 1–2, 1998.

———. *The Laws of Emotion*. Mahwah, NJ: Erlbaum, 2006.

Fromm, Erich. *Anatomy of Human Destructiveness*. New York: Holt, Rinehart and Winston, 1973.

Fujii, Lee Ann. *Killing Neighbors: Webs of Violence in Rwanda*. Ithaca, NY: Cornell University Press, 2009.

Gat, Azar. *War in Human Civilization*. Oxford: Oxford University Press, 2006.

Gerlach, Christian. "The Wannsee Conference, the Fate of German Jews, and Hitler's Decision in Principle to Exterminate All European Jews." *Journal of Modern History* 70 (1998): 759–812.

Gilly, Adolfo. *The Mexican Revolution* [1971]. Translated by Patrick Camiller. London: NLB, 1983.

Gobineau, Joseph de. *Essai sur l'inégalité des races humaines* [1853]. Paris: Firmin Didot, 1933.

Goffman, Erving. *The Presentation of Self in Everyday Life*. Garden City, NY: Doubleday, 1959.

Goldhagen, Daniel Jonah. *Hitler's Willing Executioners: Ordinary Germans and the Holocaust*. New York: Knopf, 1996.

Gomperts, Wouter. "Dysmentalization and Mentalization: A Psychoanalytical View of the Derailment of the Civilizing Process." Paper presented at the Fifteenth World Congress of Sociology, Brisbane, Australia, July 7–13, 2002.

Gong, Xiaoxia. "The Logic of Repressive Action: A Case Study of Violence in the Cultural Revolution." In Kam-yee Law, ed., *The Chinese Cultural Revolution Reconsidered: Beyond Purge and Holocaust*, 113–132. Basingstoke, UK: Palgrave Macmillan, 2003.

Gottschalk, Keith. "The Rise and Fall of Apartheid's Death Squads, 1969–1993." In Bruce B. Campbell and Arthur D. Brenner, eds., *Death Squads in Global Perspective: Murder with Deniability*, 229–260. London: Palgrave Macmillan, 2000.

Goudsblom, Johan. *Fire and Civilization*. London: Penguin Books, 1997.

——. *Stof waar honger uit ontstond: Over evolutie en sociale processen*. Amsterdam: Meulenhoff, 2001.

Gourevitch, Philip. *We Wish to Inform You That Tomorrow We Will Be Killed with Our Families*. New York: Farrar, Straus and Giroux, 1998.

Grandin, Greg. "Politics by Other Means." In Etelle Higonnet, ed., *Quiet Genocide: Guatemala, 1981–1983*. New Brunswick, NJ: Transaction, 2009.

Grossman, Dave. *On Killing: The Psychological Cost of Learning to Kill in War and Society*. Rev. ed. Boston: Little, Brown, 2009.

Haffner, Sebastian. *The Meaning of Hitler*. Cambridge, MA: Harvard University Press, 1979.

Haggard, Stephan, and Marcus Noland. *Famine in North Korea: Markets, Aid, and Reform*. New York: Columbia University Press, 2007.

Hancock, Ian. "Responses to the Porrajmos: The Romani Holocaust." In Allan S. Rosenbaum, ed., *Is the Holocaust Unique? Perspectives on Comparative Genocide*, 69–96. Boulder, CO: Westview, 2001.

Haperen, Maria van, et al. *The Holocaust and Other Genocides*. Amsterdam: NIOD/ Amsterdam University Press, 2012.

Haskell, Thomas L. "Capitalism and the Origins of the Humanitarian Sensibility, Parts 1 and 2." *American Historical Review* 90 (1985): 339–361, 547–566.

Hatzfeld, Jean. *Machete Season: The Killers in Rwanda Speak.* New York: Farrar, Straus and Giroux, 2005.

———. *The Strategy of Antelopes: Living in Rwanda After the Genocide.* London: Serpent's Tail, 2009.

Heder, Steve. "Cambodia." In Dinah L. Shelton, ed., *Encyclopedia of Genocide and Crimes Against Humanity,* 3 vols., 1:141–146. Farmington Hills, MI: Thomson Gale, 2005.

Heerma van Voss, Bas. "Report on the Case Against Zoran Žigić Before the International Criminal Tribunal for the Former Yugoslavia." Unpublished ms., 2011.

Heilbron, Johan. "Tegenoverdracht en mensenwetenschap—From Anxiety to Method in the Behavioral Sciences." *Amsterdams Sociologisch Tijdschrift* 28 (2001): 62–66.

Herzberg, Abel. *Eichmann in Jeruzalem.* The Hague: Bakker/Daamen, 1962.

Heuer, Hans-Joachim. *Geheime Staatspolizei: Über das Töten und die Tendenzen der Entzivilisierung.* Berlin: De Gruyter, 1995.

Heusch, Luc de. "Rwanda: Responsibilities for Genocide." *Anthropology Today* 11 (1995): 3–7.

Hilberg, Raul. *Perpetrators, Victims, Bystanders: The Jewish Catastrophe, 1933–1945.* New York: HarperCollins, 1993.

Hinton, Alexander Laban. *Why Did They Kill? Cambodia in the Shadow of Genocide.* Berkeley: University of California Press, 2005.

———. "Why Did You Kill? The Cambodian Genocide and the Dark Side of Face and Honor." *Journal of Asian Studies* 57 (1998): 93–122.

Hochschild, Adam. *King Leopold's Ghost: A Story of Greed, Terror, and Heroism in Colonial Africa.* New York: Mariner, 1999.

Hoetink, Harry. *The Two Variants in Caribbean Race Relations: A Contribution to the Sociology of Segmented Societies.* Translated by Eva M. Hooykaas. London: Oxford University Press, 1967.

Hoffman, Martin L. *Empathy and Moral Development.* New York: Cambridge University Press, 2000.

Horowitz, Donald L. *The Deadly Ethnic Riot.* Berkeley: University of California Press, 2001.

Hovannisian, Richard G. "The Armenian Genocide: Wartime Radicalization or Premeditated Continuum?" In Richard G. Hovannisian, ed., *The Armenian Genocide in Perspective,* 3–18. New Brunswick, NJ: Transaction, 1986.

Howard-Hassman, Rhoda E. "State-Induced Famine and Penal Starvation in North Korea." *Genocide Studies and Prevention* 7 (2012): 147–165.

Hughes, Everett C. "Good People and Dirty Work." In *The Sociological Eye: Selected Papers* [1971], 87–97. New Brunswick, NJ: Transaction, 2009.

Hughes, John. *The End of Sukarno: A Coup That Misfired, a Purge That Ran Wild.* London: Angus and Wilson, 1968.

Huizinga, Johan. *Geschonden wereld: Een beschouwing over de kansen op herstel van onze beschaving.* Haarlem: Tjeenk Willnk, 1945.

Hull, Isabel V. "Military Culture and the Production of 'Final Solutions' in the Colonies." In Robert Gellately and Ben Kiernan, eds., *The Specter of Genocide: Mass*

Murder in Historical Perspective, 141–162. Cambridge: Cambridge University Press, 2003.

Jacoby, Russell. *Bloodlust: On the Roots of Violence from Cain and Abel to the Present.* New York: Free Press, 2011.

Jaffrelot, Christophe. *Le syndrome pakistanais.* Paris: Fayard, 2013.

Jen, Yu-wen. *The Taiping Revolutionary Movement.* New Haven: Yale University Press, 1973.

Jensen, Olaf, and Claus-Christian W. Szejnmann. *Ordinary People as Mass Murderers: Perpetrators in Comparative Perspectives.* Basingstoke, UK: Palgrave Macmillan, 2008.

Joas, Hans. "Sociology After Auschwitz: Zygmunt Bauman's Work and the Problems of German Self-understanding." In *War and Modernity*, 163–170. Cambridge: Polity, 2003.

Jobson, Richard. *The Golden Trade: A Discovery of the River Gambra and the Golden Trade of the Aethiopians* [1623]. London: Dawsons of Pall Mall, 1968.

Jonas, Susanne. "Guatemala: Acts of Genocide and Scorched-Earth Counterinsurgency War." In Samuel Totten and Robert K. Hitchcock, eds., *Genocide of Indigenous Peoples*, 355–393. New Brunswick, NJ: Transaction, 2011.

Jones, James H. *Bad Blood: The Tuskegee Syphilis Experiment.* New York: Free Press, 1981.

Kaldor, Mary. *New and Old Wars.* 2nd ed. Cambridge: Polity, 2007.

Karnow, Stanley. *Vietnam: A History.* Rev. ed. New York: Random House, 1991.

Katsuichi, Honda. *The Nanking Massacre: A Japanese Journalist Confronts Japan's National Shame.* Armonk, NY: Sharpe, 1999.

Katz, Fred E. *Ordinary People and Extraordinary Evil: A Report on the Beguilings of Evil.* Albany: State University of New York Press, 1993.

Katz, Jack. *Seductions of Crime: Moral and Sensual Attractions in Doing Evil.* New York: Basic Books, 1988.

Katz, Steven T. *The Holocaust in Historical Context*, Vol. 1: *The Holocaust and Mass Death Before the Modern Age.* New York: Oxford University Press, 1994.

Keane, Fergal. *Season of Blood: A Rwandan Journey.* London: Penguin, 1995.

Keeley, Lawrence J. *War Before Civilization: The Myth of the Peaceful Savage.* Oxford: Oxford University Press, 1996.

Khan, Yasmin. *The Great Partition: The Making of India and Pakistan.* New Delhi: Routledge, 2007.

Kiernan, Ben. *Blood and Soil: A World History of Genocide and Extermination from Sparta to Darfur.* New Haven: Yale University Press, 2007.

———. *The Pol Pot Regime: Race, Power, and Genocide in Cambodia Under the Khmer Rouge, 1975–1979.* New Haven: Yale University Press, 2002.

Kimonyo, Jean-Paul. *Rwanda: Un génocide populaire.* Paris: Karthala, 2008.

Klee, Ernst, Wili Dressen, and Volker Riess, eds. *"The Good Old Days": The Holocaust as Seen by Its Perpetrators and Bystanders.* New York: Konecky and Konecky, 1991.

Kleinen, John. "Cambodja: Het gevecht om de staat." *De Gids* 146 (1983): 605–618.

Knight, Ian. "Shaka Zulu." In Dinah L. Shelton, ed., *The Encyclopedia of Genocide and Crimes Against Humanity*, 3 vols., 2:945–946. Farmington Hills, MI: Thomson Gale, 2005.

Kris, Ernst. *Psychoanalytic Explorations in Art* [1936]. New York: International Universities Press, 1952.

Kroslak, Daniela. *The Role of France in the Rwandan Genocide.* London: Hurst, 2007.

Kumar, Radha. "Settling Partition Hostilities: Lessons Learned, the Options Ahead." In Ghislaine Glasson Deschaumes and Rada Ivekovic, eds., *Divided Countries, Separated Cities: The Modern Legacy of Partitions*, 3–18. Oxford: Oxford University Press, 2003.

Kuper, Leo. *Genocide: Its Political Use in the Twentieth Century.* New Haven: Yale University Press, 1981.

Kürsat-Ahlers, Elçin. "Über das Toten in Genoziden: Ein Bilanz historisch-soziologischer Deutungen." In Peter Gleichmann and Thomas Kühne, eds., *Massenhaftes Töten: Kriege und Genozide im 20. Jahrhundert*, 180–206. Essen: Klartext, 2004.

Lacoste, Charlotte. *Séductions du bourreau: Négation des victimes.* Paris: Presses Universitaires de France, 2010.

Lame, Danielle R. de. "Une colline entre mille, ou la calme avant la tempète: Transformations et blocages du Rwanda rural." PhD diss., Free University, Amsterdam, 1996.

Langenberg, Michael van. "Gestapu and State Power in Indonesia." In Robert Cribb, ed., *The Indonesian Killings, 1965–1966: Studies from Java and Bali*, 45–61. Monash Paper on Southeast Asia, no. 21. Clayton, Victoria: Monash University, 1990.

Laponce, Jean. "Les langues comme acteurs internationaux: Phénomènes de contagion et phénomènes d'irradiation." In Bertrand Badie, ed., *Les relations internationales à l'épreuve de la science politique: Mélanges Marcel Merle*, 211–224. Paris: Economica, 1993.

Lasswell, Harold D. *Psychopathology and Politics* [1930]. Chicago: University of Chicago Press, 1960.

———. *World Politics and Personal Insecurity* [1934]. Reprinted in *A Study of Power.* Glencoe, IL: Free Press, 1950.

Leadbetter, Bill. "Genocide in Antiquity." In Israel W. Charny, ed., *Encyclopedia of Genocide*, 2 vols., 1:272–275. Santa Barbara, CA: ABC-CLIO, 1999.

Lemarchand, René. *Burundi: Ethnic Conflict and Genocide.* Cambridge: Cambridge University Press and Woodrow Wilson Center Press, 1996.

Levene, Mark. "The Changing Face of Mass Murder: Massacre, Genocide and Postgenocide." *International Social Science Journal* 54 (2002): 443–452.

———. *The Meaning of Genocide: Genocide in the Age of the Nation State*, vol. 1. London: I. B. Tauris, 2005.

Lewy, Guenter. *The Nazi Persecution of the Gypsies.* Oxford: Oxford University Press, 2000.

———. "Were American Indians the Victims of Genocide?" *History News Network*, September 2007, http://hnn.us/article/7302.

Lifton, Robert J. *The Nazi Doctors: Medical Killing and the Psychology of Genocide.* New York: Basic Books, 1986.

Lindquist, Sven. *Exterminate All the Brutes.* New York: New Press, 1996.

Lipman, Jonathan N., and Steven Harrell. *Violence in China: Essays in Culture and Counterculture.* Albany: State University of New York Press, 1990.

Lipset, Seymour Martin, and Stein Rokkan. "Cleavage Structures, Party Systems, and Voter Alignments: An Introduction." In Seymour Martin Lipset and Stein Rokkan, eds., *Party Systems and Voter Alignments: Cross-National Perspectives,* 1–64. New York: Free Press, 1967.

Lipstadt, Deborah E. *The Eichmann Trial.* New York: Nextbook/Shocken, 2011.

Lowe, Keith. *Savage Continent: Europe in the Aftermath of World War II.* New York: Viking, 2012.

MacDonogh, Giles. *After the Reich: The Brutal History of the Allied Occupation.* New York: Basic Books, 2007.

Malkki, Liisa. *Purity and Exile: Violence, Memory, and National Cosmology Among Hutu Refugees in Tanzania.* Chicago: University of Chicago Press, 1995.

Mamdani, Mahmood. *When Victims Become Killers: Colonialism, Nativism, and the Genocide in Rwanda.* Princeton, NJ: Princeton University Press, 2001.

Mandel, David R. "Instigators of Genocide: Examining Hitler from a Social-Psychological Perspective." In Leonard S. Newman and Ralph Erber, eds., *Understanding Genocide: The Social Psychology of the Holocaust,* 259–284. Oxford: Oxford University Press, 2002.

Mann, Michael. *The Dark Side of Democracy: Explaining Ethnic Cleansing.* Cambridge: Cambridge University Press, 2005.

———. "Were the Perpetrators of Genocide 'Ordinary Men' or 'Real Nazis'? Results from Fifteen Hundred Biographies." *Holocaust and Genocide Studies* 14 (2000): 331–366.

Marcus, David. "Famine Crimes in International Law." *American Journal of International Law* 97 (2003): 245–281.

Marples, David R. "Ethnic Issues in the Famine of 1932–33 in Ukraine." *Europe Asia Studies* 31 (2009): 505–18.

Marx, Karl. *Capital: A Critique of Political Economy* [1867]. In *Collected Works,* vol. 35. Moscow, New York: International Publishers, 1999, www.marxists.org/archive/marx/works.

Mascarenhas, Anthony. *The Rape of Bangla Desh.* Delhi: Vikas, [1971].

McAdam, Doug, Sidney Tarrow, and Charles Tilly. *Dynamics of Contention.* Cambridge: Cambridge University Press, 2001.

McCaa, Robert. "Missing Millions: The Demographic Costs of the Mexican Revolution." *Mexican Studies* 19 (2003): 367–400.

McCauley, Clark. "The Psychology of Group Identification and the Power of Ethnic Nationalism." In Daniel Chirot and Martin E. P. Seligman, eds., *Ethnopolitical Warfare: Causes, Consequences, and Possible Solutions,* 343–362. Washington, DC: American Psychological Association, 2001.

McNeill, William H. *Keeping Together in Time: Dance and Drill in Human History.* Cambridge, MA: Harvard University Press, 1995.

Melson, Robert. "Provocation or Nationalism: A Critical Inquiry into the Armenian Genocide of 1915." In Richard G. Hovannisian, *The Armenian Genocide in Perspective*, 61–84. New Brunswick, NJ: Transaction, 1986.

Mildt, Dick de. *In the Name of the People: Perpetrators of Genocide in the Reflection of Their Post-War Prosecution in West Germany: The "Euthanasia" and "Aktion Reinhard" Trial Cases.* The Hague: Martinus Nijhoff, 1996.

Milgram, Stanley. *Obedience to Authority: An Experimental View* [1974]. New York: HarperCollins/Perennial, 2004.

Miller, Arthur G. "Explaining the Holocaust: Does Social Psychology Exonerate the Perpetrators?" In Leonard S. Newman and Ralph Erber, eds., *Understanding Genocide: The Social Psychology of the Holocaust*, 301–324. Oxford: Oxford University Press, 2002.

Mironko, Charles K. "Social and Political Mechanisms of Mass Murder: An Analysis of the Perpetrators in the Rwandan Genocide." PhD diss., University of Michigan, 2004.

Muchembled, Robert. *Une histoire de la violence: De la fin du Moyen-Âge à nos jours.* Paris: Éditions du Seuil, 2008.

Mulisch, Harry. *Criminal Case 40/61, the Trial of Adolf Eichmann: An Eyewitness Account.* Translated by Robert Naborn. Philadelphia: University of Pennsylvania Press, 2005.

Naimark, Norman M. *Fires of Hatred: Ethnic Cleansing in Twentieth-Century Europe.* Cambridge, MA: Harvard University Press, 2001.

Naumann, Bernd. *Auschwitz.* New York: Praeger, 1966.

Neitzel, Sönke, and Harald Welzer. *Soldaten: Protokolle vom Kämpfen, Töten und Sterben.* Frankfurt: Fischer, 2011.

Newbury, Catharine. *The Cohesion of Oppression: Clientship and Ethnicity in Rwanda, 1860–1960.* New York: Columbia University Press, 1988.

Nirenberg, David. *Communities of Violence: Persecution of Minorities in the Middle Ages.* Princeton, NJ: Princeton University Press, 1996.

Olusoga, David, and Casper W. Erichsen. *The Kaiser's Holocaust: Germany's Forgotten Genocide.* London: Faber and Faber, 2010.

Orth, Karin. *Die Konzentrationslager-SS: Sozialstrukturelle Analysen und biographische Studien.* Göttingen: Wallstein, 2000.

Overy, Richard. *Interrogations: The Nazi Elite in Allied Hands, 1945.* New York: Penguin, 2011.

Parsons, Talcott. *Social Structure and Personality.* New York: Free Press, 1970.

Pinker, Steven. *The Better Angels of Our Nature: Why Violence Has Declined.* London: Penguin, 2011.

Pohl, Dieter. "Normalität und Pathologie—Sozialpsychologische Anmerkungen zur Psychogenese von Massenmördern." In Peter Gleichmann and Thomas Kühne, eds., *Massenhaftes Töten: Kriege und Genozide im 20. Jahrhundert*, 158–179. Essen: Klartext, 2004.

Port, Mattijs van de. *Gypsies, Wars, and Other Instances of the Wild: Civilisation and Its Discontents in a Serbian Town.* Amsterdam: Amsterdam University Press, 1998.

Powell, Christopher. *Barbaric Civilization: A Critical Sociology of Genocide.* Montreal: McGill-Queen's University Press, 2011.

Power, Samantha. *"A Problem from Hell": America and the Age of Genocide.* New York: Perennial/HarperCollins, 2003.

Prunier, Gerard. *The Rwanda Crisis, 1959–1994: History of a Genocide.* London: Hurst, 1995.

Reemtsma, Jan Philipp. *Trust and Violence: An Essay on a Modern Relationship.* Translated by Dominic Bonfiglio. Princeton, NJ: Princeton University Press, 2012.

Reid, Anthony. *The Contest for North Sumatra: Atjeh, the Netherlands and Britain, 1858–1898.* Kuala Lumpur: Oxford University Press, 1969.

Reid, Richard. *A History of Modern Africa: 1800 to the Present.* Chichester, UK: Wiley-Blackwell, 2009.

Reybrouck, David van. *Congo: Een geschiedenis.* Amsterdam: De Bezige Bij, 2010.

Riley-Smith, Jonathan. *The Oxford Illustrated History of the Crusades.* Oxford: Oxford University Press, 1995.

Robinson, Geoffrey. *The Dark Side of Paradise: Political Violence in Bali.* Ithaca, NY: Cornell University Press, 1995.

Robinson, Jacob. *And the Crooked Shall Be Made Straight: The Eichmann Trial, the Jewish Catastrophe, and Hannah Arendt's Narrative.* New York: Macmillan, 1965.

Roekel, Evertjan van. *Nederlandse Vrijwilligers in de Waffen SS.* Utrecht: Het Spectrum, 2011.

Roth, Paul A. "Hearts of Darkness: 'Perpetrator History' and Why There Is No Why." *History of the Human Sciences* 17 (2004): 211–251.

Rummel, Rudolph J. *China's Bloody Century: Genocide and Mass Murder Since 1900.* New Brunswick, NJ: Transaction, 1991.

———. *Death by Government.* New Brunswick, NJ: Transaction, 1994.

———. *Statistics of Democide: Genocide and Mass Murder Since 1900.* Münster: LIT, and Piscataway, NJ: Transaction, 1998.

Ruthven, Malise. "The Albigensian Crusades." In Frank Chalk and Kurt Jonassohn, eds., *The History and Sociology of Genocide: Analyses and Case Studies,* 121–133. New Haven: Yale University Press, 1990.

Sagan, Eli. *At the Dawn of Tyranny: The Origins of Individualism, Political Oppression and the State.* London: Faber and Faber, 1985.

Saideman, Stephen M. *The Ties That Divide: Ethnic Politics, Foreign Policy and International Conflict.* New York: Columbia University Press, 2001.

Sanders, Aafke. "The Evil Within: Genocide, Memory, and Myth Making in Cambodia." MA thesis, Radboud University, Nijmegen, 2006.

Sandler, Joseph, with Anna Freud. *The Analysis of Defense: The Ego and the Mechanisms of Defense Revisited.* New York: International Universities Press, 1985.

Saunders, J. J. *The History of the Mongol Conquests.* London: Routledge and Kegan Paul, 1971.

Schelling, Thomas C. *The Strategy of Conflict.* London: Oxford University Press, 1960.

Schelvis, Jules. *Vernietigingskamp Sobibor* [1993]. Amsterdam: De Bataafsche Leeuw, 2008.

Schendel, Willem van. *A History of Bangla Desh.* Cambridge: Cambridge University Press, 2009.

Schlögel, Karl. "Nach der Rechthaberei: Umsiedlung und Vertreibung als europäisches Problem." In Dieter Bingen, Wlodzimierz Borodziej, and Stefan Troebs, eds., *Vertreibungen europäisch Erinnern? Historische Erfahrungen—Vergangenheitspolitik—Zukunftskonzeptionen*, 11–33. Wiesbaden: Harrassowitz, 2003.

Schorsch, Eberhard. "Perversion, Liebe, Gewalt." *Beiträge zur Sexualforschung* 68 (1993): 53–60.

Schulte Nordholt, Henk. "A Genealogy of Violence." In Freek Colombijn and J. Thomas Lindblad, eds., *Roots of Violence in Indonesia*, 33–61. Leiden: KITLV, 2002.

Scott, James C. *Weapons of the Weak: Everyday Forms of Peasant Resistance.* New Haven: Yale University Press, 1985.

Scott, Peter Dale. "The United States and the Overthrow of Sukarno, 1965–1967." *Pacific Affairs* 58 (1985): 239–264.

Sémelin, Jacques. *Purify and Destroy: The Political Uses of Massacre and Genocide.* Translated by Cynthia Schoch. London: Hurst, 2007.

———. "Rationalités de la violence extrême." *Critique Internationale* 6 (2000): 122–124.

Sereny, Gitta. *Into That Darkness: From Mercy Killing to Mass Murder.* New York: McGraw-Hill, 1974.

Shapira, Anita. "The Eichmann Trial: Changing Perspectives." *Journal of Israeli History* 23 (2004): 18–39.

Shaw, Martin. "The General Hybridity of War and Genocide." *Journal of Genocide Research* 9 (2007): 461–473.

Shelton, Dinah L., ed. *Encyclopedia of Genocide and Crimes Against Humanity.* 3 vols. Farmington Hills, MI: Thomson Gale, 2005.

Silvester, Jeremy, and Jan-Bart Gewald. *Words Cannot Be Found: German Colonial Rule in Namibia, 1890–1923; An Annotated Reprint of the 1918 Blue Book.* Leiden: Brill, 2003.

Simmel, Georg. *Sociology: Inquiries into the Construction of Social Forms* [1908]. 2 vols. Translated and edited by Anthony J. Blasi. Leiden: Brill, 2009.

Smith, Roger W. "Human Destructiveness and Politics: The Twentieth Century as an Age of Genocide." In Isidor Walliman and Michael N. Dobkowski, eds., *Genocide and the Modern Age: Etiology and Case Studies of Mass Death*, 21–39. Westport, CT: Greenwood, 1987.

Snyder, Timothy. *Bloodlands: Europe Between Hitler and Stalin.* New York: Basic Books, 2010.

———. "Hitler vs Stalin: Who Killed More." *New York Review of Books*, March 10, 2011.

Sofsky, Wolfgang. *Die Ordnung des Terrors: Das Konzentrationslager.* Frankfurt: Fischer, 1997.

———. *Traktat über die Gewalt.* Frankfurt: S. Fischer, 1996.

Sontag, Susan. *Illness as Metaphor.* Harmondsworth, UK: Penguin, 1983.

Sorabji, C. "A Very Modern War: Terror and Territory in Bosnia-Hercegovina." In

Robert A. Hinde and Helen E. Watson, eds., *War: A Cruel Necessity? The Bases of Institutionalized Violence*, 80–90. London: Tauris Academic Studies, 1995.

Spence, Jonathan D. *God's Chinese Son: The Taiping Heavenly Kingdom of Hong Xiuquan*. London: HarperCollins, 1996.

Stannard, David E. *American Holocaust: Columbus and the Conquest of the New World*. New York: Oxford University Press, 1992.

———. "Uniqueness as Denial: The Politics of Genocide Scholarship." In Alan S. Rosenbaum, ed., *Is the Holocaust Unique? Perspectives on Comparative Genocide*, 295–340. Boulder, CO: Westview, 2009.

Staub, Ervin. "The Psychology of Bystanders, Perpetrators and Heroic Helpers." In Leonard S. Newman and Ralph Erber, eds., *Understanding Genocide: The Social Psychology of the Holocaust*, 11–42. Oxford: Oxford University Press, 2002.

———. "The Roots of Evil: Social Conditions, Culture, Personality, and Basic Human Needs." *Personality and Social Psychology Review* 3 (1999): 179–192.

Stein, Howard F. "The Indispensable Enemy and American-Soviet Relations." In Vamik D. Volkan, Demetrios A. Julius, and Joseph V. Montville, eds., *The Psychodynamics of International Relations*, Vol. 1: *Concepts and Theories*, 71–89. Lexington, MA: Lexington Books, 1990.

Steiner, John. "The SS Yesterday and Today: A Sociopsychological View." Reprinted in Joel E. Dimsdale, ed., *Survivors, Victims, and Perpetrators: Essays in the Nazi Holocaust*, 405–456. New York: Hemisphere, 1980.

Stone, Dan. "The Holocaust and Its Historiography." In Dan Stone, ed., *The Historiography of Genocide*, 373–399. Basingstoke, UK: Palgrave Macmillan, 2010.

Straus, Scott. "How Many Perpetrators Were There in the Rwandan Genocide? An Estimate." *Journal of Genocide Studies* 6 (2004): 85–98.

———. *The Order of Genocide: Race, Power, and War in Rwanda*. Ithaca, NY: Cornell University Press, 2006.

Strayer, John R. "The Albigensian Crusades: Background." In Frank Chalk and Kurt Jonassohn, eds., *The History and Sociology of Genocide: Analyses and Case Studies*, 115–120. New Haven: Yale University Press, 1990.

Su, Yang. *Collective Killings in Rural China During the Cultural Revolution*. New York: Cambridge University Press, 2011.

Suedfeld, Peter. "Theories of the Holocaust: Trying to Explain the Unimaginable." In Daniel Chirot and Martin E. P. Seligman, eds., *Ethnopolitical Warfare: Causes, Consequences, and Possible Solutions*, 51–70. Washington, DC: American Psychological Association, 2001.

Swaan, Abram de. *Bakens in Niemandsland: Opstellen over massaal geweld*. Amsterdam: Bert Bakker, 2007.

———. "Dyscivilization, Mass Extermination and the State." *Theory, Culture and Society* 18 (2001): 265–276.

———. *In Care of the State: Health Care, Education and Welfare in Europe and the USA in the Modern Era*. New York: Oxford University Press, 1988.

———. "State of Outrage: The Fading Line Between Waging War and Fighting Crime." *European Journal on Criminal Policy and Research* 2 (1994): 7–15.

————. "The Survivors' Syndrome: Private Problems and Social Repression." In *The Management of Normality: Critical Essays in Health and Welfare*, 195–204. London: Routledge, 1990.

————. "Terror as a Governmental Service." In M. Hoefnagels, ed., *Repression and Repressive Violence*, 40–50. Amsterdam: Swets and Zeitlinger, 1977.

Talbot, Ian, and Gurharpal Singh. *The Partition of India*. Cambridge: Cambridge University Press, 2009.

Temmerman, Els de. *De doden zijn niet dood: Rwanda, een ooggetuigenverslag*. Amsterdam: De Arbeiderspers, 1994.

Thurston, Anne F. "Urban Violence During the Cultural Revolution: Who Is to Blame?" In Jonathan N. Lipman and Stevan Harrell, *Violence in China: Essays in Culture and Counterculture*, 149–174. Albany: State University of New York Press, 1990.

Tilly, Charles. *Coercion, Capital, and European States, AD 990–1990*. Cambridge, MA: Blackwell, 1990.

Todorov, Tzvetan. *Face à l'extrême*. Paris: Éditions du Seuil, 1994.

Tomasello, Michael. *Why We Cooperate*. Cambridge, MA: MIT Press, 2009.

Tomasevitch, Jozo. *War and Revolution in Yugoslavia, 1941–1945*. Vol. 1: *The Chetniks*. Stanford, CA: Stanford University Press, 1975.

Totten, Samuel. "Genocide in Guatemala." In Samuel Totten, ed., *Genocide of Indigenous Peoples*, 271–298. New Brunswick, NJ: Transaction, 2011.

Totten, Samuel, and Paul R. Bartrop. *Dictionary of Genocide*. Westport, CT: Greenwood, 2008.

Trouwborst, Albert A. "The Political Economy of the Interlacustrine States in East Africa." In Henri J. M. Claessen and Pieter van de Velde, eds., *Early State Economics*, 97–108. Political and Legal Anthropology Series, vol. 8. New Brunswick, NJ: Transaction, 1991.

Üngör, Uğur Ümit. *The Making of Modern Turkey: Nation and State in Eastern Anatolia, 1913–1950*. Oxford: Oxford University Press, 2011.

Üngör, Uğur Ümit, and Mehmet Polatel. *Confiscation and Destruction: The Young Turk Seizure of Armenian Property*. London: Continuum, 2011.

Valentino, Benjamin, Paul Huth, and Dylan Balch-Lindsay. "'Draining the Sea': Mass Killing and Guerrilla Warfare." *International Organization* 38 (2004): 375–407.

Vangroenweghe, Daniel. *Rood Rubber* [1985]. Leuven: Uitgeverij Van Halewyck, 2010.

Vansina, Jan. *Antecedents to Modern Rwanda: The Nyiginya Kingdom*. Madison: University of Wisconsin Press, 2004.

Veer, Paul van 't. *De Atjeh-oorlog*. Amsterdam: De Arbeiderspers, 1969.

Vetlesen, Arne Johan. *Evil and Human Agency: Understanding Collective Evil-Doing*. Cambridge: Cambridge University Press, 2005.

Volkan, Vamik D. "An Overview of Psychological Concepts Pertinent to Interethnic and/or International Relationships." In Vamik D. Volkan, Demetrios A. Julius, and Joseph V. Montville, eds., *The Psychodynamics of International Relations*, Vol. 1: *Concepts and Theories*, 31–46. Lexington MA: Lexington Books, 1990.

Volkan, Vamik D., Gabriele Ast, and William F. Greer, Jr. *The Third Reich in the Un-*

conscious: Transgenerational Transmission and Its Consequences. New York: Brunner Routledge, 2002.

Waal, Frans de. *Chimpanzee Politics: Power and Sex Among Apes.* New York: Harper and Row, 1982.

———. *Our Inner Ape: A Leading Primatologist Explains Why We Are Who We Are.* New York: Penguin, 2005.

Wachsmann, Nickolaus, "The Dynamics of Destruction: The Development of the Concentration Camps, 1933–1945." In Jane Caplan and Nikolaus Wachsmann, eds., *Concentration Camps in Nazi Germany: The New Histories,* 17–42. London: Routledge, 2010.

Wacquant, Loïc J. D. "Elias in the Dark Ghetto." *Amsterdams Sociologisch Tijdschrift* 24 (1999): 340–348.

Walker, Robert S., and Drew H. Bailey. "Body Counts in Lowland South American Violence." *Evolution and Human Behavior* 34 (2013): 29–34.

Waller, James. *Becoming Evil: How Ordinary People Commit Genocide and Mass Killing.* New York: Oxford University Press, 2002.

———. "Perpetrators of the Holocaust: Divided and Unitary Self-Conceptions of Evildoing." *Holocaust and Genocide Studies* 10 (1996): 11–33.

Walter, Eugene V. "The Politics of Decivilization." In Maurice R. Stein, Arthur J. Vidich, and David M. White, eds., *Identity and Anxiety: Survival of the Person in Mass Society,* 291–307. New York: Free Press, 1960.

———. "The Terror Under Shaka." In Frank Chalk and Kurt Jonassohn, eds., *The History and Sociology of Genocide: Analyses and Case Studies,* 224–229. New Haven: Yale University Press, 1990.

Weiss, John. "Review of Daniel Jonah Goldhagen, *Hitler's Willing Executioners: An Historian's View.*" *Journal of Genocide Studies* 1 (1999): 257–272.

Weitz, Eric D. *A Century of Genocide: Utopias of Race and Nation.* Princeton, NJ: Princeton University Press, 2003.

Welzer, Harald. "Mass Murder and Moral Code: Some Thoughts on an Easily Misunderstood Subject." *History of the Human Sciences* 17 (2004): 15–32.

———. *Täter: Wie aus ganz normalen Menschen Massenmörder werden.* Frankfurt: Fischer Verlag, 2005.

Werth, Nicolas. "Stalinist State Violence: A Reappraisal Twenty Years After the Archival Revolution." *Tijdschrift voor Geschiedenis* 124 (2011): 481–491.

Wesseling, Hendrik L. *The European Colonial Empires, 1815–1919.* Harlow: Pearson/ Longman, 2004.

Wheatcroft, Stephen. "The Scale and Nature of German and Soviet Repression and Mass Killings, 1930–45." *Europe-Asia Studies* 48 (1996): 1319–1353.

Whitaker, Mark D. "Tonghak Rebellion (Korea)." In Andrea L. Stanton et al., eds., *Cultural Sociology of the Middle East, Asia, and Africa: An Encyclopedia,* Vol. 3: *Cultural Sociology of East and Southeast Asia; Part 2, 1200 to 1900.* Thousand Oaks, CA: Sage, 2012. DOI: http://dx.doi.org/10.4135/9781452218458.

Whyte, Lynn T., III. *Politics of Chaos: The Organizational Causes of Violence in China's Cultural Revolution.* Princeton, NJ: Princeton University Press, 1989.

Wielek, H. *De oorlog die Hitler won*. Amsterdam: Amsterdamsche Boek- en Courant-maatschappij, 1947.

Wilkinson, Steven J. "Froids calculs et foules déchaînées: Les émeutes intercommu-nautaires en Inde." *Critique Internationale* 6 (2000–2001): 125–142.

Wolf, Eric R. *Peasant Wars of the Twentieth Century*. New York: Harper and Row, 1969.

Wolfe, Tom. *The Bonfire of the Vanities*. New York: Farrar, Straus and Giroux, 1988.

Wrangham, Richard W., and Dale Peterson. *Demonic Males: Apes and the Origins of Human Violence*. New York: Houghton Mifflin Harcourt, 1996.

Wrong, Dennis H. "The Oversocialized Conception of Man in Modern Sociology" [1961]. In *Skeptical Sociology*, 31–54. New York: Columbia University Press, 1976.

Young, Kenneth R. "Local and National Influences in the Violence of 1965." In Robert Cribb, ed., *The Indonesian Killings, 1965–1966: Studies from Java and Bali*, 63–99. Monash Paper on Southeast Asia, no. 21. Clayton, Victoria: Monash University, 1990.

Zajonc, Robert B. "The Zoomorphism of Human Collective Violence." In Leonard S. Newman and Ralph Erber, eds., *Understanding Genocide: The Social Psychology of the Holocaust*, 222–240. Oxford: Oxford University Press, 2002.

Zimbardo, Philip G. *The Lucifer Effect: How Good People Turn Evil*. London: Rider, 2007.

Zwaan, Ton. "Crisis and Genocide in Yugoslavia, 1985–1995." In Maria van Haperen et al., *The Holocaust and Other Genocides*, 121–143. Amsterdam: NIOD/Amsterdam University Press, 2012.

———. "'Modernity' and 'Barbarity' in Genocidal Processes." Unpublished ms., 2007.

Index

Dikötter, Frank, 286n.32
disidentification: as absence of empathy,
    120, 200, 206, 228–29, 267, 295n.59,
    295n.63; circles of, 49; in the former
    Yugoslavia, 50, 189; ghettoization,
    129–30; in merchant towns, 60; from
    other human beings, 36, 248; in post-
    Tito Yugoslavia, 189; projection of,
    52–53; of scholars with perpetrators,
    17; socioemotional process of, 70; state
    formation, 116–17; stereotypes acti-
    vated for, 99, 100–101, 118, 119–20,
    133–34; transformation of social rela-
    tions, 69, 70, 201; of Tutsis, 99–101;
    from victims, 101, 209–10, 212, 215,
    220–24, 226, 228–29
doctors: as genocidaires, 218, 228, 248,
    296n.83
domestic pacification: through state
    monopolization of violence, 67, 84,
    115–16, 118–19, 129, 257
Donets Basin, 153
Doorn, J. A. A. van, 277n.7
doubling, 244, 245, 248–49, 250–51,
    296n.83
Dutch subjugation of the Aceh people, 22
dysmentalization: abandonment of empa-
    thy, 228–29, 236–37, 267, 295n.59,
    295n.63; doubling, 244, 245, 248–49,
    250–51, 296n.83; mentalization, 230–32,
    230–33, 238–39, 267, 294n.53; regres-
    sion in service to the regime, 10–11,
    111, 125–27, 213, 239, 251, 267–68,
    283n.22. See also loyalty; obedience

Eastern Orthodox Christianity, 184, 185
East Pakistan, 3, 171, 179, 209, 289n.85
East Pakistan, 178–79
Edhy, Sarwo, 168
Eichmann, Adolf: defense of, 21, 22;
    impressions of, 22, 23, 37, 226, 249,
    253; personality of, 21–22, 253–54,
    271n.7; testimony of, 21–22, 271n.7,
    294n.44
Einsatzkommandos, 220, 244
Elias, Norbert: on civilizing processes,
    10, 54, 116, 121–22, 126, 130, 257,
    275n.46, 282n.2; collapse of civiliza-

tion, 125; controlled decontrolling of
    emotional controls, 127; decivilizing
    processes, 10–11, 54, 125, 206; global
    identifications, 66–68
eliminationist anti-Semitism, 35, 141, 185,
    208–9, 223, 263
empathy: cruelty, 294n.48, 295n.64; dis-
    identification as absence of, 120, 200,
    206, 228–29, 234–37, 267, 295n.59,
    295n.63; dysmentalization as abandon-
    ment of, 228–29, 236–37, 267, 294n.46,
    295n.59, 295n.63; emergence in child-
    hood, 230–32, 267, 295n.59; mentaliza-
    tion, 230–33, 294n.53; in mother-child
    relationships, 232; regression in service
    to the regime, 11, 111, 125–27, 213,
    239, 251, 267; and resistance to author-
    ity in Milgram obedience experiment,
    25, 26, 30–31; suppression of, 233–34,
    274n.44, 295n.59
Endlösung (Final Solution), 42–43, 151–52,
    177, 275n.49
Enver Pasha, 173–74, 288n.71
ethnic cleansing, 45–46, 79–81, 108–13,
    149, 172–73, 180–88, 194, 279n.22
ethnic Germans, expulsion from central
    Europe, 147, 186, 191–96, 291n.113,
    291n.114
evil: banality of evil (Arendt), 13, 22–23,
    253, 254, 255, 272n.14, 274n.41;
    changing definitions of, 71; crimes
    against the environment, 71; democ-
    ratization of, 32; ordinary people who
    commit extraordinary evil, 14, 16–17,
    19, 21, 22–23, 32, 47, 220–22, 253–54,
    255, 271n.7, 274n.41; target popula-
    tions as, 51; as violence, 71, 277n.1
expulsions: of ethnic Germans, 147, 154,
    186, 191–96, 291n.113, 291n.114;
    during the Great Purge, 153–54, 156,
    286n.26
extermination camps, 42–43, 128, 152,
    176, 274n.44, 275n.49
extermination of Communists in Indone-
    sia, 165–68, 287n.46

families of genocidaires, 225, 245–46,
    249–50, 296n.80, 296n.86